CRIMINAL LAW

IN A NUTSHELL

FIFTH EDITION

By

ARNOLD H. LOEWY

Professor of Law
University of North Carolina

WEST®

A Thomson Reuters business

Mat #40755790

Nutshell Series, In a Nutshell and the Nutshell Logo are trademarks registered in the U.S. Patent and Trademark Office.

© West, a Thomson business, 1975, 1987, 2000, 2003
© 2009 Thomson Reuters

    610 Opperman Drive
    St. Paul, MN 55123
    1–800–313–9378

Printed in the United States of America

ISBN: 978–0–314–19496–1

To "Punky"

*

PREFACE

This book is designed to be a succinct exposition of substantive criminal law to which a troubled student can turn for reliable guidance. The troubled student whom I have endeavored to guide is one who finds himself in that situation in spite of his diligent effort to succeed. I have made no special attempt to aid those students who have not made a substantial effort to master the material during the semester (although candor does compel me to acknowledge that some of these students may use this book, with a few of the brighter ones even passing criminal law because of it.)

The book is also designed to serve the untroubled criminal law student (I usually find at least one or two per class) in two ways. First, for the student who likes to spend most of her study time analyzing cases and/or law review articles, but would like to see a brief textual treatment of each day's assignment, this book provides that treatment. And second, the book provides an overview or perspective to aid the student in synthesizing an entire semester's worth of material.

Although it should go without saying, I'll say it anyway—this book is not a substitute for individual analysis. One who does not develop the capacity to analyze problems will not be saved by this or any other book when he is asked to analyze a problem that neither he nor the book had previously considered.

Teachers of and books about criminal law vary widely in regard to the order in which they present the material. This book is divided into seven parts. Part I develops the purposes of punishment, an understanding of which is essential to the study of criminal law. Part II develops those specific crimes which, in the opinion of the author, need developing. In addition, it analyzes causation and self defense. Part III is concerned with the ingredients of all crimes (mens rea and actus reus), while Part IV discusses special defenses. Part V examines burden of proof and presumptions. Part VI discusses inchoate and group criminality, and Part VII analyzes limitations on the criminal law. Finally, the book concludes with a short perspective on the study of criminal law.

Throughout this book in case citations, the following abbreviations have been employed: C=Commonwealth, D.P.P.=Director of Public Prosecutions, P=People, R=Regina or Rex, S=State, and U.S.=United States. The American Law Institute's Model Penal Code, which is frequently cited in this book, has been abbreviated M.P.C. Unless otherwise indicated, all M.P.C. citations are to the proposed official draft. Whenever an M.P.C. cite is used, the section will be preceded by the M.P.C. designation (*e.g.*, M.P.C. § 210.6 substitutes aggravating and mitigating circumstances for degrees of murder). Hopefully, this will avoid confusion between references to M.P.C. sections and the frequent internal nutshell section references that are made throughout the book.

VI

PREFACE

Because this is not intended to be a source book, case citations are illustrative rather than exhaustive and secondary sources (other that the M.P.C.) have been intentionally omitted save for those few instances where their inclusion was unavoidable. Without intending to disparage the many outstanding works in the field of criminal law that I have found helpful, I would like to especially note the aid I received from reading LaFave and Scott, *Handbook on Criminal Law*, and Dressler, *Understanding Criminal Law*.

In the forty-five years since I began teaching criminal law, I have received many helpful insights into the criminal law from my colleagues and students. Some of these insights are in this book. In addition, I would like to thank the several secretaries and research assistants who at one time or another have aided me in the preparation of the book. Finally, I would like to particularly thank seven research assistants from three generations of law students. The first edition (1975) was enhanced by the efforts of Kathleen C. Barger, Jack Drum and A. W. Turner, Jr. Joanna G. Hansen and Timothy C. Holm contributed significantly to the second edition. For the third edition, I thank Dameron Page and Deborah Stencel. For the fourth edition, I am grateful to William Cross and for the fifth edition I am grateful to Kyle Winter.

A.H.L.

Lubbock, Texas
July 2009

*

OUTLINE

PART II. SPECIFIC CRIMES

PART III.   INGREDIENTS OF A CRIME

PART IV. SPECIAL DEFENSES

TABLE OF CASES

References are to Pages

TABLE OF CASES

TABLE OF CASES

TABLE OF CASES

TABLE OF CASES

*

CRIMINAL LAW

IN A NUTSHELL

FIFTH EDITION

*

PART I

PUNISHMENT

CHAPTER I

PUNISHMENT

§ 1.01 The Distinguishing Feature of the Criminal Law

Before an intelligent study of criminal law can be undertaken, it is necessary to focus on the single characteristic that differentiates it from civil law. This characteristic is punishment.

Generally, in a civil suit, the basic questions are (1) how much, if at all, has defendant injured plaintiff, and (2) what remedy or remedies, if any, are appropriate to compensate plaintiff for his loss. In a criminal case, on the other hand, the questions are (1) to what extent, if at all, has defendant injured society, and (2) what sentence, if any, is necessary to punish defendant for his transgressions.

Since the criminal law seeks to punish rather than to compensate, there should be something about each course of conduct defined as criminal that renders mere compensation to the victim inadequate. This follows from the truism that no human

1

being should be made to suffer if such suffering cannot be justified by a concomitant gain to society.

No rational assessment of the kinds of activity that should be punished can be undertaken without some analysis of the purposes of punishment. Those purposes most frequently mentioned are reformation, restraint, retribution, and deterrence (perhaps more easily remembered as the three "R"s and a "D" of punishment).

§ 1.02 Purposes of Punishment

A.   REFORMATION

Without question, it is desirable for punishment to reform. Certainly, society gains and nobody loses if an individual who has transgressed against society's standards is rehabilitated.

There is, however, serious difference of opinion as to the relative importance of reformation. Some believe that since criminals represent the worst in society, it is unjust to take tax dollars from those they consider more worthy to finance the rehabilitation of those they deem less worthy. Others believe that reformation, while desirable, should be subordinated to other purposes, such as deterrence. See § 1.03A *infra*.

Generally speaking, however, reformation is regarded by criminologists as a worthwhile goal of punishment. The real objection to reformation is simply that it doesn't work. This observation can be supported by the high degree of recidivism among those who have been imprisoned. Moreover, it can be persuasively argued that the very nature of the prison system runs counter to the goal of reformation. One doesn't break a criminal of criminal tendencies by requiring him to associate exclusively with other criminals.

Notwithstanding the above analysis, it would be unfair to dismiss the noble concept of reformation as a total failure. All of us are familiar with instances in which unskilled, uneducated and apparently incorrigible criminals have developed skills in prison which have transformed them into highly useful citizens. Perhaps the real tragedy of the penal system is that this happens so infrequently that when it does occur, we hear about it.

B. RESTRAINT

That some individuals need to be restrained is hardly a debatable proposition. Even the staunchest advocate of reformation would not contend that a convicted unreformed dangerous criminal ought to be without restraints while he is being reformed. As one court put it: "To permit a man of dangerous criminal tendencies to be in a position where he can give indulgence to such propensities would be a folly which no community should suffer itself to commit, any more than it should allow a wild animal to range at will in the city streets." C. v. Ritter, 13 Pa.D. & C. 285, 291 (Oyer and Terminer 1930).

Although the above quotation overstates the case for restraint (people are imprisoned for committing

crimes, not for having "dangerous criminal tendencies"), the thrust of the observation is beyond dispute. There is considerable dispute, however, as to
who should be restrained and for how long. For
example, a persuasive argument could be made that
a community needs more protection from the town
bully who constantly picks fights with members of
the local citizenry than it needs from one who after
years of frustration kills her unfaithful spouse and
promptly confesses in a manner which indicates
considerable remorse. Yet the odds are that the
town bully, if jailed at all, will be at liberty much
earlier than the spouse killer.

Whether (and for how long) imprisonment for
restraint is necessary will depend on the dangerousness manifested by the defendant in perpetrating
his crime. Society needs more physical protection
from armed robbers than embezzlers. Another factor is the amenability *vel non* of the particular
offender to a lesser restraint. For example, a thief
who violates the terms of his probation or an intoxicated driver who continues to drive after the suspension of her driver's license may need to be
incarcerated whereas a thief or driver who adheres
to the terms of the original punishment needs no
further restraint.

An argument against emphasizing restraint as a
purpose of punishment is not directed towards restraint per se, but towards restraint without reformation. This argument suggests that unless restraint is either permanent (life imprisonment
without possibility of parole) or coupled with a

meaningful rehabilitative program, imprisonment will not restrain criminal conduct, but will merely postpone it. Although there is some force to this argument, it cannot justify the total abolition of immediate restraint for the protection of society. It does, however, emphasize the societal value of effective reformation.

C. RETRIBUTION

Unlike restraint, there is some difference of opinion as to the propriety of considering retribution as a legitimate purpose of punishment. Opponents contend that it is barbaric and unfit for a civilized society. Proponents, however, maintain that it is morally right to hate criminals, and to inflict retribution upon them for their misdeeds. Less vigorous proponents of retribution note that in fact people think society should get even with those who commit crimes against it. Thus, regardless of whether retribution is or is not morally justifiable in an ideal world, it is demanded by the citizenry of this world. Furthermore, proponents contend that the availability of institutionalized retribution is necessary to prevent private or personal retribution.

A closely related, if not identical, purpose to retribution is expiation. Rather than focusing upon seeking revenge against the criminal, expiation aims at cleansing or purifying society by removing the criminal from its midst.

Whether or not one believes that retribution and/or expiation are morally justifiable, the evidence seems to show that they are significant factors in allocating punishment. Cliches such as "the criminal owes a debt to society" and "make the punishment fit the crime" are essentially retributive in nature. Perhaps the most realistic hope for those opposed to retributive punishment is not that it be eliminated entirely, but that it not be allowed to become (or remain) the dominant force in punishment, subordinating other goals, such as reformation, to a secondary status.

D. DETERRENCE

(1) Individual Deterrence

The concept of individual deterrence, like reformation, aims at precluding further criminal activity by the particular defendant who is before the court. Unlike reformation, it emphasizes the negative. Specifically, it says to a convicted criminal: "This is what happens to you when you commit a crime. Remember that when you get out of prison." It can be argued that to some extent, this is at cross-purposes with reformation, inasmuch as poor prison conditions are conducive to individual deterrence, but inconsistent with a meaningful rehabilitative program. It is possible, of course, to run a prison which is sufficiently unpleasant to discourage return visits, but which nevertheless has a meaningful rehabilitative program.

(2) General Deterrence

The theory of general deterrence is that punitive sanctions which are imposed upon one convicted criminal will deter others with similar propensities from engaging in such conduct.

Critics of this position maintain that most prospective criminal defendants are unaware of the sentences that courts in fact impose, and that even those that are aware do not tend to be the type of people who carefully calculate possible loss as well as potential gain. Furthermore, there is evidence that factors apart from the law, such as religious indoctrination or peer expectations tend to influence a person's behavior to a greater extent than the criminal law. Finally, opponents of the deterrent theory point to the actual crime rate to show how ineffective deterrence really is. The classic illustration from earlier times is the number of pickpockets who were said to have preyed upon people who had come to watch other pickpockets being hanged.

Proponents of the deterrence theory maintain that prospective criminals have at least a general idea as to how their crimes will be punished and that this knowledge does influence their thinking, at least to some degree. They further contend that the importance of non-legal factors in shaping a person's conduct does not negate the importance of the law but simply suggests that the law is not the only factor governing a person's conduct. Finally, they suggest that the efficacy of the deterrent theory can be measured not by the number of criminals it has failed to deter, but can be measured by the number it has in fact deterred. Specifically, the question is not how many pickpockets exist in spite of the penalty against them, but how many more would there be without such a penalty.

It is unlikely that a clear resolution to the deterrent question can be found due to the absence of a control group. Simply stated, we are not willing to abolish the criminal law in order to ascertain its significance in deterring criminal conduct. The closest thing we have to such an experiment occurred during World War II in Denmark when the Germans arrested the entire Danish police force and substituted a far less effective policing system. There, the rate of at least some crimes increased tenfold. Other data indicate that certainty of punishment is more significant than severity in deterring crime. See Andenaes, *The General Preventive Effects of Punishment,* 114 U.Pa.L.Rev. 949 (1966).

In conclusion, it seems fair to say that the prospect of punishment does deter crime, at least to some degree. Obviously, the more that the crime is calculated, the greater the deterrent potential of punishment. Nevertheless, because of our unwillingness to create a meaningful control group, we cannot precisely calibrate the extent of this deterrent effect.

§ 1.03 Punishment in Practice (Some Hard Cases)

A. CONFLICTING PURPOSES

Occasionally a case will arise in which one purpose of punishment seems to suggest lengthy im-

[handwritten margin notes: "conflicting purposes influence sentencing"]

prisonment, whereas another purpose suggests no imprisonment at all. The resolution of such a conflict will depend upon a judge's assessment of the relative efficacy of the competing purposes.

An illustrative case, R. v. Jones, 115 Can.Crim. Cas.Ann. 273 (Ont.App.1956), involved a thirty-five year old defendant who pleaded guilty to three counts of indecent assault against young girls. Psychiatric testimony suggested "that there [was] not much likelihood of a recurrence of the offence ... and that a prison term [would] be definitely detrimental to the [defendants'] condition." *Id.* at 275. Thus, the court was forced to balance the value of reformation on the one hand with restraint, deterrence, and retribution on the other.

At least three possible alternatives suggest themselves:

First, the court could have imposed substantial sentences such as five years per offense, the sentences to run consecutively. This would have restrained him for fifteen years or until age fifty. Furthermore, to the extent that this type of crime is deterrable, such a sentence would have maximized this value, as well as expressing society's revulsion for this type of crime in the form of retribution or expiation. In fact, none of the judges opted for this alternative. Presumably, this was due to the societal revulsion against taking a man with a previously spotless record who from the evidence appears to be reformable, and turning him into a permanent parasite, languishing in prison with no real hope of ever becoming a useful member of society.

Second, the court could have placed him on probation for a period of time, and imposed a fine sufficiently substantial that he would have been deterred from committing such a crime in the future. This course of action, which commended itself to the trial judge and a dissenting appellate judge (actually they would have imposed a fine only, evidently without probation), has considerable merit. Clearly, it is the punishment most compatible with defendant's rehabilitation. Additionally, a substantial fine for a family man of modest means seems to be an adequate individual deterrent.

Obviously, such a penalty is inadequate for those who believe in retribution and is no more of a deterrent to one who pursues little girls than a prostitute's high price tag is to a man who pursues such women. In addition, such a penalty totally ignores restraint. Although the evidence indicated that defendant was unlikely to repeat such depredations, this would hardly seem to be sufficient assurance to satisfy those of his neighbors with small children.

In defense of this approach, however, it can be argued that retribution is particularly inappropriate when the defendant is mentally unbalanced. By the same token, sex perverts hardly rank high on the list of potential criminals likely to be deterred by punitive sanctions. Failure to restrain the defendant may be a justifiable risk if the court is persuaded that the chances of his ultimately committing another crime are reduced by non-imprisonment.

The third and final possible approach to sentencing (and the one actually adopted by the majority of the Court of Appeal) is to sentence the defendant to a relatively light (in the actual case, six to eighteen months), but active prison term. The court conceded that this would probably be detrimental to his recovery, but concluded that in view of the uncertainty of recovery and the importance of general deterrence, an active sentence was required.

At first glance, this seems like a reasonable enough compromise among the competing punitive purposes. Yet, it may be the worst alternative. First, as the court's opinion concedes, such a prison term is likely to retard the rehabilitative process. Second, when the brevity of his prison term is coupled with his failure to be rehabilitated, the adequacy of his restraint is open to question to an even greater degree than if he had not been sentenced at all. Finally, since criminals of this type tend to be relatively non-deterrable, a six to eighteen month sentence is not likely to have a significant impact upon them.

The real lesson to be derived from *Jones*, however, is not that the Ontario Court of Appeal was wrong, but that decisions regarding punishment are tremendously complex and that all too frequently there is no right answer.

B. NO APPARENT PURPOSE

Even more difficult than a case involving conflicting purposes of punishment is one in which no
punitive purpose is apparent. The classic example of
such a case is R. v. Dudley and Stephens, 15 Cox
Crim.Cas. 624 (Q.B.1884), in which the defendants,
while adrift on a lifeboat about a thousand miles
from land, killed the weakest and sickliest of those
on the boat, and fed upon his body to avoid death
by starvation. The Queen's Bench found that this
act constituted wilful murder and sentenced the
defendants to death, the only penalty then available
for murder. Later, the Crown commuted the sentence to six months imprisonment.

Assuming for the moment that the court was
correct substantively (see § 11.04 *infra*), it remains
to be seen what, if any, punitive purpose was served
by its decision.

Deterrence does not seem to be served. The possibility of execution many months later, contingent
upon being saved and the act being discovered, will
hardly deter one from killing at the very moment he
is about to lose his life. Indeed, the only conceivable
penalty that might deter in this situation would be
death by torture. Yet, the Crown took precisely the
opposite tact in humanely reducing the penalty to
six months imprisonment.

Restraint hardly seems appropriate. While some
may hesitate to ride on a boat with these defendants in the future, there is no reason to believe

that they will be any more dangerous as free citizens than other members of the community.

Similarly, reformation has no place in this case. As the court noted: "It must not be supposed that in refusing to admit temptation to be an excuse for crime it is forgotten how terrible the temptation was; how awful the suffering; how hard in such trials to keep the judgment straight and the conduct pure. We are often compelled to set up standards we cannot reach ourselves, and to lay down rules which we could not ourselves satisfy." *Id.* at 637. Defendants whose only failing is an inability to exceed the moral standards of the Queen's Bench are not particularly good candidates for reformation.

Retribution does not seem apposite either. Quite simply, these are not the kind of defendants upon whom society needs or wants to wreak vengeance. Arguably expiation (the cleansing of crime from society) justifies the penalty. Yet the court never explained why society must be cleansed of conduct in which most of its members would have engaged under similar circumstances. Certainly this is not normally deemed to be the policy of the criminal law.

§ 1.04 Equality—An Unexpressed Theory of Punishment

Cases like *Dudley* and *Jones* which seem inexplicable under the traditional purposes of punishment are substantially more explicable when considered in light of the great Anglo–American tradition of equality. This tradition (another aspect of which is embodied in the Equal Protection clause of the United States Constitution) suggests that there should be some degree of uniformity of treatment for those who commit crimes against society. Of course, to some extent, this concept is contrary to the theory of individualized justice. Nevertheless, both considerations (equality and individualization of justice) are relevant, and a sentence will generally reflect a conscious or subconscious effort on the part of the court and/or legislature to balance these frequently conflicting factors.

If one accepts the Queen's Bench's conclusion that Dudley and Stephens were guilty of wilful murder, equality serves as a rationale for their punishment. Although Dudley and Stephens do not need to be punished for any of the four reasons which generally justify punishment, other wilful murderers do. Because others who commit the same crime need to be punished and since principles of equality suggest substantial uniformity of treatment, Dudley and Stephens must also be punished. Of course, one could counter the logic of this argument by noting with the United States Supreme Court that "things which are different in fact or opinion [need not] be treated in law as though they were the same." Tigner v. Texas, 310 U.S. 141 (1940). Still, one should not be too harsh on a court or legislature for wanting to treat all wilful murderers somewhat equally. Compare Furman v. Georgia, 408 U.S. 238, 306–14 (1972) (concurring opinions of Stewart and White, JJ.) § 1.08 *infra*.

Equality does not always require complete uniformity of punishment. Like any other factor, it is merely one consideration to be balanced against others. Thus, in *Dudley,* the Crown commuted the sentence to six months. Considerations of equality demanded that some punishment be imposed on the adjudged murderers, but since no other reason for punishment was present, six months was thought to be appropriate.

Similarly, the sentence in *Jones* (six to eighteen months) is not really explicable in terms of deterrence and is counter-productive in regard to reformation. Yet when considerations of equality enter the picture (imprisonment is generally required for child molesters, such as this defendant), the prison term makes more sense.

§ **1.05** Compensation

In recent years, several jurisdictions have adopted a more literal "debt to society" approach to criminal liability by requiring convicted criminals to perform uncompensated community service in lieu of or in addition to imprisonment. Unlike imprisonment which costs society money, community service really is calculated to give something back to the society upon which the criminal has transgressed.

A variant of this approach is victim compensation, under which the criminal is required to pay or perform services for his victim. Conditioning a thief's probation on restitution or an assaulter's probation on the payment of medical bills are common illustrations of victim compensation. The Thirteenth Amendment to the Constitution supports compensatory service or payments: "Neither slavery nor involuntary servitude, *except as punishment for crime* whereof the party shall have been duly convicted shall exist within the United States...." (emphasis added).

Obviously an incarcerated defendant is not in a position to perform services or earn money. Consequently, compensatory sentences are not generally imposed in cases requiring substantial imprisonment. Newer methods of restraint, such as intensive probation or even house arrest (complete with electronic controls, such as a bracelet, which sounds an alarm in the police station when the arrestee either removes the bracelet or leaves her home) reduce the necessity for restraint by imprisonment, thereby increasing the opportunity for societal or victim compensation.

Such an approach may well be workable in future cases such as *Jones* or *Dudley* (§ 1.03, *supra*). In a case such as *Jones,* electronically enforced house arrest should adequately restrain the defendant while he is earning money to finance the psychiatric or physical care required by his victims. Defendants such as Dudley and Stephens presumably would not even need to be under house arrest while they atoned for their crime by performing community service or aiding the family of their victim.

§ 1.06 Judicial Discretion in Sentencing

At one time in our Nation's history, judges had virtually unlimited sentencing discretion. Thus, if a robbery statute provided for incarceration of from one to thirty years, it was exclusively within the unfettered discretion of the trial judge to assess the penalty. Although this system had the advantage of allowing maximum sentencing flexibility, it has several disadvantages, including lack of predictability and excessive variation from judge to judge. For these reasons, several States and the Federal Government, in varying degrees, have tightened judicial discretion.

The Federal Government has gone to the other extreme by virtually eliminating judicial discretion. For Federal offenses there is a presumptive sentence which must be given unless there are factors that justify an upward or downward deviation. Even then, the judge can only deviate in accordance with the very limited discretion allowed in each upward or downward category.

Those states that have eliminated discretion vary greatly in how they have done so. Some list specific aggravating and mitigating circumstances. Others require that certain purposes of punishment be taken into account. Some appellate courts seriously monitor the performance of trial judges by regularly reversing sentences thought to be out of line. (E.g. Alaska). Others do not, thereby functionally leaving trial judges pretty close to having unfettered discretion.

§ 1.07 Disproportionality

The Eighth Amendment to the United States Constitution forbids cruel and unusual punishment.

In Weems v. U.S., 217 U.S. 349 (1910), the Supreme Court held that punishment which is cruelly disproportionate to the crime offends this clause. *Weems* so categorized a sentence of fifteen years of hard labor in leg irons for a public official who falsified a minor document.

In recent years, the Court has invoked this principle to invalidate capital punishment when cruelly disproportionate to the crime. The five leading cases are Coker v. Georgia, 433 U.S. 584 (1977) Enmund v. Florida, 458 U.S. 782 (1982), and Atkins v. Virginia, 536 U.S. 304 (2002), Roper v. Simmons, 543 U.S. 551 (2005), and Kennedy v. Louisiana, 128 S.Ct. 2641 (2008)

Coker disallowed the death penalty for rape notwithstanding extremely aggravating circumstances (he raped a 16 year old in the presence of her husband, robbed them both at knifepoint, kidnapped his rape victim, and threatened her with death; all after having escaped from prison while serving three life, two twenty year and one eight year consecutive sentences which had been imposed for the rape and murder of one young woman, and the rape, kidnapping and assault of another) because the crime was not sufficiently serious to warrant the death penalty.

In *Enmund,* the Court held that the death penalty was disproportionately cruel when applied to a minor participant in a felony murder (see § 2.09, *infra*) who defendant neither personally killed, attempted to kill, intended that there be a killing, nor intended that lethal force be employed. Consequently, the death penalty could not be imposed on Enmund, who planned the robbery and drove the getaway car but lacked the requisite homicidal state of mind. *Enmund* does not apply to a major participant in a felony who acts with reckless indifference to human life. Tison v. Arizona, 481 U.S. 137 (1987).

Atkins held that evolving standards of decency are such that it is constitutionally impermissible to sentence a mentally retarded person to death, regardless of the severity of his crime. While agreeing that mental retardation does not negate the defendant's culpability, the Court concluded that it diminishes it to the point that capital punishment is cruel and unusual. In *Simmons*, the Court extended *Atkins* reasoning to those under eighteen, at the time of the crime.

Finally, *Kennedy*, relying on prior decisions, especially *Coker*, held that capital punishment could not be imposed for the crime of rape of a child. Although recognizing that *Coker* had left the question opened, the Court concluded that any crime short of aggravated murder, treason, or activity creating a great risk to many (e.g. air piracy) could not be subject to capital punishment.

Apart from capital cases, the Supreme Court has been extremely reluctant to second-guess State legislatures or judges on the proportionality of their sentences. For example, in Rummel v. Estelle, 445 U.S. 263 (1980), the Court upheld a life imprisonment sentence for a man who had been convicted of his third nonviolent theft offense. Although the amounts obtained from each of his thefts were relatively trivial ($80, $28.36, and $120.75), each was a felony under Texas law. In Hutto v. Davis, 454 U.S. 370 (1982), the Court upheld a forty year sentence for the crimes of possession of nine ounces of marijuana with the intent to sell (20 years) and the sale of three of those ounces (20 additional years). In both cases, the Court emphasized that "successful challenges to the proportionality of particular [noncapital] sentences should be exceedingly rare."

The only successful "exceedingly rare" challenge came in Solem v. Helm, 463 U.S. 277 (1983), decided just one term after *Davis*. *Helm* invalidated a life without parole sentence imposed on a defendant who wrote a no account check for $100. Helm was sentenced so severely because he had six prior felony convictions, including three for burglary and one for a third offense of drunk driving. Although one might have thought that *Rummel* foreclosed Helm's challenge, the Court did not agree. Emphasizing the permanence of Helm's penalty (as opposed to Rummel, who had the probability of parole), the Court refused to allow a penalty whose harshness grossly exceeded the gravity of the offense. Among the factors that the Court deemed relevant were the sentences typically imposed by the jurisdiction at bar on other more serious offenders (*e.g.* murderers, kidnappers, and rapists) and the penalty imposed by other jurisdictions on recidivists who write no account checks.

Any thought that *Helm* might open the floodgates to rethink *Rummel* and *Davis* was dashed in Harmelin v. Michigan, 501 U.S. 957 (1991), wherein the Court upheld a sentence of life without parole for possession of 672 grams of cocaine. Justices Scalia and Rehnquist would have rejected *Helm*'s analysis and read disproportionality analysis out of the Eighth Amendment. Justices Kennedy, O'Connor, and Souter would have retained *Helm*, but applied it sparingly. In their view, Harmelin's offense was sufficiently serious to justify the penalty. Justices White, Blackmun, Marshall, and Stevens dissented.

Finally, in Lockyer v. Andrade, 538 U.S. 63 (2003), the Court considered the constitutionality of California's three strikes law as applied to a petty thief who on two separate occasions stole less than $100 worth of videotapes from K–Mart stores. Although ordinarily each offense would have been a misdemeanor, because of Andrade's prior strikes, each was treated as a felony subject to a life imprisonment with no parole eligibility for twenty-five years, the sentences to run consecutively. Thus, for his two petty thefts, Andrade was compelled to spend a *minimum* of fifty years in prison before he could be considered for parole. The Court found this sentence to be consistent with the *Rummel*, *Helm*, and *Harmelin* line of cases, and therefore constitutionally permissible.

Notwithstanding *Andrade*, states are be free to apply proportionality analysis more strictly than the Supreme Court requires. Some state courts seem willing to do this. See *e.g.* S. v. Hayes, 739 So.2d 301 (La.App.1999).

§ 1.08   Capital Punishment

There are several arguments in favor of and opposed to capital punishment. Advocates of the death penalty contend, among other things, that it is sometimes necessary for restraint, retribution, and/or deterrence.

Unquestionably, death is a superior restraining device to any other punishment, a point vividly demonstrated when a convicted murderer sentenced to life imprisonment escapes and kills again. The principal contrary argument is that the infrequency with which this happens coupled with the low rate of recidivism by murderers in general renders this type of super-restraint unnecessary. Furthermore, the really dangerous murderers could be restrained in super-max prisons, if only we could identify them in advance.

Literal retribution (eye for an eye, etc.) is consistent with capital punishment for murder. In addition to "giving the killer what he deserves," some would argue that society is thereby cleansed or expiated. Those opposed to capital punishment argue either that retribution is an impermissible purpose of punishment or alternatively that this much retribution is unnecessary.

Finally, those favoring the death penalty argue that it is necessary to deter murder. In the usual case, this is probably the weakest argument for capital punishment. Even assuming the calculating criminal, it is difficult to imagine one saying: "I'm willing to risk life imprisonment to kill this person, but I'm not willing to risk death." Perhaps in a few cases, the added deterrence of the death penalty may be meaningful (a classic illustration is the life termer who kills a prison guard).

Abolitionists (those favoring the abolition of the death penalty) contend that far from being a deterrent, capital punishment encourages violent crime. This contention is based on the social approval executions give to killing (*i.e.,* if the state believes in killing people, killing can't be totally wrong). In addition, it is not unheard of for potential killers to be mentally unbalanced with suicidal tendencies. Such persons may subconsciously desire to die, and kill in order to be executed. Although some studies seem to indicate that death deters, other countries which have abolished the death penalty appear to have a lower homicide rate than the United States. Furthermore, on average states in the United States without capital punishment have a lower homicide rate than states with capital punishment.

Perhaps a more telling argument against capital punishment is its finality. An erroneous guilty verdict, and they do occur, with disturbing frequency, cannot be corrected after execution. For example, a recent Illinois study showed that more than half of the death row inmates (14 out of 27) were innocent, causing the Governor to call for a moratorium on the death penalty. Because of this possibility, more procedural safeguards are employed in capital cases than in non-capital cases, thereby rendering them longer and more costly. Furthermore, appellate courts at least appear more apt to reverse convictions when the death penalty is imposed, sometimes making arguably bad law in the process. *See e.g.* P. v. Anderson, 447 P.2d 942 (Cal.1968). Thus, in addition to the possibility of executing an innocent person, capital punishment increases the probability that a guilty one will go free.

Another argument against capital punishment is that its cruelty renders it morally unjustifiable. We do not normally tolerate dismemberment, stockades, or even whipping [See Jackson v. Bishop, 404 F.2d 571 (8th Cir.1968); but see S. v. Cannon, 190 A.2d 514 (Del.1963)] because of their cruelty. Intentionally leading a man to his death after months (or years) on death row is arguably more cruel and barbaric than any of these punishments.

In Furman v. Georgia, 408 U.S. 238 (1972), the United States Supreme Court ruled (5–4) that the death penalty as then administered in most states violated the Eighth Amendment's prohibition against cruel and unusual punishments. The scope of its decision was limited, however, because each member of the majority wrote a separate concurring opinion. Only Justices Brennan and Marshall totally condemned the death penalty. Mr. Justice Douglas rejected the death penalty because it was administered in such a way as to discriminate against unpopular minorities. Justices Stewart and White found that the death penalty was administered so infrequently and so arbitrarily as to lose any punitive value it might otherwise have. This coupled with the fact that the legislative will would not be frustrated if the death penalty were never imposed was enough to render it unconstitutional.

After *Furman,* States desiring to retain the death penalty either made it mandatory for certain offenses (thereby apparently eliminating arbitrariness and infrequency) or provided a series of aggravating and mitigating circumstances, permitting the infliction of death only when the aggravating circumstances outweighed the mitigating ones and warranted the supreme penalty. The Court invalidated the mandatory approach, holding that such automatic imposition of the death penalty constituted cruel and unusual punishment. Woodson v. North Carolina, 428 U.S. 280 (1976). It upheld the "aggravating and mitigating" approach, however. Gregg v. Georgia, 428 U.S. 153 (1976). Notwithstanding *Gregg,* several commentators have argued that the "aggravating and mitigating" approach has not eliminated arbitrariness or discretion. Some State appellate courts attempt to monitor the process by comparing each death sentence with other first degree murder cases that did and did not inflict capital punishment. The Supreme Court, however, does not require such appellate review, Pulley v. Harris, 465 U.S. 37 (1984).

The Supreme Court has insisted that the aggravating circumstances be meaningful. Thus, when

Georgia applied its "outrageously or wantonly vile, horrible, or inhuman" standard to justify imposing the death penalty on a murderer whose murder was not demonstrably more vile than most, the Court reversed the death sentence for want of a meaningful aggravating circumstance. Godfrey v. Georgia, 446 U.S. 420 (1980). The Court has been even more serious about mitigating circumstances, reversing every death sentence in which the State rendered any potentially meaningful mitigation irrelevant. Perhaps the most extreme illustration of this principle was Sumner v. Shuman, 483 U.S. 66 (1987), wherein the Court overturned the death penalty of a man serving life without parole for the murder of a prison guard on the ground that Nevada refused to allow evidence of mitigation in that one narrow situation. And, of course, some circumstances, such as mental retardation, can be sufficiently mitigating to per se preclude the imposition of the death penalty. See § 1.07, *supra*.

Although it once thought otherwise, The Court now allows victim impact evidence to be introduced in death penalty cases. See Payne v. Tennessee, 501 U.S. 808 (1991).

PART II
SPECIFIC CRIMES

CHAPTER II
HOMICIDE

§ 2.01 Introduction

The principal problem facing a student of the law of homicide is ascertaining the degree of criminality that attaches to various types of unlawful killing. At early common law, this was no problem inasmuch as all such homicides were punishable by death. Later, they were divided into murder (the more heinous) and manslaughter. Still later, legislatures divided murder into degrees, and manslaughter into voluntary and involuntary categories. In addition, many states created the separate crime(s) of reckless homicide, negligent homicide, and/or vehicular homicide.

The legal term of art employed to distinguish murder from manslaughter is "malice aforethought." It is important to remember that "malice aforethought" is a legal term of art and is not always used in its ordinary dictionary sense. Specifically, a killing need not be malicious (in the usual sense of the term) nor thought of beforehand in order to qualify as an unlawful killing with "malice aforethought" and therefore murder. To illustrate, in most states, a man who kills his dying, beloved wife upon her request would be guilty of murder, as would a woman who, without thinking, intentionally pushes a boy in the water thereby drowning him.

The kinds of killings which courts have characterized as heinous enough for murder (and therefore with "malice aforethought") are varied. They include:

(1) intentional killings except those that are lawful (for example those committed in self-defense, see Chapter 6 *infra*) or mitigated to manslaughter (for example those committed in the heat of passion, see § 2.04 *infra*);

(2) killings in which the defendant intentionally inflicts serious bodily harm (or in some states, intentionally perpetrates an assault with a deadly weapon) subject to the exceptions noted above (see § 2.03 *infra*);

(3) killings resulting from outrageously reckless conduct (see § 2.08 *infra*);

(4) certain killings arising out of the perpetration of particular felonies (see § 2.09 *infra*).

Degrees of murder are determined exclusively by statute. Thus, one must expect substantial variation from state to state, if indeed a particular state even divides murder into degrees. The most common types of murder generally classified as first degree, however, include those which are premeditated (see § 2.02, *infra*) and those which are perpetrated during the course of certain enumerated and highly dangerous felonies, usually arson, burglary, kidnapping, rape and robbery (see § 2.09 *infra*). If there are only two degrees of murder, as there are in most states, all murders which are not first degree are of course second degree. A few states, however, (*e.g.,* Minnesota, Minn.Stat.Ann. §§ 609.185, 609.19, 609.195), have more than two degrees of murder.

The types of unlawful killings frequently classified as manslaughter include:

(1) a killing in the heat of passion (see § 2.04 *infra*);

(2) certain killings perpetrated in defense of one's person, but under circumstances which preclude self-defense from justifying or excusing the act entirely (see § 6.05 *infra*);

(3) killings caused by reckless (or in some states, grossly negligent) conduct (see § 2.07 *infra*);

(4) certain killings arising out of the perpetration of particular misdemeanors (see § 2.10 *infra*).

Like murder, manslaughter is usually divided into degrees, generally voluntary and involuntary. Where such a division is employed, voluntary manslaughter is frequently used to denote those killings described in (1) and (2) above. Involuntary manslaughter usually includes those homicides described in (3) and (4) above.

Lesser homicides have been created in some states, principally to deal with highway fatalities where juries might be reluctant to convict a driver of a crime as serious as murder or manslaughter (see § 2.07 *infra*).

§ 2.02 Willful, Deliberate, and Premeditated

Frequently, statutes elevate murder to first degree on the basis of its willful, deliberate, and premeditated character. Typical of such statutes is California Penal Code § 189 which provides: "All murder which is perpetrated by means of a destructive device or explosive, knowing use of ammunition designed primarily to penetrate armor, poison, lying in wait, torture, or by any other kind of willful, deliberate, and premeditated killing ... is murder of the first degree...."

"Willful," as used in this type of statute, means a specific intent to kill. Thus, an intent to scare, to wound, or even to cause grievous bodily harm will not suffice. On the other hand a jury is permitted to infer intent from the surrounding circumstances. Thus, if the State proves beyond a reasonable doubt that defendant aimed a loaded revolver at her victim's body and hit her victim in the heart killing him instantly, the jury may (but need not) infer that defendant intended to kill her victim even if defendant contends that she only intended to scare or wound him but was a poor shot.

"Deliberation" is seldom defined separately from the other terms in this type of statute. To the extent that it adds anything, however, it appears to require that the defendant act in a cool state of blood. Thus, when a defendant is dominated by passion or fear, it may be impossible for him to deliberate to the degree necessary to render him a first degree murderer. *E.g.,* Wells v. C., 57 S.E.2d 898 (Va.1950). Decisions can be found, however, where lack of cool deliberation did not preclude an intentional murder from being classified as first degree. *E.g.,* C. v. McAndrews, 430 A.2d 1165 (Pa. 1981).

By far the most difficult of the concepts in this formulation of first degree murder is premeditation. The term itself simply means "thought of beforehand." The real problem lies in ascertaining how much beforehand the thought must have been formulated. The classic judicial language is that the time must be "appreciable." But this could merely mean capable of being appreciated, which can be a matter of seconds. For example, in S. v. Misenheimer, 282 S.E.2d 791 (N.C. 1981), the court held that "some period of time, however short, before the actual killing" will suffice. One court went even further, holding that any intentional killing qualified as a wilful, deliberate, and premeditated killing. See C. v. O'Searo, 352 A.2d 30 (Pa. 1976). In response to *O'Searo*, the Pennsylvania Legislature, which first created the premeditation deliberation formula, now defines "an intentional killing" as first degree murder (although the Legislature [somewhat circularly] defined intentional as wilful, deliberate, and premeditated).

Because decisions such as this tend to obfuscate the difference between first and second degree murder, some jurisdictions have sought to require more meaningful premeditation. The California Supreme Court, for example, has held that for the premeditation element to be satisfied, there must be evidence of planning or motive. Consequently, the court reversed the first degree murder conviction of a man for the apparently unplanned and motiveless brutal murder of his housemate's ten year old daughter. P. v. Anderson, 447 P.2d 942 (Cal.1968). Arizona has insisted that the distinction between premeditated and non-premeditated murders be meaningful in order to avoid a serious constitutional question. S. v. Thompson, 65 P.3d 420 (Ariz. 2003).

Sometimes states have had difficulty deciding how much premeditation to require. For example, the Washington Supreme Court held that a strangulation death was not first degree murder even though the defendant had to hold the victim's neck for several minutes before causing her death. S. v. Bingham, 719 P.2d 109 (Wash.1986). But a couple of years later, the same court held that a man who repeatedly stabbed a taxi driver *could* be guilty of first degree murder on the theory that each additional stab constituted premeditation. S. v. Ollens, 733 P.2d 984 (Wash.1987).

If a killing is by poison or torture, does it also have to be premeditated? Assuming the statute says (as most do) "*other* willful, deliberate, or premeditated killing," one would think that premeditation (or at least intent to kill) would be required, but the courts have not always agreed. For example, in S. v. Johnson, 344 S.E.2d 775 (N.C.1986), the North Carolina Supreme Court held that murder by poisoning was first degree, whether or not it was otherwise wilful, deliberate, or premeditated.

Some authorities have attacked the premeditation test on a more fundamental level. They contend that there is no necessary correlation between premeditation and the need for a relatively severe penalty. The authors of the Model Penal Code, for example, have suggested that one who on the spur of the moment for no particular reason kills somebody has committed a more heinous offense than another who after much brooding decides in favor of a euthanasia type demise for a terminally ill beloved spouse. These authors have concluded, borrowing from the Royal Commission on Capital Punishment, "that there are not in fact two classes of murder but an infinite variety of offenses which shade off by degrees from the most atrocious to the most excusable." Thus, the M.P.C. (M.P.C. § 210.6) opted for abolition of degrees of murder entirely, in favor of a series of aggravating and mitigating circumstances to be employed as factors in assessing punishment. Compare section § 1.08 *supra*. Some States have followed the M.P.C. in abandoning the premeditation/deliberation formula. *E.g.* New Jersey, N.J.S.A. 2C:11–3.

§ 2.03 Intent to Cause Serious Bodily Injury

According to most jurisdictions, one who kills while attempting to inflict serious bodily injury has demonstrated sufficient malice aforethought to be guilty of murder. Where murder is divided into degrees, this type of murder is generally denominated second degree.

Differences of opinion exist as to the definition of serious bodily injury. Some jurisdictions define it as "creat[ing] a substantial risk of death or ... caus[ing] serious, permanent disfigurement, or protracted loss or impairment of the function of any bodily member or organ." 18 Pa.C.S.A. § 2701(a)(1). Others merely require it to "be grave, not trivial.... It is not, however, required that the injuries be such as result in death." Jackson v. S., 323 S.W.2d 442, 443 (Tex.Crim.App.1959). In those jurisdictions adopting the former approach, this category of murder can probably be subsumed under depraved heart murder (§ 2.08 *infra*) inasmuch as one who is found to have intentionally done an act "creat[ing] a substantial risk of death" will most likely be found to have acted with a depraved heart. On the other hand, one can intend to cause non-trivial injury without creating an outrageous risk of death, for example by intending to break another's leg.

A popular variant of the intent to inflict serious bodily injury basis for murder is that based upon assault with a deadly weapon. Under this test, proof beyond a reasonable doubt that death resulted from an assault with a deadly weapon is sufficient to justify a conviction for second degree murder. *E.g.*, S. v. Boyd, 180 S.E.2d 794 (N.C.1971). Inasmuch as a common definition of deadly weapon is "a weapon likely to cause death or serious bodily injury" the principal prosecutorial advantage in employing this rule lies in obviating the necessity to prove that defendant in fact intended to inflict serious injury. As a practical matter, however, it will not normally make much difference since a jury which has found that defendant assaulted another with a deadly weapon is likely also to find that he intended to inflict serious injury.

§ 2.04 Provocation

Under some circumstances, provocation can reduce a killing which would otherwise be murder to voluntary manslaughter. For such a reduction to transpire, two conditions must be satisfied: first, defendant must be so governed by passion that he is unable to reason to the extent necessary to form a deliberate purpose to take a life; and second, the circumstances arousing this passion must be such that a reasonable person would be similarly governed. Occasionally, a court will require the provocative circumstances to be such as would justify a reasonable person in killing. *E.g.*, Girouard v. S., 583 A.2d 718 (Md. 1991). This position has been denounced by most courts and commentators, however, on the grounds that the reasonable person does not kill regardless of how much he is provoked, and that if he would kill under some circumstances, the crime should be excused rather than treated as manslaughter, a serious felony.

Ascertaining whether a particular defendant subjectively killed "in the heat of passion" is not usually a difficult question. Determining whether the provocation was adequate from an objective (reasonable person) vantage point, however, can be extremely difficult. Two criteria must be met: first, the provocative act must have been sufficient to engender such passion in the heart of a reasonable person, and second, there must not have been a sufficient passage of time to create a "cooling off period" for the reasonable person. Some courts hold that the duration of a reasonable "cooling off period" is a question of law to be determined by the court, whereas others permit the jury to make this determination. Compare Peagler v. S., 93 So. 536 (Ala.1922) with P. v. Harris, 134 N.E.2d 315 (Ill. 1956).

A similar dichotomy exists with regard to adequacy of provocation. Some states have categories of provocation known as legally sufficient. If the provocative act does not fall within one of these enumerated categories, it will not mitigate the killing to manslaughter regardless of the passion actually or even reasonably engendered thereby. Some of the more common illustrations of legally sufficient provocation (this varies substantially among states) include adultery, fear, battery, assault, mutual combat, and illegal arrest. Most states that adopt the legally sufficient provocation rule hold that "mere words", however insulting, will not mitigate a killing to manslaughter. Under such a rule, one who kills a provoker, who intentionally called him an s.o.b for the purpose of provoking him and with knowledge that it would provoke him, is guilty of murder, not manslaughter, Freddo v. S., 155 S.W. 170 (Tenn.1913). Some, but not all, jurisdictions do not apply this limitation to informational (e.g. I just raped your wife) as opposed to insulting words. (E.g. You are an s.o.b.). See Toler v. S., 260 S.W. 134 (Tenn. 1924). Because of the difficulty of developing all-encompassing categories of "legally sufficient", some courts have rejected this concept by permitting the jury, as the embodiment of the reasonable man, to rule upon the adequacy of the provocation in all but the clearest cases of inadequate provocation. *E.g.*, P. v. Berry, 556 P.2d 777 (Cal.1976). Even here, however, not any provocation will get the question to the jury. See e.g. P. v. Oropeza, 59 Cal.Rptr.3d 653 (Cal.App. 4 Dist. 2007), holding that ordinary road rage will not justify a manslaughter instruction.

In most jurisdiction, while legally sufficient provocation is necessary to get the case to the jury, it does not guarantee a jury verdict in favor of the defense. The jury still has to determine that in its view the provocation was adequate. Thus, even if the provocation question goes to the jury, the jury can still return a verdict of guilty of murder. There are, however, a few jurisdictions that differ, contending that if the provocation is legally sufficient, a verdict of murder cannot be sustained. See S. v. Thornton, 730 S.W.2d 309 (Tenn. 1987).

A final consideration in this area is the extent to which individual peculiarities are relevant in ascertaining the reasonableness of passion. The tendency of the courts has been to refuse to consider such factors. For example, in Bedder v. D. P. P., [1954] 2 All E.R. 801 (H.L.), where an impotent man killed a prostitute who had jeered at him and kicked him in the private parts upon his inability to perform, the court held that the proper test for determining passion was the effect of the provocative act upon a reasonable man, and not its effect upon a reasonable impotent man.

The M.P.C. takes a slightly different tack with a provision that is a remarkable hybrid of subjectivity and objectivity:

> "Criminal homicide constitutes manslaughter when ... a homicide which would otherwise be murder is committed under the influence of extreme mental or emotional disturbance for which there is reasonable explanation or excuse. The reasonableness of such explanation or excuse shall be determined from the viewpoint of a person in the actor's situation under the circumstances as he believes them to be." M.P.C. § 210.3.

A substantial minority of States have adopted this approach. Two major issues have arisen therein. One is how extreme must the disturbance be. The courts seem clear that it need not be the outermost possible extremity inasmuch as that would be insanity. See S. v. Ott, 686 P.2d 1001

(Ore.1984). The other issue is the reasonableness of the explanation or excuse. Although not quantifiable into a precise rule, it is clear that some extreme and unwarranted jealousies will not suffice. See P. v. Casassa, 404 N.E.2d 1310 (N.Y.1980). On the other hand, cases can be found in which extreme emotional disturbance can get to the jury when common law provocation probably would not have. See P. v. Harris, 740 N.E.2d 227 (N.Y. 2000).

§ 2.05 Assisted Suicide

Although it was a common law crime (punished by forfeiture of estate and an ignominious burial), suicide is not a crime in any jurisdiction. However, assisting suicide is. Some jurisdictions punish assisting suicide as a common law crime. Others punish it by statute. Although under some circumstances, there may be a constitutional right to refuse medical treatment (Cruzan v. Director, Missouri Dep't of Health, 497 U.S. 261 (1990)), there is, as of yet, no general right to assisted suicide (physician or otherwise) even (or perhaps, especially) if the assistant is Dr. Jack Kevorkian. See P. v. Kevorkian, 527 N.W.2d 714 (Mich.1994). See generally Washington v. Glucksberg, 521 U.S. 702 (1997).

Several cases have pushed the line between murder and assisted suicide. The line, fine though it may be in some cases, is whether the defendant actually participated in the final act. Thus, if George gives Sue rope to help her hang herself, he is guilty of assisted suicide (assuming that he gave her the rope with the purpose of facilitating suicide). But if he helps her balance herself so that she can get the rope around her neck, he may be guilty of murder. See P. v. Cleaves, 280 Cal.Rptr. 146 (Cal.App.1991).

§ 2.06 Involuntary Manslaughter

Most unlawful unintentional killings are involuntary manslaughter. Involuntary manslaughter usually requires either recklessness or gross negligence. The basic difference in these terms goes to subjective appreciation. A reckless person is aware of a substantial and unjustifiable risk, and chooses to take it. A grossly negligent person ought to be aware of a substantial and unjustifiable risk. Whether she is or is not aware is immaterial when gross negligence is the standard.

Proponents of objectivity argue that a person who creates a homicidal risk that materializes is dangerous whether he realized it or not. Furthermore, they contend that it is such an unusual case in which a person engaging in such conduct does not appreciate the risk that any marginal utility in a subjective test is outweighed by the temptation to a defendant to falsely claim lack of foresight.

Those supporting pure subjectivity, however, contend that a fabricated claim of lack of foresight is no more likely to be believed than any other false claim. Further, they argue that there is a real difference in culpability between one who in fact recognized a risk and took it anyway as opposed to one who merely should have but did not recognize the risk.

Those jurisdictions which employ an objective test use a variety of epithets to describe the quantum of negligence necessary to constitute manslaughter. Typical of these are "criminal negligence," "gross negligence," and "culpable negligence." About the only certainty of meaning one can ascribe to these epithets is that they require more than ordinary negligence, *i.e.*, more than would be required in a civil case. Undesirable as this lack of certainty may be, it is probably unavoidable. Nobody has yet devised a formula which more precisely describes the degree of negligence necessary for involuntary manslaughter.

Occasionally a court will permit ordinary negligence to suffice for involuntary manslaughter. *E.g.*, S. v. Williams, 484 P.2d 1167 (Wash.App.1971). More frequently, ordinary negligence will suffice under limited circumstances, such as negligent handling of inherently dangerous instrumentalities. See P. v. Sandgren, 98 N.E.2d 460 (N.Y.1951) (vicious dogs). The rationale for this appears to be that ordinary negligence in the handling of dangerous instrumentalities is tantamount to gross negligence.

Jurisdictions applying a subjective test generally employ terms such as "reckless" or "wanton." Whatever term is in fact used, the significant distinguishing facet of subjectivity is that the defendant must have personally appreciated a risk and have chosen to take it anyway. The M.P.C., which requires recklessness for involuntary manslaughter, defines "reckless" as "[a] conscious disregard [of] a substantial and unjustifiable risk.... the risk must be of such a nature and degree that, considering the nature and purpose of the actor's conduct and the circumstances known to him, its disregard involves a gross deviation from the standard of conduct that a law-abiding person would observe in the actor's situation." M.P.C. § 2.02(2)(c).

Not all jurisdictions can be categorized as objective or subjective. Some have not spoken directly to the question. Others employ standard subjective language ("reckless" or "wanton"), eschew standard objective language ("gross negligence" or "criminal negligence"), yet appear to apply an objective test. For example, in C. v. Welansky, 55 N.E.2d 902 (Mass.1944), the Supreme Judicial Court of Massachusetts held that the test for determining manslaughter culpability was "wanton or reckless conduct" and not negligence or gross negligence. *Id.* at 910. Indeed, the court went so far as to say that "[t]here is in Massachusetts at common law no such thing as 'criminal negligence.' " *Id.* at 911. Yet, in defining wanton or reckless conduct, the court said that it "is at once subjective and objective." *Id.* at 910. To illustrate, the court opined that " 'even if a particular defendant is so stupid [or] so heedless ... that in fact he did not realize the grave danger, he cannot escape the imputation of wanton or reckless conduct in his dangerous act or omission, if an ordinary normal man under the same circumstances would have realized the gravity of the danger. A man may be reckless within the meaning of the law although he himself thought he was careful.' "

An important lesson to be derived from *Welansky* is that judges are not bound to ascribe the same meaning to terms as text writers do. Therefore, it is imperative that the student analyze how a court employs particular terminology and not merely accept the terminology it employs.

§ 2.07 Reckless Homicide (Negligent Homicide, Vehicular Homicide)

Some states have adopted a category of homicide less severe than involuntary manslaughter. *E.g.* Michigan M.C.L.A. § 28.557. These homicides, generally denominated "reckless homicide" or "negligent homicide", usually require a lesser quantum of negligence to establish culpability. Sometimes "reckless" or "negligent" homicide is limited to certain types of activity, most frequently the operation of motor vehicles (in which case, the crime may be called "vehicular homicide"). One reason for this crime is the reluctance of juries to convict automobile drivers of manslaughter.

The M.P.C. defines negligent homicide simply as "[c]riminal homicide ... when it is committed negligently." M.P.C. § 210.4. It defines acting negligently as the situation in which one "should be aware of a substantial and unjustifiable risk that [another's death] will result from his conduct. The risk must be of such a nature and degree that the actor's failure to perceive it, considering the nature and purpose of his conduct and the circumstances known to him, involves a gross deviation from the standard of care that a reasonable person would observe in the actor's situation." M.P.C. § 2.02(2)(d).

Jurisdictions that define involuntary manslaughter in subjective terms, like the M.P.C., tend to follow the Code's lead in having a lesser offense of negligence homicide. Negligent homicide, in those jurisdictions, looks a lot like involuntary manslaughter in jurisdictions employing an objective test.

§ 2.08 Depraved Heart Murder

When a death results from outrageously reckless conduct, most courts hold that the requirement of malice aforethought is satisfied. To illustrate, a motorist who drives through the center of a large city at rush hour at 80 m.p.h., or a workman who hurls a brick from the top of a large building into an area where several people are standing is said to have demonstrated by his "depraved heart" sufficient malice to categorize as murder any death caused by his actions. The most significant problems in this area are the degree of outrageousness necessary to render one's heart "depraved," and the extent to which objectivity vis-a-vis subjectivity is determinative of the question.

It is probably not possible to quantify the outrageousness necessary to transform recklessness into malice. Courts rarely talk in terms of percentage figures, such as a 25% chance of death being sufficient and a 15% chance being insufficient. A relevant factor in assessing conduct is the social utility sought to be achieved by defendant. For example, a doctor who performs an operation from which there is a 75% chance that the patient will die, but without which he would surely die within six months, is very unlikely to be convicted of murder if the patient dies. On the other hand, a person who drives wildly through a crowd of people purely for the fun of it is likely to be convicted of murder for a resulting death, even if objectively speaking there was a less than a 20% probability of death occurring. This same driver would be less likely to be convicted of murder if her wild driving were not for fun, but to get her critically ill husband to the hospital.

The arguments in regard to subjectivity versus objectivity are similar to those in regard to involuntary manslaughter, although the arguments favoring subjectivity are somewhat more powerful when a murder conviction is at stake. Although some jurisdictions do permit a conviction of murder for one who was outrageously reckless by the standards of a reasonably prudent person, regardless of whether the defendant realized the magnitude of the risk. See C. v. Malone, 47 A.2d 445 (Pa.1946). Most, however, require that the defendant be subjectively aware of the risk when a murder conviction is at stake. Sometimes, it is not clear which standard the court is applying.

In 1967, England legislatively enacted a subjective test (Criminal Justice Act, 1967, c. 80, § 8), thereby rejecting the objective test that previously had been judicially approved in D.P.P. v. Smith, [1960] 3 All E.R. 161 (H.L.) The M.P.C. also requires that a defendant "consciously disregard" the risk. M.P.C. §§ 2.02(2)(c) and 210.2.

Some jurisdictions will permit a conviction for "depraved heart" murder only when the defendant subjects more than one person to an outrageous risk of death from his depraved conduct. Under this approach (called "universal malice"), an unintentional killing resulting from an extraordinarily outrageous risk to a particular victim (e.g. failure to feed a baby) can be no more than manslaughter. Northington v. S., 413 So.2d 1169 (Ala.Cr.App. 1981). Most jurisdictions do not impose this limitation. C. v. Malone, *supra*. "Depraved heart" murder is usually murder in the second degree.

Many jurisdictions permit second degree murder for extraordinarily reckless drunk driving, but some do not. (compare Pears v. S., 672 P.2d 903 (Alaska App.1983) [allowing such a conviction] with Essex v. C., 322 S.E.2d 216 (Va.1984)). Even cases like *Pears*, require an extraordinary level of recklessness. (Pears had several warnings and near misses before his fatal collision.) But revulsion to drunk driving, especially recidivist drunk driving, may be causing some courts to require less extreme recklessness than was formerly the case. See Jeffries v. S., 169 P.3d 913 (Alaska 2007).

§ 2.09 Felony Murder

At early common law, felony murder was a simple proposition: any death resulting from a felony is murder. Thus a totally unforeseeable death resulting from an apparently non-dangerous felony would be murder. Today most jurisdictions do not apply felony murder this harshly. Rather, the doctrine is usually limited to dangerous felonies, foreseeable deaths, or both.

Frequently, statutes classify felony murder as murder in the first degree when the felony is one of a specifically enumerated group, usually arson, burglary, kidnapping, rape, or robbery. Under such a statute, all other felony murders are second degree. Determining whether a particular felony qualifies for second degree murder (or first degree if a particular jurisdiction doesn't limit first degree murder to the enumerated felonies) can be difficult. Some jurisdictions impose the limitation that the felony be inherently dangerous, *i.e.* similar to the enumerated felonies. *E.g.*, P. v. Phillips, 414 P.2d 353 (Cal. 1966). Other states demand that the act done during the course of the felony be dangerous. See Jenkins v. S., 230 A.2d 262 (Del.1967). These tests are not synonymous. A felony may be dangerous, but the act which caused death apparently not, such as putting one's hand over the mouth of a rape victim and accidentally suffocating her. On the other hand, a felony may be not inherently dangerous, but the means of committing it extremely dangerous, such as when a person obtains money by the false pretense that he can cure a sick person better than a doctor could.

Besides being dangerous, the felony must also be intentional. Thus, one who recklessly assaults another person (see §§ 5.01,5.02) and in the process kills a third person will not be guilty of felony murder. For example, a drunk driver whose car recklessly crashes into another car thereby killing one person and injuring another is guilty of felonious assault on the injured person, but is not guilty of felony murder because he neither intended the killing or the underlying felony. See S. v. Jones, 538 S.E.2d 917 (N.C.2000).

Another limitation usually, but not always, imposed on felony murder is the merger doctrine. Under this doctrine, if the underlying felony merges with the killing, the felony will not suffice for felony murder. The classic example is assault and battery with a deadly weapon. Assault and battery with a deadly weapon is not independent of the killing since all of the elements of this crime (see § 5.03 *infra*) are included in murder (see § 2.03 *supra*). Robbery, on the other hand, is independent of the killing because it includes an element (larceny, see § 7.08 *infra*) which is not an element of murder. Therefore, robbery, unlike assault and battery, does not merge with murder. P. v. Burton, 491 P.2d 793 (Cal.1971). Cases can be found, however, in which the merger doctrine has been extended to burglary where the only reason for the entry being criminal was the intent to commit an assault. *E.g.*, P. v. Wilson, 462 P.2d 22 (Cal.1969). (Burglary is discussed in § 7.11 *infra*). In a jurisdiction which treats a death resulting from a felonious assault as murder (see § 2.03, *supra*), the felony murder doctrine in general, and the merger doctrine in particular, are important only to fix the degree of murder, or to prevent provocation from reducing the murder to manslaughter (see § 2.04, *supra*). Provocation is not usually permitted to negate the malice created by the felony murder doctrine.

Of course, manslaughter, although a dangerous felony, cannot form a basis for felony murder. It would be foolish to reduce a killing to manslaughter because of adequate provocation (see § 2.04 *supra*) and then increase it to murder on a felony murder theory. Even the law isn't this much of an ass.

Some jurisdictions limit felony murder by insisting that the killing actually be perpetrated by the felon or his cohort. Thus, in C. v. Redline, 137 A.2d 472 (Pa.1958), the Supreme Court of Pennsylvania reversed a first degree murder conviction that had been predicated on a police officer's justifiably shooting and killing defendant's cohort to prevent their (defendant's and cohort's) escape from a robbery. The Supreme Court reasoned that the felony murder rule was designed to impose liability on a felon for his own act or that of a cohort, but not for that of a third party who is retarding rather than aiding the commission of the felony. Consequently, the court held that the felony could not be found to be the proximate cause of death.

Presumably, in such a case a defendant could be found guilty of murder if the jury finds that under all circumstances, his conduct was so outrageously reckless as to evidence a "depraved heart" (see § 2.08 *supra*). California, which follows *Redline,* has so held, at least when defendant's conduct involves something more outrageous than mere participation in an armed robbery [Taylor v. Superior Court of

Alameda County, 477 P.2d 131 (Cal.1970), wherein defendant's cohort verbally threatened to use his gun and acted edgy throughout the robbery whereupon the robbery victim shot him]. In such a case, the felony (robbery) would elevate the "depraved heart" murder to murder in the first degree.

Not all states follow *Redline*. For example in P. v. Dekens, 695 N.E.2d 474 (Ill.1998), the Illinois Supreme Court upheld a felony murder conviction on the theory that the felony proximately caused the killing. Two judges dissented: one on the *Redline* ground that neither of the felons did the killing; the other on the ground that the felony murder rule was not intended to protect the lives of felons.

Another factor affecting the scope of the felony murder rule is the time period surrounding the felony upon which liability can be predicated. In one extreme case, a court held that even if defendant hit his victim with a brick and then formed an intent to rob him, he could be convicted of felony murder. C. v. Stelma, 192 A. 906 (Pa.1937). In another case, a court found felony murder when a policeman who had stopped two robbers for speeding two hours, several miles, and one state away from the scene of the robbery was shot to death by one of the robbers. S. v. Metalski, 185 A. 351 (N.J.Err. & App.1936). Most cases are between these extremes. a typical example is P. v. Gladman, 359 N.E.2d 420 (N.Y. 1976), where the court upheld a felony murder conviction for a defendant who had walked a few blocks from the scene of the robbery, but before

reaching a point of safety shot and killed a policeman who was looking for him.

It is difficult to calculate the future of felony
murder. England, where the doctrine began, has
abolished it. The M.P.C. recommends its rejection
except for the purpose of creating a rebuttable
presumption of malice for killings perpetrated during the course of a felony. M.P.C. 210.2. Michigan
has held that all *murders* committed during a felony
are first degree murders, but that a killing perpetrated during the course of a felony that would not
otherwise be murder, does not become murder by
virtue of the felony. P. v. Aaron, 299 N.W.2d 304
(Mich.1980).

Not all states, including those that generally follow the M.P.C. have been willing to reject felony
murder. *See e.g.* NY CLS Penal Law § 125.25(3).
And, recent decisions such as *Dekens* seem to indicate a resurgence in the rule. In most states it is
probably unlikely that many people would be convicted of murder under the felony murder rule, who
did not at least act with a depraved heart. But, it is
not improbably that there will be some.

§ 2.10   Misdemeanor Manslaughter

The misdemeanor manslaughter rule (sometimes
called the unlawful act doctrine because it can be
broad enough to encompass violations of local law
or administrative regulations that do not rise to the
level of misdemeanors as well as certain felonies
which for one reason or another are not included in
the felony murder rule) has a history that is quite

similar to its big brother, the felony murder rule. Like felony murder, it once imposed absolute homicidal liability for a death resulting from an unlawful act. And like felony murder, it has since been subjected to a number of limitations.

One such limitation is the nature of the misdemeanor. Most jurisdictions will not permit an involuntary manslaughter conviction to be predicated upon a strict liability offense (see § 8.04 *infra*) because of the defendant's lack of culpability. In addition, some states require that the misdemeanor be *malum in se* (that is wrong in itself) as opposed to merely *malum prohibitum* (that is wrong merely because the legislature says it is wrong). See S. v. Means, 211 N.W.2d 283 (Iowa 1973). This distinction has been criticized by some courts on the ground that many *malum prohibitum* statutes, such as traffic regulations, are passed to protect the public from serious injury or death. Some of these courts employ the test of whether the statute was designed to protect the public from such a risk. *See e.g.* S. v. Cope, 167 S.E. 456 (N.C.1933).

Another limitation sometimes put on misdemeanor manslaughter is proximate cause. Thus, a driver who non-negligently kills another while unlawfully driving with an expired driver's license will not be guilty of manslaughter because the failure to renew the license did not proximately cause the death. C. v. Williams, 1 A.2d 812 (Pa.Super.1938). On the other hand, a number of cases have sustained manslaughter convictions when a simple assault caused an unanticipated death. *E.g.,* S. v. Frazier, 98

S.W.2d 707 (Mo.1936). The theory (analogous to the tort "take your victim as you find him" rule) seems to be that one who intentionally injures another must assume the risk of even an unforeseeable death. Obviously, these jurisdictions do not apply the "merger" doctrine (see § 2.09 *supra*) to misdemeanor manslaughter.

Some jurisdictions effectively reject the misdemeanor manslaughter rule by holding that in addition to the misdemeanor there must be proof of criminal negligence. *E.g.,* S. v. Strobel, 304 P.2d 606 (Mont.1956). The M.P.C. rejects the misdemeanor manslaughter rule entirely. M.P.C. § 210.3.

It would not, however, be accurate to think of the misdemeanor manslaughter rule as dead. New Jersey, relatively recently, upheld a homicide conviction on evidence that the defendant had procured cocaine for himself and his girlfriend, and she died from it. The court reasoned that his distributing the cocaine to her caused her death. S. v. Ervin, 577 A.2d 1273 (N.J.Super.1990). And, even more recently, the Ohio Supreme Court upheld the prosecution of a woman for involuntary manslaughter for non negligently crossing the centerline (after being rendered unconscious by a heart attack) and causing the death of three people. S. v. Weitbrecht, 715 N.E.2d 167 (Ohio 1999).

CHAPTER III

CAUSATION

§ 3.01 Introduction

Causation problems are not limited to homicide cases. They exist whenever the law requires a particular result as a condition of criminal liability. Thus, in arson, for example, it is not enough to prove that defendant lit a torch intending to burn another's dwelling house and the house in fact burned. The state must also prove that defendant's act caused the burning. If, in the above illustration, defendant had thrown the torch inside the house, but the house was struck by lightning and burned while the torch flickered and died without burning anything, defendant would not be guilty of arson (although he would be guilty of attempted arson, see Chapter XIV *infra*). Because most causation problems do arise in the homicide context, however, these problems will be explored at this time, and the remainder of the chapter will be devoted to such cases.

The usual homicide case does not involve a causation problem. A defendant who intentionally shoots his victim in the heart for the purpose of causing the victim's instant death is guilty of murder when he successfully accomplishes that purpose. Similarly, a defendant who knows that he is creating an unreasonable risk of death to his passenger by driving 90 miles per hour in a 50 mile per hour zone is guilty of at least involuntary manslaughter if his passenger dies instantly in a crash attributable to his excessive speed. Unfortunately, not all cases are so clear. Many times a death is attributable to more than one cause. In such a case, a court must determine whether the manner of death is sufficiently related to the defendant's conduct that the death can be fairly attributed to him. When a court concludes that the death is fairly attributable to the defendant's conduct, it uses the term "proximately caused" to describe that conclusion. *E.g.*, Stephenson v. S., 179 N.E. 633 (Ind.1932). Because the defendant's conduct is a factor in questions of causation, we will consider intentional killings separate from unintentional killings. The causation problems in felony murder and misdemeanor manslaughter cases have been considered elsewhere (§§ 2.09, 2.10 *supra*) and will not be considered in this chapter.

§ 3.02 Intentional Killings

At a minimum, the state must prove simple "but for" causation, *i.e.*, "but for" defendant's act, the victim would not have died at the time and in the manner that he did. One exception to this rule is when two forces simultaneously inflict an injury, each of which, standing alone, would have been instantly fatal. In this situation, it is not true that "but for" defendant's act, the victim would have lived longer than he did. Nevertheless, an intentional act which produces such a result is deemed to be a cause of death.

Although proof of "but for" causation is essential to establish liability, it is not, standing alone, sufficient to establish proximate cause. The real question in determining proximate cause is the extent to which it is justifiable to hold a defendant liable for a death occurring in an unanticipated manner. As an illustration, suppose a defendant shoots at a potential victim intending to kill him but in fact misses. The victim then enters a building (which he otherwise would not have entered) in order to avoid being shot. As he enters, the building explodes (because of a bomb put there by a third person) thereby killing the victim. In such a case the original defendant would not be guilty of murder even though the victim would not have been killed "but for" the original shooting. Unfortunately, the result in other situations is not this clear. When a defendant intends to cause death (or to a lesser extent when she intends to inflict serious injury), the courts tend to hold her liable for the ultimate death unless there is a very clear break in the causal link. For example, A shoots at B intending to kill him, but misses. B, who unbeknown to A had a weak heart, dies of a heart attack. Assuming that "but for" the shot B would not have died of a heart attack at that time, A will be guilty of murder. *Cf.* S. v. Luther, 206 S.E.2d 238 (N.C.1974). Defendant, who intended to kill the victim, was guilty of murder even if the victim's death resulted from the conjunction of the victim's heart disease with the excitement and shock of defendant's assault.

Cases involving intervening causes are somewhat more difficult. When A shoots B, leaving her to die and C comes along and stabs B thereby hastening her death, it is clear that C is guilty of murder (intentionally shortening the life of another). Nevertheless, most courts would also hold A liable, on the ground that at the time of death both wounds were contributing to the life shortening process. If C had decapitated B, it would be harder to hold A responsible for the resulting death. See S. v. Luster, 182 S.E. 427 (S.C.1935). Most likely, C's supervening act would limit A's liability to attempted murder. Even here, however, A might be held liable on the ground that his intent to kill B rendered B unable to defend herself against C, thereby proximately causing her death. *Cf.* Henderson v. Kibbe, 431 U.S. 145 (1977). (Defendants guilty of second degree murder when, after robbing a thoroughly intoxicated man and abandoning him on an unlighted road on a cold night, the man was hit by a truck and killed.)

The "negligent treatment of a wound" cases present substantially the same problem. When A seriously wounds B in an attempt to kill him and B dies from negligent medical treatment, A is guilty of murder. Hall v. S., 159 N.E. 420 (Ind.1928). If the treatment is outrageously negligent, however, and it is clear that the treatment is the primary cause of death, there is some authority holding the defendant not guilty of murder. *E.g.,* R. v. Jordan, 40 Crim.App. 152 (1956).

Another category of case where courts frequently find liability is where the victim in some manner contributes to her own death after the defendant's attack. When the attack was still contributing to the victim's death, courts don't care if the victim's own lack of desire to live contributes to her death. D is still liable. P. v. Brackett, 510 N.E.2d 877 (Ill.1987). Even when the death was a suicide, if it can be fairly said that D drove V to it, courts tend to impose liability. Stephenson v. S., 179 N.E. 633 (Ind.1932).

Obviously, these examples can be multiplied (and doubtless most criminal law professors will do precisely that), but in a book this size, these examples should suffice to demonstrate the bias in favor of homicidal liability for deaths which would not have occurred "but for" the defendant's intentional act. The "but for" must be taken seriously. Thus if there is not evidence that the defendant's reprehensible act caused or accelerated the victim's death, he will not be liable. See Oxendine v. S., 528 A.2d 870 (Del. 1987).

§ 3.03 Unintentional Killings

Courts seem less willing to attribute a victim's death to defendant's wrongful conduct when the defendant does not intend to kill. When the defendant intends to inflict serious injury, but in fact causes death, there is not likely to be a great distinction made in causation terms from an intent to kill case that results in death. When the defendant intends no harm, however, but is merely reckless, grossly negligent, or ordinarily negligent, there is a tendency to carefully scrutinize the circumstances of the death before concluding that they are fairly attributable to the defendant's wrongful conduct.

A good illustration is a modified version of one of the situations presented in § 3.02 *supra*. Assume that A is driving his automobile at 90 miles per hour in a 50 mile per hour zone, and B, his passenger, who unbeknown to A has a weak heart, dies of a heart attack brought on by the fear of an accident which never transpires. Unless A should have reasonably foreseen that his culpably negligent driving would cause a heart attack, a persuasive argument can be made that he should not be guilty of manslaughter. See S. v. Hall, 299 S.E.2d 680 (N.C.App. 1983) (to find proximate cause in a homicide case, one must find that a person of ordinary prudence could have reasonably foreseen that such a result, or some similar injurious result, was *probable* under the facts as they existed).

Of course, this is contrary to the situation in which the killing was intentional, *e.g.* the shooting illustration in § 3.02 *supra*. Nevertheless, since the purpose of criminal law is punishment rather than compensation (§ 1.01 *supra*), there is some reluctance on the part of courts to hold a defendant criminally liable for an unintended and unanticipated death. Some courts, however, have carried this reluctance to an extreme. For example, in C. v.

Root, 170 A.2d 310 (Pa.1961), the court exculpated a defendant automobile highway racer from liability for the death of his opponent occasioned by the opponent's attempt to pass in a highly dangerous manner. The court reasoned that the opponent's reckless act was a sufficiently superceding cause of death that the defendant's original conduct in entering the race was not a substantial factor in producing death. Its opinion emphasized that it was requiring a stricter standard of proximate cause than it would require in a tort case.

Some courts reject *Root* reasoning and would impose liability in that kind of a situation. See S. v. McFadden, 320 N.W.2d 608 (Iowa 1982). Where the defendant's behavior is outrageously reckless, causation principles are arguably closer to intentional killing. (See P. v. Russell, 693 N.E.2d 193 (N.Y. 1998) where the court imposed murder liability on all participants in a gun battle, even though it was unclear which side fired the fatal bullet that killed a passerby.)

§ 3.04 Year and a Day Rule

At common law, death could not be attributed to defendant's wrongful conduct unless it occurred within a year and a day of the conduct. The rationale for this rule was the lack of medical precision in determining cause after such a long period of time, coupled with the very real probability of an intervening cause being responsible for the death. In view of the medical advances of the twentieth century, it can be argued that the year and a day rule is obsolete and should be discarded. Indeed, many jurisdictions have done so. In fact, so many jurisdictions have discarded the rule either by legislation or judicial decision, that the Tennessee Supreme Court felt free to refuse to apply the rule in the context of a murder conviction predicated on the death of a victim fifteen months after being stabbed by the defendant. The defendant argued that changing the rules in his case amounted to a due process violation. But because so many other jurisdictions had rejected the year and a day rule, a closely divided United States Supreme Court concluded that the defendant had not been unfairly surprised. See Rogers v. Tennessee, 532 U.S. 451 (2001). See also § 18.02, *infra*.

CHAPTER IV

RAPE

§ 4.01 The Traditional View

At common law, rape was defined as unlawful sexual intercourse with a woman against her will by force or threat of immediate force. Each of these terms requires some explication.

The term "unlawful" precluded conviction of a husband for forcibly engaging in sexual intercourse with his wife against her will. The victim of a rape had to be female, and the term "sexual intercourse" was limited to penile-vaginal contacts. The slightest penetration of the vulva was sufficient, and when the victim was a virgin, there was no requirement that the hymen be broken. Of course, the emission of semen was not necessary.

The common law excluded from rape, acts of forcible homosexual contact and forcible heterosexual contact with some body cavity other than the vagina (although each of these was, and in most jurisdictions still is, a serious felony sometimes called sodomy). The common law rules also made it impossible for a woman to ever be convicted of rape as a participating first degree principal (see § 15.07 *infra*) even if she forced a man to have intercourse with her at gun point.

Various imprecise terms might be employed to describe the quantum of force necessary for rape. Because rape is such a serious offense, a threat to do very mild injury will not suffice. Perhaps as good a definition as any is that the force or threat of force must be sufficient to overcome any resistance she might make.

The phrase "against her will" means that she must affirmatively resist (at least in the usual situation). Further, the resistance must be substantial. Thus, her "I'd really rather not" will not suffice. See C. v. Berkowitz, 641 A.2d 1161 (Pa.1994). On the other hand, when the force or threat of force is overwhelming, the victim is neither required to risk death or serious injury nor do an obviously useless act. *Cf.* S. v. Rusk, 424 A.2d 720 (Md.1981).

One reason for rape laws requiring substantial resistance is that at early common law, all forms of sexual intercourse outside of marriage were unlawful. Consequently, substantial resistance was required to prove that the rape victim was not an adulteress or fornicatress. See Anne M. Coughlin, *Sex and Guilt*, 84 Va. L. Rev. 1 (1998).

§ 4.02 Statutory Changes

Some states prefer to lump all sexual assaults under one category called "sexual assault." Others, including the M.P.C. (§ 213), still treat penile-vaginal contact differently and more seriously than other forms of forcible sexual contact. Most states and the are gender neutral, allowing for the possibility of female defendants and male victims. The MPC, however, opted to preserve gender discrimination in regard to rape, allowing only females to be victims and only males to be perpetrators. Most jurisdictions allow prosecutions of husbands when the parties are separated. Some, but not the MPC, allow such prosecution even when the parties are living together. New York allows such a prosecution on constitutional grounds. See P. v. Liberta, 474 N.E.2d 567 (N.Y.1984).

Following a provocative article by Susan Estrich, there is some, but not much, tendency to accept a "no means no" rule. 95 Yale L.J. 1087 (1986). Indeed, one state, New Jersey, went further and held that the absence of yes means no unless the defendant has reason to believe that the victim had consented. In re M.T.S., 609 A.2d 1266 (N.J.1992). While other states do not go that far, there is a tendency to treat nonconsensual sexual intercourse as a lesser included offense. See C. v. Berkowitz, 641 A.2d 1161 (Pa.1994).

§ 4.03 Rape by Fraud or Coercion

Whether one can commit rape by fraud depends on the nature of the fraud. Courts classically distinguish fraud in the factum (rape) from fraud in the inducement (no rape). Fraud in the factum occurs when a doctor purports to be examining a victim with a medical instrument that turns out to be the doctor's penis. Fraud in the factum can also occur when a person pretends to be the victim's husband, and, under that pretense, has intercourse with her. Some, but not all, courts apply similar reasoning to one who impersonates the victim's boyfriend. Compare P. v. Hough, 607 N.Y.S.2d 884 (1994), with U.S. v. Hughes, 48 M.J. 214 (1998).

Fraud in the inducement consists of statements like "Sleep with me and I'll get you a part in a movie" uttered by one who has no intention of so acting. In one well known California case, the defendant pretended to be a doctor's representative hired to inject the victim with a drug designed to cure a disease that defendant fraudulently represented she had. Because she knew that she was consenting to sexual intercourse, the court found the fraud to be in the inducement and the defendant not guilty of rape. See Boro v. Superior Ct., 210 Cal.Rptr. 122 (Cal.Dist.Ct.App.1985). Of course, because the victim believed that she was receiving a medical injection, a willing court could have found that she believed she was engaging in an entirely different kind of activity. But the *Boro* court did not see it that way.

Sex by nonphysical coercion was not rape at common law. Some states now punish coercive sexual intercourse. See, *e.g.*, In re M.T.S., 609 A.2d 1266 (N.J.1992). Others seem unsure. See C. v. Mlinarich, 542 A.2d 1335 (Pa.1988) (where an equally divided court affirmed a refusal to convict a defendant, who as guardian for a delinquent girl threatened to have her sent back to reform school if she did not have sex with him). Still others do not. For example, in one case, a high school principal was found not guilty of rape when he obtained sexual intercourse from a student by threatening to not let her graduate unless she complied. See S. v. Thompson, 792 P.2d 1103 (Mont.1990). Fortunately, some states have specific statutes designed to impose liability in cases like *Mlinarich* and *Thompson*.

§ 4.04　Post-Penetration Withdrawal of Consent

Our new millennium has seen a surprisingly large number of cases in which rape is predicated upon a refusal to discontinue sex after the victim, who had originally consented, affirmatively withdraws her consent. The prevailing view seems to be to impose liability in these cases. Indeed, Maryland, which had initially refused to impose liability in such a case, has recently reversed its position, and now imposes liability. See S. v. Baby, 946 A.2d 463 (Md. 2008). In many of these cases (including *Baby),* one could have argued that the original consent was not valid. But where the original consent was ambiguous, but the protests after penetration was clear, it may be easier for the prosecution to rely on withdrawal of consent.

A related issue for those jurisdictions allowing conviction under these circumstances, is how much time the defendant must be given to discontinue the intercourse. The general view seems to be a reasonable time, which can be considerably less than the time necessary to ejaculate. See S. v. Bunyard, 133 P.3d 14 (Kan. 2006).

§ 4.05 Statutory Rape

Non-forcible sexual intercourse with a minor is generally punished as rape, sometimes called "statutory rape." In some states, the victim must be below the age of puberty to be a victim of statutory rape. In most of these states, there is a lesser offense, sometimes called obtaining carnal knowledge of a child, which is applicable to older children, through somewhere between 15 and 18. Some, but not all states require the perpetrator to be a specified number of years older than the victim in order for the activity to be deemed criminal. States vary as to whether prior chastity is a requirement. Mental defectives are frequently protected under this type of statute also.

In most states, statutory rape is a gender neutral crime. In a few states, however, only females can be victims, and only males can be perpetrators. The United States Supreme Court upheld such a statute from California against an equal protection challenge, reasoning that since only females bear the burden of potential pregnancy, it was equitable for only males to bear the burden of potential criminal liability. Michael M. v. Superior Court of Sonoma County, 450 U.S. 464 (1981).

Because only males could be prosecuted, the Court viewed the statute as one favoring females. In fact, the statute discriminates against young women by rendering them legally incapable of consenting to sexual intercourse at the same age as their brothers. Although only men can be convicted of this crime, the triggering event is the legislatively presumed incapacity of teenage girls, but not of teenage boys. Had the Court viewed the statute as one discriminating against women, it might have been less willing to uphold it. See Loewy, *Returned to the Pedestal—The Supreme Court and Gender Classification Cases: 1980 Term* 60 N.C. L. Rev. 87, 97–102 (1981).

"Statutory rape" is generally a strict liability offense (see § 8.04 *infra*). Thus, even an honest and reasonable mistake as to age (or mental capacity) will not serve to exculpate the defendant. For a particularly egregious example, see Garnett v. S., where the defendant, himself a mentally defective person, believed a thirteen year old girl who told him that she was sixteen. 632 A.2d 797 (Md.1993). There is, however, some authority to the contrary. P. v. Hernandez, 393 P.2d 673 (Cal.1964). (See § 8.06 *infra*). Arguably, because sex outside of marriage is now constitutionally protected (See sec. 18.04, *infra*), it is arguable that the Constitution compels the states to recognize an honest and reasonable mistake of age. See Loewy, *Statutory Rape in a Post Lawrence v. Texas World*, 58 SMU L. Rev. 77 (2005). Whether that argument will ultimately prevail, remains to be seen.

CHAPTER V

OTHER CRIMES AGAINST THE PERSON

§ 5.01 Battery

Battery is generally defined as an intentional bodily injury or offensive touching of another. Thus, a man who intentionally punches another in the nose or fondles a woman without her consent is guilty of this offense. In some jurisdictions, criminal negligence (see § 8.01 *infra*) will suffice in lieu of intent for this offense. See Saunders v. S., 345 S.W.2d 899 (Tenn.1961). Also, there are some cases sustaining battery convictions based on violations of the law. However, in most of these cases, the defendant appeared to be in fact criminally negligent [*e.g.,* unlawfully discharging a firearm to frighten children and accidentally hitting one, S. v. Lehman, 155 N.W. 399 (Minn.1915)].

§ 5.02 Assault

Classically, there are two types of assault, encompassing overlapping, but not necessarily identical offenses. One is an attempted battery, that is, a serious effort to commit a battery which fails. The other is intentionally causing another to fear an immediate battery. Thus, if unbeknown to B, A shoots a loaded gun at B's back and misses, he has committed the first type of assault, but not the second. Conversely, if A, for the purpose of frightening B, threatens B with a gun which A knows to be unloaded he is guilty of the second type of assault, but not the first. See Harrod v. S., 499 A.2d 959 (Md.App.1985) Some jurisdictions criminally punish only attempted battery type assaults whereas others punish both. See S. v. Wilson, 346 P.2d 115 (Ore. 1959).

In addition to the classic definitions of assault, some jurisdictions have used assault as a generic term to describe either assault or battery. Thus, a defendant who intentionally injures somebody may be convicted of assault rather than battery.

§ 5.03 Aggravated Assault and Battery

The crimes of assault and battery can be aggravated in several ways. One of the most common means of aggravation is based on intent to commit a more serious crime. Thus, assault or battery with intent to commit murder, mayhem, or rape is generally punished more severely than simple assault or battery. Although one can find an occasional case to the contrary, it usually is essential that the defendant actually intend to commit the more serious crime, and not merely be reckless or even outrageously reckless towards committing it. For example, if A intends to and actually does shoot B within an inch of his heart, he would not be guilty of assault and battery with intent to commit murder. Actually this rule is simply an illustration of the more general rule that an attempt requires a specific intent to commit the attempted crime. (For fuller discussion of this rule, see § 14.02 *infra*). Like other attempts, an assault and battery with intent to commit murder merges with the completed crime so that if the assault successfully culminates in murder, the defendant is not also guilty of assault with intent to commit murder (See § 14.01 *infra*).

Another basis for aggravating an assault or a battery is the means used to perpetrate the offense. The most common illustration is assault with a deadly weapon. Resultant harm is another basis of aggravation. Assault and battery inflicting serious bodily injury is an illustration of this classification. Another frequently recognized aggravating factor is the special status of the victim. An example is assault and battery of a police officer in the performance of his duty. Finally, in some states, assault and battery can be aggravated more severely by a combination of these factors than by any of them standing alone. *E.g.,* N.C.Gen.Stat. §§ 14–32 to 14–34.2. See Loewy, Culpability, Dangerousness and Harm: Balancing the Factors on Which Our Criminal Law Is Predicated, 66 N.C. L. Rev. 283 (1988).

§ 5.04 Mayhem

Although logically mayhem is a form of aggravated battery and is treated as such by some states, *e.g.,* Hawaii, S. v. Sorenson, 359 P.2d 289 (Haw. 1961), and apparently by the M.P.C., see M.P.C. §§ 211.1(2)(a), 210.0(3), the common law and most states treat it as a separate offense. Its essence is permanent dismembering or disabling of another.

At common law mayhem was limited to those injuries which rendered a man less able to fight for the king. Since preserving the king's army was the rationale of the crime, consent of the victim was no defense. Indeed, in such a case, the victim was as guilty as the perpetrator inasmuch as both contributed to the diminution of the king's fighting forces. See S. v. Bass, 120 S.E.2d 580 (N.C.1961).

Modern mayhem statutes are designed to punish the infliction of serious permanent injury. Although definitions vary widely, serious permanent injury to such things as eyes, noses, ears, lips, and limbs are generally covered by these statutes. In addition, dismembering of a sex organ will normally be punishable under a mayhem statute or under a specialized type of mayhem statute, sometimes called malicious castration.

The degree of intent necessary for this offense varies substantially. Of course, intent to maim will suffice. Generally, the more serious intent to kill is also sufficient. Beyond that, there is so much diversity that an attempted capitulation in a nutshell seems unwarranted.

§ 5.05 Kidnapping and Related Offenses

At early common law, kidnapping required a forcible asportation of the victim to another country. Under modern statutes, the asportation need not be this extensive. Jurisdictions vary as to how extensive it must be. One case, P. v. Adams, 192 N.W.2d 19 (Mich.App.1971), held that the asportation of a prison guard from one portion of the prison to another was not sufficient because the asportation did not significantly increase the danger to which he was subjected. Because many violent crimes (e.g. rape, robbery, assault) usually involve some movement of the victim, kidnapping potentially could be superimposed upon all of these crimes. To prevent this, many jurisdictions require the asportation to be substantially greater than that which would normally occur as an incident to the underlying crime. See P. v. Levy, 204 N.E.2d 842 (N.Y.1965).

Some jurisdictions allow restraint (which constituted a misdemeanor called false imprisonment at common law) to suffice for kidnapping. Such jurisdictions have even a harder job of distinguishing restraint or movement inherent in a robbery from the additional serious offense of kidnapping. One jurisdiction, North Carolina, requires greater restraint or movement than is inherent in a robbery, but not all that much greater. (See S. v. Beatty, 495 S.E.2d 367 (N.C.1998), holding that pointing a gun at one robbery victim was not kidnapping, but kicking and tying the hands of another was.)

Kidnapping can be accomplished by fraud as well as by force such as when a man induces a girl into his car ostensibly for some legitimate purpose such as babysitting, but in fact for the purpose of taking her elsewhere to engage in sexual activity. See S. v. Missmer, 435 P.2d 638 (Wash.1967).

Kidnapping requires an intent to act without authority of the law. Thus, a person who takes another from one place to another, believing (however unreasonably) that the law has so authorized him, is not guilty of kidnapping. P. v. Weiss, 12 N.E.2d 514 (N.Y.1938).

Many jurisdictions have different degrees of kidnapping. Kidnapping for ransom usually aggravates the crime. On the other hand, it is usually a lesser form of kidnapping for a parent to kidnap his child in violation of a custody order.

CHAPTER VI

SELF–DEFENSE AND RELATED DEFENSES

§ 6.01 Introduction

Most special defenses to crime, such as insanity, intoxication, necessity, and duress are at least theoretically relevant to all crimes and are therefore presented later (Part IV *infra*). However, self-defense and related defenses (defense of others, defense of property, prevention of crime) are relevant only to crimes against the person (*e.g.,* murder, mayhem, and assault) and will therefore be presented here.

§ 6.02 In General

As a general rule, a person may use whatever force reasonably appears to be necessary, *short of deadly force,* to prevent the immediate unlawful imposition of harm to himself. *E.g.,* S. v. Fair, 211 A.2d 359 (N.J.1965). But see § 6.06 *infra*.

The phrase "reasonably appears to be necessary" is a compromise between "actually is necessary" and "honestly appears to be necessary." Thus, if A threatens to strike B with what appears to be a rock, B is justified in punching A to prevent the battery even though the rock was in fact papier-mache and A's only intent was to scare B. Of course, if the test were "actually is necessary" (which it is not), B would have no defense. On the other hand, if A does not seriously threaten B, but B, because of unusual timidity, honestly but unreasonably believes that he is in danger from A, B's punching A would not be privileged, and he would be guilty of assault and battery. A few jurisdictions [*e.g.*, Indiana, Gunn v. S., 365 N.E.2d 1234 (Ind. App.1977)] reject this rule and would exculpate a defendant who honestly, albeit objectively unreasonably, acts in self-defense.

Deadly force, that is force likely to inflict death or serious bodily injury, may not normally be employed even when reasonably necessary to prevent injury. For example, B may not shoot A in order to avoid a minor beating. The law deems it better that one suffer minor injury than that another's life be needlessly spent.

Normally, deadly force may be used only when it reasonably appears necessary to prevent immediate death or serious injury [see S. v. Norman, 378 S.E.2d 8 (N.C.1989)], or to prevent the commission of a serious felony (see § 6.09 *infra*) or to apprehend the felon (see § 6.08 *infra*). Some jurisdictions permit the use of deadly force when it is immediately necessary to prevent harm, even if the harm isn't imminent. Compare the majority and dissenting opinions in S. v. Schroeder, 261 N.W.2d 759 (Neb. 1978). In some jurisdictions, when a strong person threatens unspecified harm to a much weaker person, the weaker person may reasonably fear death or serious bodily harm, and may respond with deadly force. See S. v. Wanrow, 559 P.2d 548 (Wash. 1977).

§ 6.03 Battered–Spouse Syndrome

In recent decades, a growing number of self-defense cases have recognized the relevance of battered-spouse syndrome. This is an issue when a spouse or lover (disproportionately often female) kills her spouse or lover after a (or to prevent another) beating. When the battering spouse is in the process of inflicting serious injury (or perhaps death), no special rule is necessary, she has a classic case of self defense. Even then, it may be helpful to the defense to introduce evidence of learned helplessness.

In some cases, the immediate necessity to kill is not readily apparent. Indeed, in some instances, the victim had finished beating his spouse and was sleeping when he was killed. In such cases, jurisdictions that employ strict objectivity in assessing reasonableness will not consider battered-spouse syndrome evidence. See S. v. Norman, 378 S.E.2d 8 (N.C.1989). Other jurisdictions, however, that take a more subjective view of reasonableness have been willing to consider battered spouse evidence in cases where without such evidence, the need for immediately deadly force may not have been apparent. See S. v. Hickson, 630 So.2d 172 (Fla.1993).

§ 6.04 Retreat Rule

The "retreat" rule, which is adopted by many jurisdictions and the M.P.C. [M.P.C. § 3.04(2)(b)(ii)], requires a defendant who can safely retreat to do so before using deadly force. The rationale for this rule is that it is not reasonably necessary to kill when a person can avoid the danger by running away. The rationale for the conflicting "no retreat" rule is that a person should not be required to resort to what some might deem cowardice in order to spare the life of the one who precipitated the difficulty in the first place. Thus, the "retreat" rule might be accurately though pejoratively called the "coward's" rule. On the other hand, it is just as accurate (and pejorative) to describe the "no retreat" rule as the "uncivilized" rule.

When adopting the retreat rule, the M.P.C. acknowledged that it was clearly the minority rule. Today a significant number of jurisdictions adopt the rule, while many others do not. Compare S. v. Jackson, 382 P.2d 229 (Ariz.1963), advocating the "no retreat" rule, with P. v. Russell, 693 N.E.2d 193 (N.Y.1998), advocating the "retreat" rule. *Russell* presents an unusually good look at the virtues (or, I suppose, depending on your philosophical perspective, vices) of the retreat rule. The case involved two groups of shooters at a Brooklyn housing project. Each claimed that the other was the aggressor. It was unclear whose bullet killed the passerby. The Court held that neither side could rely on self defense because whichever side was the non-aggressor was required to take advantage of a safe retreat, and neither side did.

Jurisdictions which follow the "retreat" rule generally subject it to several important limitations. First, it is limited to those occasions upon which the defendant would otherwise be compelled to use deadly force. Thus, a person may defend himself from a non-deadly attack even though the necessity for doing so could have been avoided by running. Indeed, a person may defend himself from even deadly force without retreating, provided that he himself does not plan to use deadly force. For example, if A runs at B with a knife threatening to kill him, B is privileged to manually disarm A rather than take an obviously safe retreat. However, B is not privileged to shoot A.

Another limitation sometimes imposed on the "retreat" rule is that the defendant must *know* that he can retreat in *complete safety*. Unlike normal self-defense rules, this rule is subjective. Even though a reasonable person might have known that he could retreat in complete safety, if this defendant did not know it, he would be under no duty to retreat rather than use deadly force. (Of course, it still must be reasonably necessary to employ this quantum of force apart from the issue of retreat.) In addition, under this limitation, the defendant is not required to calculate the extent of his injury. Unlike the rule that requires a defendant to absorb a minor beating rather than resort to deadly force, a defendant who is murderously attacked need not retreat if he believes that doing so will subject him to even minor injury.

Most jurisdictions employing the "retreat" rule make an exception for an attack in one's own home. The obvious rationale for this exception is that one's home (or "castle") has always been thought of as a person's ultimate bastion of security. In short, there is no place to retreat once one has been forced out of his own home. Courts have varied on the scope and limitation of the "home exception." Attacks in such places as offices and automobiles have rendered conflicting decisions. Also, the effect of the victim/initial attacker's right to be on the premises may affect the scope of the "home exception." However, the prevailing view is that even if both parties live on the premises retreat is not required. Part of the rationale for this is to avoid exacerbating the difficulty that battered spouses face in making their defense. See Weiand v. S., 732 So.2d 1044 (Fla. 1999).

§ 6.05 Imperfect Self–Defense

Imperfect self-defense is a concept which is applicable only when the person claiming self-defense kills the attacker. Its function is to reduce what would otherwise be murder to voluntary manslaughter. Obviously, it is applicable only when, for one reason or another, the defendant cannot succeed with a claim of perfect self-defense. Analytically, imperfect self-defense is akin to "provocation" as a justification for reducing murder to manslaughter (see § 2.04 *supra*). Both proceed on the assumption that the defendant's killing was unlawful, but because of a mitigating circumstance, lacked malice aforethought.

One type of imperfect self-defense occurs when a defendant who non-feloniously precipitated an attack is forced to kill in self-defense. For example, if A punches B in the nose and B retaliates by attempting to kill A with a knife whereupon A in self-defense kills B, A would not have a perfect self-defense since his original battery precipitated the altercation. Accordingly, A would be guilty of manslaughter rather than murder. See S. v. Norris, 279 S.E.2d 570 (N.C.1981). [The M.P.C. in this type of case would allow A to raise a perfect self-defense although, of course, A would still be guilty of the original battery. M.P.C. § 3.04(2)(b).] It should be noted, however, that this defense is not available when the original attack is felonious. For example, suppose A attacks B with a knife. B successfully repels the attack and turns to kill A whereupon A shoots and kills B. A is guilty of murder, not manslaughter. See C. v. Blackman, 285 A.2d 521 (Pa. 1971).

In either of the above cases (non-felonious or felonious attack), it is possible for the aggressor to regain the right of perfect self-defense. To do this, there must be total withdrawal (not merely strategic retreat) from the confrontation, and this withdrawal must be communicated to the other party in such a manner that the other party can perceive it. To illustrate, A attacks B (either feloniously or non-feloniously), B then gets the better of the fight, whereupon A announces that he wants to totally discontinue the fight. A attempts unsuccessfully to get away and finally as a last resort kills B in self-defense. *E.g.,* S. v. Mayberry, 226 S.W.2d 725 (Mo. 1950). There is room for abuse under this rule in that the victim is not around to tell his side of the story as to the communication of good faith total withdrawal. Thus it is understandable that juries sometimes will reject a defendant's argument that he really did totally withdraw from the confrontation. [Indeed, Mayberry was convicted upon retrial. S. v. Mayberry, 272 S.W.2d 236 (Mo.1954).]

Another type of imperfect self-defense occurs when the defendant honestly, but unreasonably, believes that deadly force is necessary to prevent death or grievous bodily harm. See Shuck v. S., 349 A.2d 378 (Md.App.1975) The unreasonableness, of course, renders the resulting killing unlawful [at least in most jurisdictions (see § 6.02 *supra*)], while the honesty of the belief negates malice. Some jurisdictions do not recognize imperfect self-defense in this situation and would condemn this type of killing as murder. *E.g.,* P. v. Manzo, 72 P.2d 119 (Cal.1937).

The M.P.C. has its own version of "imperfect self-defense" although it does not employ that terminology. Rather, it takes the position that the degree of a defendant's guilt ought to depend on culpability as to each element. Thus, a defendant who honestly and unreasonably (*i.e.* negligently) believes that it is necessary to kill could be guilty of negligent homicide. M.P.C. § 3.09(2).

§ 6.06 Defense of Others

At early common law, one was privileged to defend those to whom he stood in a special protectorate position (*e.g.* child, spouse, etc.). Most modern jurisdictions ignore this qualification and allow any citizen to come to the aid of another. The major question dividing jurisdictions today is the scope of the privilege.

Some states hold that an intervenor stands in the shoes of the party on whose behalf the intervention takes place. Other states say that the question is whether the amount of force the intervenor used would have been justified if the circumstances were as he reasonably believed them to be. This dichotomy is only significant when the person being aided is not privileged to use force.

An illustrative case is P. v. Young, 183 N.E.2d 319 (N.Y.1962), in which the defendant reasonably thought that an eighteen year old boy, who in fact was being lawfully arrested by two plainclothes policemen, was being attacked by them. Consequently, he defended the boy and in the course of that defense injured one of the policemen. The court sustained the defendant's conviction of assault on the ground that his right to use force was no greater than the arrestee's right, which of course was nonexistent.

Undoubtedly to encourage greater citizen involvement in such matters, New York legislatively overruled *Young* and provided that "[a] person may . . . use physical force upon another person when and to the extent that he reasonably believes such to be necessary to defend himself or a third person from what he reasonably believes to be the use or imminent use of unlawful physical force by such other person...." N.Y.—McKinney's Consol. Laws of N.Y. Penal Law § 35.15.

§ 6.07 Resisting Unlawful Arrest

Although some cases permit one to employ reasonable non-deadly force to resist an unlawful arrest [*e.g.,* S. v. Lopez, 235 So.2d 394 (La.1970)] and a few even permit deadly force [*e.g.,* S. v. Robertson, 5 S.E.2d 285 (S.C.1939)], most jurisdictions have accepted the M.P.C. position [M.P.C. § 3.04(2)(a)(i)] which outlaws even moderate force when the arrestee knows that a police officer is making the arrest.

There is much to be said in favor of the M.P.C. position. A policeman, who is trained to overcome resistance, is likely to escalate force until the arrestee cannot escape without employing deadly force. In that event serious injury to the policeman, arrestee, or both is probable. Furthermore, because the lawfulness of the arrest depends on information which the policeman has and of which the arrestee may be ignorant, it is not likely that the arrestee would know whether the arrest was lawful or not. Indeed, most arrestees do not even know what constitutes an unlawful arrest. (*Note:* The fact that the arrestee knows he is innocent is not tantamount to knowing that the policeman lacks probable cause to arrest him.) Finally, any rights which the arrestee loses by submission can (at least theoretically) be vindicated in court.

On the other side, the M.P.C. rule is subject to abuse. An unscrupulous policeman could arrest an enemy without any basis whatever, and then add an assault and battery charge when the enemy tries to resist. While such an extreme case may be rare, it is not unthinkable that an otherwise innocent protest demonstrator might be convicted in this manner.

Ordinarily, the unlawfulness of the arrest is relevant even in those jurisdictions adopting the M.P.C. rule. First of all, it precludes aggravating an assault and battery conviction to assault and battery on a police officer in the lawful performance of his duties because making an unlawful arrest is not within the lawful performance of his duties. And second, a defendant under these circumstances cannot be convicted of the additional offense of resisting arrest because that crime presupposes a lawful arrest. See P. v. Curtis, 450 P.2d 33 (Cal.1969).

It should also be noted that whether or not the State adopts the M.P.C. rule, an arrestee may defend against excessive force used to effectuate an arrest in order to protect against physical injury which cannot be rectified by the legal process. This rule is not applicable to an arrestee who knows that submission to arrest will terminate the officer's use of force. See S. v. Mulvihill, 270 A.2d 277 (N.J. 1970).

§ **6.08** **Apprehension of Criminals**

At common law, a police officer could use whatever force reasonably appeared to be necessary to arrest a felon and whatever force, short of deadly force, reasonably appeared to be necessary to arrest a misdemeanant (assuming of course that the arrest was otherwise lawful, a matter discussed at some length in criminal procedure books and courses.) See Sauls v. Hutto, 304 F.Supp. 124 (E.D.La.1969).

This dichotomy has been criticized by the M.P.C. (M.P.C. § 3.07) and others on several grounds. First of all, some felonies are less dangerous than some misdemeanors (e.g., felonious tax fraud vis-a-vis the misdemeanor of drunken driving). Second, it is not always possible for the arresting officer to know whether the crime with which the arrestee will ultimately be charged will be a felony or a misdemeanor. And third, since most (if not all) felonies today are not punishable by death (see §§ 1.06, 1.07 supra), much of the rationale for allowing deadly force in the capture of felons is eliminated.

The M.P.C. would limit the use of deadly force in effectuating an arrest to a policeman (or a private citizen assisting him) who believes that the arrestee used or threatened deadly force in the commission of his crime or that there is a substantial risk that he will cause death or serious bodily harm if not immediately arrested. In addition, the M.P.C. would deny the use of deadly force when there is a substantial risk of injuring bystanders.

Substantially influenced by the M.P.C., the Supreme Court held that the Fourth Amendment precludes the use of deadly force to effectuate the arrest of an apparently unarmed escaping felon unless "the officer has probable cause to believe that the suspect poses a significant threat of death or serious physical injury to the officer or others." Tennessee v. Garner, 471 U.S. 1 (1985). Because this decision was based on the United States Constitution, it is binding on all jurisdictions in the United States.

More recently, the Supreme Court has backtracked a bit from *Garner,* holding that whether deadly force is appropriate depends on balancing a number of factors. Scott v. Harris, 549 U.S. 991 (2006). In *Scott*, the Court upheld as reasonable a deadly (but not in fact fatal) maneuver for forcing the object of a high speed chase off of the road. Even though the plaintiff's original crime was merely speeding, and it was at least plausible that he would have discontinued his highly dangerous driving if the police had given up the chase, the Court found that for the protection of the public, it was permissible to force the plaintiff off the road, resulting in his permanent paraplegia.

Although deadly force ordinarily may not be employed to effectuate the arrest of a misdemeanant or a non-dangerous felon, there are circumstances in which the policeman's right of self-defense will effectively secure the right to use deadly force. For example, A (a policeman) arrests B for throwing litter in a park. B forcibly refuses to submit to arrest. A then uses force to subdue B's resistance. B follows with deadly force, whereupon A, in self-defense, uses deadly force against B. It should be noted that jurisdictions adopting the "retreat" rule

(§ 6.04 *supra*) do not apply it to this type of situation. Thus, a misdemeanant who can outrun a policeman need not fear deadly force (except in a *Scott v. Harris* situation), but a misdemeanant who can out-wrestle a policeman is not so fortunate. This dichotomy is not so anomalous as it appears at first glance in that the resister is manifesting substantially more disrespect for the law than the runner. See Durham v. S., 159 N.E. 145 (Ind.1927).

A private citizen, not acting pursuant to a policeman's orders, may use moderate non-deadly force to effectuate the arrest of a person whom he reasonably believes has committed a crime. He may not, however, use deadly force to apprehend a suspected criminal unless the arrestee has *in fact* committed a felony. Thus, a private citizen who kills a person whom he honestly and reasonably believes to be an escaping felon who cannot be detained in any other way is guilty of at least manslaughter if the victim in fact did not commit a felony. *Cf.* U.S. v. Hillsman, 522 F.2d 454 (7th Cir.1975). Some states go further and permit a private citizen to use deadly force only when the arrestee committed a specified dangerous felony (*e.g.* armed robbery). See C. v. Chermansky, 242 A.2d 237 (Pa.1968). The M.P.C. never permits a private citizen, acting on his own, to use deadly force to effectuate an arrest. M.P.C. § 3.07(2)(b)(ii).

An interesting anomaly flowing from Tennessee v. Garner, *supra,* is that in some states a private citizen may be permitted to use deadly force to prevent the escape of an unarmed burglar (private citizens are not governed by the Fourth Amendment) whereas a policeman under similar circumstances would not be so privileged. See S. v. Clothier, 753 P.2d 1267 (Kan.1988).

§ **6.09** **Protection of Property and Crime Prevention**

Although the right to use force to protect property theoretically is different from the right to forcibly prevent crime, practically speaking they are the same because a person taking property is almost always committing a crime. Once again, the general rule is that a person can use whatever force, short of deadly force, reasonably appears to be necessary to protect the property and/or prevent the crime. See Shepperd v. C., 322 S.W.2d 115 (Ky.1959).

At common law, deadly force was justifiable wherever it reasonably appeared necessary to prevent the commission of a felony. Today, most jurisdictions limit this justification to the prevention of dangerous felonies. *E.g.,* S. v. Nyland, 287 P.2d 345 (Wash.1955).

A person is permitted to use deadly force, however, when reasonably necessary to protect the sanctity of his home from a burglar. But when the owner or occupant of the home knows that the intruder only intends to temporarily use the home (such as to make a phone call or as shelter from a storm), deadly force is not permissible. When the burglar intends only to steal property, jurisdictions are split on whether to allow deadly defensive force. See Gainer v. S., 391 A.2d 856 (Md.App.1978) (does not allow deadly force); Kent v. S., 367 So.2d 508 (Ala. Cr.App.1978) (allows deadly force). Of course even those jurisdictions allowing such force require exhaustion of nondeadly alternatives before resorting to deadly force.

A person is criminally liable for injury or death caused by a trap such as a spring gun. Some jurisdictions exempt from liability those who would have been privileged to use such force if present. *E.g.,* S. v. Childers, 14 N.E.2d 767 (Ohio 1938). The M.P.C. rejects this exemption because of its fortuity and thus its lack of relationship to non-culpability. M.P.C. § 3.06(5). See also P. v. Ceballos, 526 P.2d 241 (Cal.1974).

CHAPTER VII

CRIMES AGAINST PROPERTY

§ 7.01 Introduction

The law of theft as it stands today is explicable if not justifiable because of its historical development. At early common law, larceny (as well as robbery, which is larceny by force) was the only theft crime and it was punishable by death. Judges concerned about the death penalty were naturally reluctant to expand this capital crime. Consequently, certain kinds of thefts which bore striking similarities to larceny were not punished as such. At the same time, other judges, equally concerned about allowing thieves to go free, were holding other kinds of thefts to be larceny even though they bore even closer similarities to the thefts that were not so punished.

Finally, the whole situation was altered by patchwork legislation which attempted to fill in the gaps left by the common law judges. See M.P.C. Tent. Draft 1, pp. 101–106. Most of this chapter is concerned with the law of theft as it now stands after this legislation.

§ 7.02 The Elements of Larceny

A. INTRODUCTION

Larceny can be defined as the trespassory taking and carrying away of the valuable personal property of another with the intent to permanently deprive the person entitled to possession of that possession.

B. TRESPASSORY TAKING

In many respects, this aspect of larceny is the most troublesome (see § 7.03 *infra*). To satisfy this element it is necessary for the thief to take possession from the rightful possessor without his consent. (However, as will be apparent from § 7.03 *infra,* the terms "possession" and "consent" are far from self-defining.) For example, if A pays B $100 today for B's diamond ring which by agreement B is not to deliver to A until next week, B's subsequent failure to deliver the ring would not render her guilty of larceny. See C. v. Tluchak, 70 A.2d 657 (Pa.Super.1950). This is because B has not trespassed on A's possession. Rather, she has simply refused to turn the ring over to A's possession. The difference is that taking something from another which he is entitled to retain is a trespass, but failure to give something to another which he is entitled to receive is not a trespass.

Similarly, if A, knowing that B intends to steal her merchandise, instructs an employee to give B what he wants, B will not be guilty of larceny. See

Topolewski v. S., 109 N.W. 1037 (Wis.1906) A's employee's conduct pursuant to A's orders amounts to consent, thereby exculpating B. If the employee merely shows B where the goods are, however, but neither gives them to B nor gives B permission to take them, B's taking would be without consent and trespassory, thereby justifying a conviction for larceny. See R. v. Egginton, 126 Eng.Rep. 1410 (C.P. 1801).

C. ASPORTATION (CARRYING AWAY)

In addition to the trespassory taking, most jurisdictions require that the property be carried away. Any asportation, however slight, is sufficient. Thus, a pickpocket who moves a wallet six inches prior to being captured will have satisfied this requirement. Adams v. C., 154 S.W. 381 (Ky.1913). The purpose of the asportation requirement is to verify objectively the thief's dominion over the property. Thus, it may be possible to treat starting the engine of a car as sufficient asportation even though the thief had not yet driven the car away. P. v. Alamo, 315 N.E.2d 446 (N.Y.1974). A technical problem can arise where A, seeing B's property on a table, sells it to C who then carries it away himself. Although there is a split of authority, some courts hold this to be larceny by treating C as A's innocent agent thereby attributing C's asportation to A. *E.g.,* S. v. Patton, 271 S.W.2d 560 (Mo.1954). *Contra,* S. v. Laborde, 11 So.2d 404 (La.1942).

D. VALUABLE PERSONAL PROPERTY

Larceny only protects personal property from theft. Thus, the theft of growing crops or trees (which are real property) does not constitute larceny unless they have been severed prior to the theft (which would make them personal property). Adams v. S., 48 So. 795 (Ala.1909). Similarly, at common law it was impossible to steal services such as another's labor. See Chappell v. U.S., 270 F.2d 274 (9th Cir.1959). The M.P.C. (M.P.C. § 223.7) and a few states have rejected this rule, treating the theft of services as larceny. At common law a chose in action could not be stolen; however, today tangible evidence of a chose in action (*e.g.,* a deed or a check) can be the subject of larceny. See P. v. Allen, 446 P.2d 223 (Colo.1968).

Similarly, absent a special statute, one cannot be punished for wrongfully appropriating a trade secret. If one steals the paper upon which the trade secret is printed, however, a larceny conviction can be obtained. *Cf.* P. v. Kunkin, 507 P.2d 1392 (Cal. 1973). Obviously with the advent of the computer age and cyber crimes, such statutes have become essential. Their scope and variety, however, is such that recapitulation in a book this size is impossible. (Some law schools have separate courses dealing with such issues.)

The requirement that the personal property be valuable would not seem to be much of a limitation since valuable only means of the value of one cent or more. Yet at common law, this requirement precluded dogs from being the subject of larceny. See S. v. Arbogast, 57 S.E.2d 715 (W.Va.1950).

The concept of value is significant insofar as degrees of larceny are concerned. In most states, grand larceny, that is, larceny of more than a specified amount (usually between $50.00 and $500.00), is punishable more severely (usually as a felony) than larceny of the smaller amount, called petit larceny. In determining value, scienter is irrelevant. Thus, if A steals a $210 watch, it is no defense to grand larceny that he thought it was worth $190 (assuming, of course, that $200 is the dividing line). See Hedge v. S., 229 S.W. 862 (Tex.Crim.App.1921).

E.   OF ANOTHER

In most cases, the "of another" element seems obvious. Of course a person can't steal from himself. The principle, however, has also been invoked to preclude convicting one partner for stealing from the partnership on the ground that the thieving partner had an interest in that which was taken. *E.g.,* Maloney v. C., 95 S.W.2d 578 (Ky.1936). A few states [*e.g.,* Minnesota, S. v. MacGregor, 279 N.W. 372 (Minn.1938)] and the M.P.C. (M.P.C. § 223.0) reject this rule, reasoning that the thieving partner's interest was not an undivided one. Interspousal thefts were subject to the same difficulty at common law. Since husband and wife were recognized as one, quite naturally neither could steal from the other. Some jurisdictions, deeming this rule a throwback to the days of female subservience, have rejected it. *E.g.,* Fugate v. C., 215 S.W.2d 1004 (Ky.1948). The M.P.C. [M.P.C. § 223.1(4)] has partially rejected it, distinguishing between household goods normally available to both spouses (no theft) and the purely personal property of the other spouse (theft).

Since larceny is a crime against possession, it is possible to steal one's own property from another with a superior possessory interest. For example, if A takes his own car from B, knowing that B has a statutory lien, he may be convicted of larceny. See S. v. Etape, 699 P.2d 532 (Kan.1985). Similarly, a person can be guilty of larceny by stealing property from another thief. This is because the first thief has possessory rights superior to all except the rightful possessor. Therefore, the second thief has trespassed on this right. *E.g.,* Levin v. U.S., 338 F.2d 265 (D.C.Cir.1964).

F.   INTENT TO PERMANENTLY DEPRIVE THE PERSON ENTITLED TO POSSESSION OF THAT POSSESSION

Larceny, being the serious offense that it is, does not concern itself with unauthorized borrowing of property. Rather, it requires that the defendant intend a permanent deprivation. Some courts have held that an intent to subject the property to a substantial risk of loss suffices for this element. *E.g.,* S. v. Smith, 150 S.E.2d 194 (N.C.1966). Consequently, a defendant who without authority "borrows" another's car hoping to win the local demolition derby with it, is guilty of larceny (rather than the less serious statutory offense of unauthorized use of an automobile or "joyriding," which is also a crime in most jurisdictions). Furthermore, he is guilty of larceny whether or not he in fact wrecks the car since the test is his intent at the time of the trespass. On the other hand, if he should form his intent to drive in the demolition derby after his unauthorized taking of the car, he can still be convicted of larceny in most states on the theory that the trespass was a continuing one. See S. v. Boisvert, 236 A.2d 419 (Me.1967).

Intent to pay for property or return equivalent property (other than property for sale for which the defendant is in fact able to pay or substitute equivalent property) will not normally save the defendant from a larceny conviction. *E.g.,* Kelley v. P., 443 P.2d 734 (Colo.1968). To illustrate, A, seeing a car belonging to B with a hundred dollar bill on the front seat, takes the car and the money to the race track intending to return both (with an extra $100 for B's trouble) after winning big at the track. A is not guilty of larceny of the car since he intends to return it (although of course he is guilty of unauthorized use of the car), but he is guilty of larceny of the $100 since (1) he did not intend to return the same hundred dollars that he took and (2) he subjected the hundred dollars to a substantial risk of loss. Even if A in fact were to win $1000 at the race track and in his ecstasy over his good fortune were to accidentally wreck the car, the legal result would be the same—larceny of the money, but not the car.

See Saferite v. S., 93 P.2d 762 (Okla.Crim.App.
1939).

Because a defendant must *intend* to deprive the
person *entitled* to possession of that possession, a
defendant who honestly (albeit wrongly or unreasonably) believes that he is entitled to the property
cannot be guilty of larceny. This "claim of right"
negates the requisite intent. The defense is usually
applied to a person believing himself to be a creditor
who takes the amount of money that he believes is
owed him from the person he believes to be his
debtor. Some jurisdictions require the debt to be
liquidated and others require the defendant to believe that he is legally entitled to collect the debt in
this manner. Still others impose no such limitations.

§ 7.03 Types of Larceny

A. LARCENY BY STEALTH

Larceny by stealth is the most traditional form of
larceny. It occurs where unbeknown to the victim,
the defendant takes and carries away his property
with the requisite larcenous intent.

B. LARCENY BY AN EMPLOYEE
(SERVANT)

Larceny by an employee (or in former days, larceny by a servant) occurs when an employee who has
been given custody of property by an employer
appropriates the property to his own use. At first

glance, the trespass element would appear to be lacking in that the employee presumably rightfully obtained the property and only later decided to misappropriate it. The common law courts, however, would have none of this argument. Rather, they concluded that at all times the employer retained something called "constructive possession" while the employee obtained only "custody." Thus, at the very moment the employee appropriated the property to his own use, he trespassed on the constructive possession of his employer and satisfied the trespass requisite for larceny.

There are two caveats to keep in mind in conjunction with this rule. First, the defendant must really be an employee, that is, an agent with limited power over the disposition of the property. If he has discretion in regard to disposition of the property, as would an investment broker, he would have possession rather than custody of the property and any subsequent misappropriation would not be trespassory. Thus, he would not be guilty of larceny. See Morgan v. C., 47 S.W.2d 543 (Ky.1932).

A second limitation on larceny by an employee (at least at early common law) was that the employer must have given him the property. When a third party, such as a customer, gave the property to the employee, he was said to have obtained possession rather than mere custody. The employer could not retain constructive possession because he never had possession. R. v. Bazeley, 168 Eng.Rep. 517 (Cr.Cas. Res.1799). With one exception (which virtually swallows the rule), this is still the law. The exception is when the employee deposits the property in a place designed for that purpose by the employer, such as a cash box. Thus, when a bank teller gets money from a customer, he has possession of it. But when he deposits the money in a drawer set aside for that purpose, constructive possession returns to the bank. Therefore, if the teller later takes the money from the cash drawer, he has trespassed upon the bank's constructive possession and is guilty of larceny. Nolan v. S., 131 A.2d 851 (Md. 1957). If, however, he intended to steal it at the time he put it in the cash drawer, some courts say possession was never returned to the rightful owner and the defendant is not guilty of larceny. See, C. v. Ryan, 30 N.E. 364 (Mass.1892).

C. LARCENY BY A FINDER

At common law, a person who found lost or mislaid property was guilty of larceny if at the time of the finding he intended to appropriate the property to his own use rather than return it to its rightful owner, at least when knowledge of ownership or reasonable means of ascertainment were available. (At very early common law this rule applied only to mislaid property, on the ground that the possessor of lost property, unlike the possessor of mislaid property, relinquished constructive possession when he lost the property thereby preventing the subsequent taking from being trespassory.) The critical time was the time of the finding. A person who found a wrist watch which he intended to keep, but after a change of heart returned, was guilty of larceny; whereas one who found a watch which he intended to return, but later kept for himself, was not guilty. *E.g.,* Brewer v. S., 125 S.W. 127 (Ark.1910). The M.P.C. reverses this rule and punishes failure to make a reasonable effort to return the property regardless of initial intent (M.P.C. § 223.5).

In most states, failure to register unidentified found property with the proper authority (*e.g.,* a magistrate or town clerk) and/or in some other way publicly disclose the finding (*e.g.,* advertise the fact in a newspaper) is a criminal offense. *E.g.,* Alaska Stat. 11.20.260.

Property delivered by mistake can be the subject of larceny if, but only if, the defendant is aware of the mistake at the time she receives it. See U.S. v. Rogers, 289 F.2d 433 (4th Cir.1961). If she did not discover the mistake until later (*e.g.* upon opening her pay envelope at home), there would be no trespassory taking and no larceny.

D.   LARCENY BY A BAILEE

Early in the development of the common law (1473), the crime of larceny was applied to a bailee who broke open the contents of a bailment and stole them. This case [Carrier's Case, Y.B. Pasch. 13 Edw. 4, f. 9, pl. 5 (Star Ch.)], which was decided without opinion, has been construed to require a "breaking of the bulk" for larceny. The theory is that when the bulk was broken, the bailment terminated, thereby reverting constructive possession to the bailor and rendering the bailee's taking trespassory. Of course, the extraordinary part of this rule is that if the bailee does not break bulk (*i.e.,* steals the whole thing), he is not guilty of larceny.

Modern statutes in virtually all jurisdictions have abrogated the dichotomy suggested by the Carrier's Case. In some states a defendant is guilty of larceny by a bailee whether or not he breaks bulk. In other states thievery by a bailee is punishable as embezzlement (see § 7.04 *infra*).

E. LARCENY BY TRICK

A person who obtains property subject to a known obligation to dispose of it in a particular way, but who at the time of obtaining it intends to misappropriate it, is guilty of larceny if he in fact misappropriates it. To illustrate, in the leading case of R. v. Pear, 168 Eng.Rep. 208 (Cr.Cas.Res.1779), defendant who leased a horse with the intent to sell it (as the jury found) which in fact he did, was convicted of larceny by trick. The theory behind larceny by trick is that because of the trick, the owner retains constructive possession giving the trickster mere custody. Thus, when the trickster misappropriates the property, he trespasses on constructive possession.

It is important to note that it is the misappropriation and not the original taking that is the essential criminal act. Thus, if Pear had returned the horse to its rightful owner, he would not have been guilty of larceny despite his original intent. However, the original wrongful intent is necessary for constructive possession to remain in the owner. Had Pear not formed his wrongful intent until after renting the horse, his subsequent misappropriation would not have been trespassory and he would not have been guilty of larceny by trick. [As to his possible guilt for larceny by a bailee see § 7.03D *supra,* or for embezzlement see § 7.04 *infra*].

Larceny by trick is not established by a misappropriation or nonappropriation of anything other than the property obtained by trick. For example, suppose A gives B fifty dollars upon B's promise to leave the premises and return with B's wrist watch, which A has just purchased. B is not guilty of larceny by trick upon his failure to return (regardless of his original intent) because A intended for B to have the money. [*Note:* if this were all deemed to be part of one face to face transaction, B might be guilty of larceny on yet another theory of constructive possession, see Atkinson v. U.S., 289 Fed. 935 (D.C.Cir.1923)]. But if B tells A that the money is to go to C who will give B the watch to bring to A, B will be guilty of larceny by trick if he never intended to and does not take the money to C. See Bourbonnaise v. S., 248 P.2d 640 (Okl.Cr.App. 1952).

§ 7.04 Embezzlement

Embezzlement (sometimes called fraudulent conversion) is a wholly statutory offense. It was first created in response to R. v. Bazeley, 168 Eng.Rep.

517 (K.B.1799), in which a bank teller, who pocketed money given to him for deposit by a customer, was found not guilty of larceny due to the absence of a trespass.

Embezzlement can be defined as the fraudulent conversion of the property of another by one who has lawful possession of the property and whose fraudulent conversion has been made punishable by the statute. Because embezzlement is wholly statutory, the last phrase of this definition is especially important. If the statute punishes as an embezzler, anybody who fraudulently converts another's property of which he is lawfully possessed, this phrase obviously presents no problem. More frequently, however, statutes define only certain classes of people, typically agents, fiduciaries, public officials (sometimes as a separate crime), attorneys, and the like as those whose defalcations constitute embezzlement. Under such a statute, a finder of property who intended to return it when he found it but subsequently chose to keep it (and thus would be not guilty of larceny at common law, see § 7.03C *supra*) would not be guilty of embezzlement. Similarly, an independent contractor acting as a collection agent for a great number of people with the authority to commingle funds who fails to account for the debts he has collected may or may not be subject to an embezzlement conviction depending on the state court's definition of agent. Compare the majority and dissenting opinions in P. v. Riggins, 132 N.E.2d 519 (Ill.1956).

Although most of the rules applicable to larceny also apply to embezzlement, there are some differences. Since the alleged embezzler is entitled to possess the property, it is obvious that slight asportation does not constitute a deprivation. For example, suppose a fiduciary carries his principal's money home with him one night intending to misappropriate it. If he has a change of heart and brings it back the next day, he has not committed embezzlement. Many jurisdictions, however, deem secretion of property with intent to embezzle sufficient for embezzlement. *E.g.*, S.D. Compiled Laws 22–38–5. One state, California, has held that real property can be the object of embezzlement (unlike larceny). See P. v. Roland, 26 P.2d 517 (Cal.App. 1933). Of course, in such a case, no asportation is required.

The claim of right defense is generally applicable to embezzlement as well as larceny. Just as it nullifies the "trespass" element in larceny, it negates the "fraudulent" element in embezzlement. It can be argued that the defense should have less applicability to embezzlement (at least when the defendant's claim is that he is owed an unliquidated amount) in that the essence of this crime, breach of trust, is present even when the defendant claims he is owed part of the property. *Cf.* S. v. Liliopoulos, 10 P.2d 564 (Wash.1932). Most courts, however, have not adopted this distinction. *E.g.*, Lewis v. P., 60 P.2d 1089 (Colo.1936).

In one instance, it is theoretically possible for larceny and embezzlement to overlap, *i.e.*, when a principal conveys money to a fiduciary who at the time she receives it intends to appropriate the money to her own use. Under the *Pear* decision [§ 7.03E *supra*], the fiduciary, upon her subsequent misappropriation, should be guilty of larceny by trick. Yet, her being in lawful possession would seem to give rise to embezzlement. In this situation, some courts say that the crime is larceny by trick (she had mere custody, not possession). Other courts would say she can be convicted of either crime (but of course not both with cumulative sanctions). See S. v. Griffin, 79 S.E.2d 230 (N.C.1953). Some states avoid the problem by defining possession for purposes of embezzlement broadly enough to include both common law custody and possession, thereby subsuming much of common law larceny under their embezzlement statute.

Embezzlement is generally punished as severely as larceny. Like larceny, it is generally divided into degrees based on the value of property embezzled. In addition, some states treat certain kinds of embezzlers (the kinds, of course, vary from state to state) less severely than others.

§ 7.05 False Pretenses

A. INTRODUCTION

The crime of obtaining property by false pretenses, like embezzlement, originated as a statutory attempt to plug a common law loophole. Obtaining property by false pretenses can be defined as ob-

taining title to property by knowingly or recklessly
making a false representation of a presently existing fact of pecuniary significance which is intended
to and does defraud the victim, thereby causing him
to part with his property. Although the impetus to
make the sort of conduct criminal at common law
never materialized because of the caveat emptor
concept, there was an indiscriminate kind of common law false pretenses called "cheats." "Cheats"
was applicable to those merchants who used false
weights and measures, thereby indiscriminately
cheating the public. This was thought to be very
different from the person who simply made a fool of
another in a one to one transaction. Although it was
once regarded as less serious than larceny, today
obtaining property by false pretenses is usually
punished with the same severity.

B. OBTAINING TITLE TO PROPERTY

The requirement that title be obtained serves to
distinguish this crime from larceny by trick
(§ 7.03E *supra*). To be guilty of larceny by trick, the
thief obtains mere possession (a type of possession
called "custody" so that "constructive possession"
can remain with the defrauded owner) and subsequently disposes of the property. The crime of false
pretenses, on the other hand, requires no subsequent disposition of the property—it is complete
upon obtaining title. Some have thought it anomalous that the greater fraud (obtaining title as opposed to possession) gave rise to the lesser offense

(at least in earlier times), of false pretenses. This dichotomy was explicable if not justifiable by the fact that larceny by trick punishes two wrongs (deceitful obtaining of property and subsequent misappropriation) whereas obtaining property by false pretenses punishes only deceitfully obtaining property.

C. KNOWINGLY OR RECKLESSLY MAKING A FALSE REPRESENTATION

An unintentional false representation will not suffice for this crime. To illustrate, assume that in 1948, A has bet B ten dollars that Thomas Dewey would defeat Harry Truman in that year's presidential election. (Dewey led early in the evening, and one newspaper printed a headline that Dewey had won the election. In fact, Truman won.) If A reads in the newspaper that Dewey won and collects his money from B by relaying that news to him, A would not be guilty of obtaining money by false pretenses. Indeed, negligence will not suffice. Thus, if A's friend C, who A should know has been wrong about such things in the past, tells A that Dewey had won, A's negligent reliance on C's statement in collecting the money from B would not render A guilty.

The most obvious illustration of a knowing false statement would be if A witnessed Dewey's concession statement and falsely told B that Dewey won. A belief short of knowledge will also suffice. Thus, if C tells A that Truman had won, whereupon A, believing this to be probably but not certainly true, tells B that Dewey had won and thereby collects his money, A's belief in the falsity of the statement would render him guilty.

Reckless disregard as to truth or falsity as well as knowledge or belief of falsity will suffice. Hence, if, after the election, A tells B that Dewey won, knowing that he has no information one way or the other on the matter, his obtaining B's ten dollars would be by false pretenses. For a full discussion of this subject see P. v. Marsh, 376 P.2d 300 (Cal.1962).

D.   OF A PRESENTLY EXISTING FACT

Because the false representation must be of a presently existing fact, many jurisdictions will not permit a false promise to do something in the future to satisfy this element. For example, if A buys ten pounds of meat from B promising to pay B twenty dollars next week, A's failure to pay B will not render him guilty of false pretenses, even if he never intended to pay. See R. v. Goodhall, 168 Eng.Rep. 898 (K.B.1821). Some jurisdictions [*e.g.,* California, P. v. Ashley, 267 P.2d 271 (Cal.1954)] and the M.P.C. [M.P.C. § 223.3(a)] would convict A when he never intended to pay, on the theory that his statement was false as to his *present* intention. The traditional view, however, holds that one's intention is not a fact thereby precluding the statement from being false as to a presently existing *fact*. *E.g.,* Chaplin v. U.S., 157 F.2d 697 (D.C.Cir.1946).

The majority rationale (requiring a false statement of a fact rather than of an intention) is based on a revulsion towards debtors' prison, coupled with the inability to determine with certainty whether or not a non-paying debtor ever intended to pay. This rationale has been criticized on the ground that since a false statement of intention will suffice for larceny by trick [recall Pear's being convicted for selling the horse after falsely claiming that he intended to return it, § 7.03E, *supra*]. Although there is surface logic in this argument, the dichotomy usually drawn (false promise o.k. for larceny by trick, but not for false pretenses) is probably sound. In larceny by trick (Pear's case), failure to return the horse is itself pretty good evidence of wrongful intent. Furthermore, even if the jurors should guess wrong and convict somebody of larceny by trick who didn't form the intent to keep the horse until after he rented it, they would not have convicted an innocent person—rather they would have convicted somebody who is probably guilty of statutory embezzlement (§ 7.04 *supra*) or statutory larceny by a bailee (§ 7.03D *supra*), or at very least, one who has wilfully misappropriated another's property. On the other hand, failure to pay what one owes (A's failure to pay B in the meat hypothetical) is no more consistent with an original wrongful intent than with an original rightful intent and a subsequent change of heart. In addition, should the jury guess wrong and convict a person whose original intent was rightful, we would *pro tanto* be returned to the days of debtors' prisons. The M.P.C., which would allow a conviction based on a false statement of intention, attempts to minimize this problem by not allowing the jury to infer such falsity solely from the fact that the promise was not performed (M.P.C. § 223.3).

Even in jurisdictions where false statements of intention do not suffice for false pretenses, bad checks usually do. The theory is that a check is a present representation of the *fact* that the drawer has sufficient funds at the bank to pay the check. *E.g.,* S. v. Davis, 336 P.2d 692 (Idaho 1959). Whether or not a bad check qualifies for false pretenses (it will not when nothing of value is obtained for it), one knowingly issuing it can be convicted under a bad check statute. *E.g.,* West's Ann.Cal.Pen.Code § 47a.

False opinions of value usually do not qualify for false pretenses. This is especially so when the opinion is given in vague terms (*e.g.,* "a great value" or "the best car on the road"). There is some authority, however, for the proposition that a false statement of value given in such a way as to appear to be a statement of fact rather than opinion will qualify for false pretenses. See Herrick v. S., 196 A.2d 101 (Me.1963). The M.P.C. accepts as a basis for false pretenses, false statements of value except for "puffing by statements unlikely to deceive ordinary persons in the group addressed." M.P.C. § 223.3.

There is a split of authority in regard to misstatements of law (*e.g.,* "Buy this car and you won't have to pay property taxes on it for the next two years."). Some courts reason that since everyone is presumed to know the law, a false statement in regard thereto cannot be deceptive. S. v. Edwards, 227 N.W. 495 (Minn.1929). Others hold that the maxim "ignorance of the law is no excuse" was not coined to shield reprehensible defrauders. S. ex rel. Hull v. Larson, 277 N.W. 101 (Wis.1938). The M.P.C. adopts the latter view [M.P.C. § 223.3(a)].

E.   OF PECUNIARY SIGNIFICANCE

The false statement must be of pecuniary significance, or, in the words of some courts, material. Thus, a salesperson in a store who induces another to buy a product by falsely claiming to be a famous person, such as a movie star, would not be guilty of false pretenses. On the other hand, one who obtains a loan by such a claim would be guilty. The difference is that the identity of the salesperson (at least in the usual case) has nothing to do with the value of the product, whereas the identity of the borrower is very important in assessing the wisdom of making a loan.

Sometimes the pecuniary significance of a representation is open to question. For example, assume that a person borrows $500 and for security gives a $2000 car which is in fact encumbered with a $1000 mortgage, but which he knowingly misrepresents as being unencumbered. Some courts would hold this to be a false statement of pecuniary significance if it is established that the loan would not have been made had the true facts been known. However, a persuasive argument can be made to the contrary. Compare majority and dissenting opinions in Nelson v. U.S., 227 F.2d 21 (D.C.Cir.1955).

F.   WHICH IS INTENDED TO AND DOES DEFRAUD THE VICTIM

Because the defendant must intend to defraud, the defense of claim of right would appear to negate this intent (compare §§ 7.02F, 7.04 *supra*). Although most cases so hold, there is some authority to the contrary. The contra authority holds that the fraudulent intent is still present notwithstanding the defendant's belief that his ultimate ends are justifiable. See S. v. Emerson, 259 P.2d 406 (Wash. 1953).

The false statement must actually defraud the victim. For example, if a used car salesman says, "This car has only gone 40,000 miles," and the customer buys it even though he knows the car has gone 80,000 miles, the salesman is not guilty of obtaining property by false pretenses. See S. v. Bohannon, 193 N.W.2d 153 (Neb.1971). Nevertheless, he may be guilty of an attempt to obtain property by false pretenses. See § 14.08 *infra*.

Occasionally courts hold that the misrepresentation must be such as to defraud a reasonable person. This view is usually rejected, on the ground that unreasonable people need special protection from this type of crime. See *e.g.,* Rowe v. S., 51 S.W.2d 505 (Tenn.1932).

§ 7.06 Forgery and Related Offenses

Forgery is the false making or altering of a legally significant instrument with the intent to defraud. Jurisdictions vary as to what instruments are legally significant. The most common instrument to be so included is a check.

When a defendant has insufficient funds in the bank, his writing a check on that bank is not forgery [although, if done intentionally, it is a violation of a bad check statute in practically all jurisdictions, and, if property is obtained thereby, it is usually obtaining property by false pretenses, see § 7.05D *supra*]. Indeed, most jurisdictions would not deem it forgery even if he had no account at all because the instrument would nevertheless be genuine, *i.e.,* exactly what it purports to be: an order to the bank to pay money. See Winston v. Warden, 464 P.2d 30 (Nev.1970). But see In re Clemons, 151 N.E.2d 553 (Ohio 1958).

Claiming a false authority generally will not suffice for forgery, *e.g.,* John Jones without authority signs a check, "John Jones as agent for John Smith." Gilbert v. U.S., 370 U.S. 650 (1962). Fraudulently and materially altering a receipt, invoice, or other similar instrument will suffice, *e.g.,* altering a credit card invoice for three dollars to twenty-three dollars. S. v. Cowley, 439 P.2d 567 (N.M.App.1968). However, changing the figures on a negotiable instrument without also changing the written sum is usually held not to be a material alteration and thus not forgery. *E.g.,* S. v. Nelson, 82 N.W.2d 724 (Iowa 1957).

Forgery is generally punished more severely than the other non-violent theft crimes. The rationale for this appears to be the impact that a forged instrument has on the entire commercial system as well as the impact on the person whose name is forged (even though, absent negligence, that person is not financially liable).

Uttering a forged instrument consists of negotiating or attempting to negotiate an instrument which the defendant knows to be false. Unlike receiving stolen goods (§ 7.07 *infra*), one can be guilty of both forging and uttering the same check. This fact, coupled with there being no petit forgery (at least in most jurisdictions) means that a person who forges and cashes five ten dollar checks can be convicted of ten felonies. See Barker v. Ohio, 328 F.2d 582 (6th Cir.1964).

§ 7.07 Receiving Stolen Goods

Receiving stolen goods can be conceptualized as a kind of aggravated form of accessory after the fact to larceny. Unlike a true accessory after the fact type of crime, however, it is usually punished as severely as larceny (compare § 15.01 *infra*). One person cannot be guilty of stealing and receiving the same item. If he were in fact involved in stealing the item, he would not be guilty of receiving it even if his fellow thieves left it with him exclusively.

To be guilty of receiving stolen goods, the receiver must know or believe that the goods were stolen. It is not enough that a reasonable person would have so believed. Of course, a jury may (though it need not) infer from the fact that a reasonable person would have known or believed that the goods were stolen, that the person on trial in fact had such knowledge or belief. Belief rather than knowledge is sufficient (although some courts do not talk in these terms) because it is rare that anybody will have certain knowledge of a theft. For example, when A in a whisper asks B, a jeweler, if he would like to buy a $300 wrist watch for $25, B does not know that the watch is stolen, but he has a pretty good idea that it is and this belief will suffice for the crime. See, *e.g.,* Samples v. S., 337 P.2d 756 (Okla. Cr.App.1959).

The goods must be received for a dishonest purpose. Thus, when one accepts stolen goods for the purpose of returning them he is not guilty.

Receiving stolen goods is usually divided into degrees on the basis of the amount received (compare larceny § 7.02D *supra*).

§ 7.08 Robbery

Robbery is larceny from a person or in his presence by force or by the threat of immediate force. In a sense, robbery can be thought of as aggravated assault as well as aggravated larceny. It is the presence of the larceny which aggravates the assault and vice versa. The person assaulted, however, need not be the same person from whom the property is taken. For example, A can rob B of his money by threatening to shoot C.

An analytical difficulty surrounding robbery concerns distinguishing it from panhandling. if a big mean looking man says to a frail woman stranger in a no nonsense voice: "Let me have your money," it may be difficult to ascertain whether she acquiesced to his begging or to his threats. The question for the jury is whether or not he obtained the money by threat of force. similarly, one must ascertain when a purse snatcher is guilty of robbery as opposed to larceny from the person (pickpocket). If he takes the purse stealthily, he is thief. if he takes it forcefully, he is a robber. See P. v. Patton, 389 N.E.2d 1174 (Ill.1979). (Compare the issues surrounding use of force in rape. Ch. 4, *supra*).

Some jurisdictions apply the "claim of right" defense to robbery as readily as they do to larceny (compare § 7.02F *supra*). see P. v. Butler, 421 P.2d 703 (Cal.1967). Others do not, however, on the ground that no person can claim a right to collect his debts by force. *E.g.,* P. v. Reid, 508 N.E.2d 661 (N.Y.1987). Even when such a defense is recognized for robbery, it is not a defense to the assault inherent therein. Thus, if A points a gun at B, saying "give me that $100 you owe me or I'll kill you," he is, at least, guilty of assault with a deadly weapon. See P. v. Rosen, 78 P.2d 727 (Cal.1938).

In all other respects, the elements of larceny (§ 7.02 *supra*) are also required for robbery. Degrees of robbery, however, do not normally vary with the value of the property taken. Rather, they vary with the amount of force that is used or threatened. For example, armed robbery and/or robbery in which someone is seriously injured are usually punished more severely than common law robbery. *E.g.,* Minn.Stat.Ann. §§ 609.24, 609.245.

§ 7.09 Extortion (Blackmail)

Extortion (blackmail) is defined in two different ways. Some jurisdictions say that one who makes threats for the purpose of obtaining money or property is an extortionist. *E.g.,* 13 Vt.Stat.Ann. § 1701. Others give the crime a more restrictive definition, saying that to be guilty of extortion the person must actually obtain money or property by means of the threats. *E.g.,* N.Y.—McKinney's Penal Law § 155.05(e). Thus if A threatens B by saying "Give me $1000 or I'll kidnap your child," some courts would convict him of extortion, while others would not convict unless, due to the threat, A actually obtained money from B. [Even in the latter jurisdictions, however, he could be guilty of attempted extortion (see Ch. XIII, *infra*)]. In jurisdictions applying the more restrictive definition, extortion is similar to robbery, differing only in that for extortion the threats need not be of immediate bodily harm. For example, one who obtains money by saying, "Give me $1000 or I'll cut off your ear next week," is an extortionist rather than a robber.

The threats need not be of physical injury or even to do something unlawful. For example, if A says to B, "Give me $1000 or I'll tell your wife of your affair with C," he is an extortionist even though it is not unlawful for A to tell B's wife about the affair. In fact, extortion can be predicated upon the threat to perform a duty which the extortionist is compelled by law to perform. To illustrate, A, a policeman, threatens to arrest B, a thief caught in the act, unless B gives to A all of the money that he stole. S. v. Barts, 38 A.2d 838 (N.J.1944), affirmed 40 A.2d 639 (N.J.Err. & App.1945).

A baseless threat to sue for civil damages may not be enough for extortion on the theory that the courts will ultimately resolve the question and that therefore the victim has not been harmed. See Rendelman v. S., 927 A.2d 468 (Md. App. 2007). But, a threat to file criminal charges, even if well founded, may be a basis for extortion. See S. v. Harrington, 260 A.2d 692 (Vt. 1970)

There are four possible views in regard to the claim of right defense. For example, consider the following: A, a supermarket manager, tells B that she will have him arrested for larceny unless he pays her $50 to compensate her for the $50 worth of merchandise which she claims he has stolen.

The most lenient test invoked is whether A honestly believes that B has taken that much merchandise. Under this test, A merely has to think that B owes her the money to avoid being an extortionist.

A somewhat more stringent test is reasonable belief. To avoid an extortion conviction under this test, A must not only believe that B owes this much money, but that belief must be founded upon circumstances which would cause a reasonable person to so believe. Obviously, the rationale for this additional requirement is to protect innocent people in B's position from being importuned in this manner.

A third and even more stringent test is whether B in fact owes A the money. Under this test, even an honest and reasonable claim of right will not exculpate A if B does not in fact owe that much money.

The fourth and most stringent test rejects claim of right entirely. This view would hold A liable even if B had in fact stolen the property in A's presence. The rationale for this position is that threatened prosecution should not be used as a means of collecting debts. Rather, A's duty is to file a criminal complaint against B. For A to fail to so report upon payment of funds compounds B's original offense (compare § 15.01, *infra*) and subverts justice. In opposition to this view, one can assert persuasively that criminal courts are sufficiently busy without adding the burden of those cases in which the victim can be satisfied simply by being paid, particularly since restitution and a small fine is likely to be the only sentence imposed on the thief anyway. For a discussion of all of these views, see majority and dissenting opinions in P. v. Fichtner, 281 A.D. 159 (N.Y.App.Div.1952), affirmed 114 N.E.2d 212 (N.Y.1953), N.Y.—McKinney's Penal Law § 155.15 (1967).

§ 7.10 Consolidation of Theft Offenses

Because of the similar criminological significance among many of the theft offenses, some states and

the M.P.C. (M.P.C. § 223.1) have consolidated
many of the separate offenses into one crime, frequently called theft. The consolidation states vary
as to which theft crimes are included in this new
omnibus crime. The most inclusive states combine
larceny (all forms), embezzlement, false pretenses,
bad checks, receiving stolen goods, and extortion.
Robbery and forgery are usually recognized as separate and more serious offenses. Extortion is sometimes accorded this same treatment. Bad checks are
sometimes treated separately and less severely than
the omnibus theft crimes.

Where consolidation has occurred, a defendant
usually has the right to a bill of particulars. See,
e.g., Wis.Stat.Ann. 263.32, 971.36. Where this requirement is too stringent, much of the advantage
of consolidation can be abrogated. For example, if
the bill of particulars charges the defendant with
embezzling the property but the evidence discloses
that he purloined it in a larcenous manner, he may
be entitled to an acquittal. On the other hand,
where the requirements for the bill of particulars
are lax, a defendant may be put on trial without any
real understanding of the nature of the charge
against him.

An alternative to substantive consolidation is procedural consolidation. *E.g.,* Iowa Code Ann. § 813.2
R.6. States adopting this form of consolidation retain the independent theft crime nomenclature
("larceny," "embezzlement," etc.) but permit the
prosecutor to join several different theft crimes in
the same indictment. Although this device is some-

what effective in ameliorating the problems of the separate offenses, it does not resolve all of the problems. One reason it does not is that in some jurisdictions the prosecutor must elect at the close of the trial which crime to submit to the jury. If the prosecutor and court (or jury) differ as to the type of theft, the defendant is likely to be acquitted. Even where the prosecutor is permitted to let all counts go to the jury, a hung jury is possible when the jurors cannot agree on the type of theft.

A hybrid (between substantive and procedural) type of consolidation permits conviction for one type of crime even though the evidence establishes another. The most common examples of this are false pretenses statutes which state that a person is guilty of false pretenses even if the evidence establishes that his crime was larceny. So long as false pretenses is punished the same as larceny, this type of statute is capable of effectuating a substantive consolidation.

Canada adopts a variant of this position. Crim. Code of Can. § 592(3). It permits appellate courts to reverse a theft conviction when the evidence discloses a crime at variance with the verdict, and substitute a guilty verdict for the proper crime. Such a procedure might not pass constitutional muster in the United States because "[c]onviction upon a charge not made would be sheer denial of due process." *Cf.* De Jonge v. Oregon, 299 U.S. 353 (1937).

§ 7.11 Burglary

At common law, burglary was defined as the trespassory breaking and entering of the dwelling house of another in the nighttime with the intent to commit a felony. As with larceny (§§ 7.02, 7.03 *supra*), technicalities abound in this crime. For example, the term "breaking" requires the removal of anything blocking entry. Opening a closed but unlocked door has always sufficed for this element, whereas further opening an already partially opened door at one time did not suffice, *e.g.,* Carter v. C., 244 S.W. 321 (Ky.1922), but now usually does, *e.g.,* S. v. Mower, 275 A.2d 584 (Me.1971). Just as larceny has its constructive possession, common law burglary has its constructive breaking. This could be accomplished by fraudulently obtaining entry by means of a ruse (*e.g.,* falsely stating, "Let me in to inspect the house for termites").

Just as the intent to steal in larceny must accompany the trespass, burglary requires the intent to commit a felony to accompany the breaking and entering. Thus a defendant who breaks and enters with the intent only to take a nap in the building is not guilty of burglary even if upon entry he changes his mind and steals something. Conversely, a defendant who breaks and enters with the intent to steal is a burglar, even if after entry he has a change of heart and steals nothing. See P. v. Hill, 429 P.2d 586 (Cal.1967).

Modern burglary statutes are so diverse as to render a thorough analysis or even survey of them impossible in a book of this size. It is significant, however, that in one state or another for one degree of burglary or another (or the lesser statutory offense of breaking and/or entering), practically every one of the elements has been eliminated.

To illustrate, in some states, a breaking without an entry or an entry without a breaking will suffice for some forms of burglary. A store or other such building or even a vehicle sometimes will suffice in lieu of a dwelling house. Daytime burglaries are often punished, though usually less severely than the more traditional nighttime burglaries. The intent to commit a felony has been abrogated for some forms of burglary. Even the trespassory element has been abolished in some states under some circumstances. For example, a person who enters a store which is open to the public, intending at that time to commit a theft, can be guilty of statutory burglary. Probably, the requirement that the premises be that of another has not been abrogated. Even here, however, it is noteworthy that many modern burglary statutes do not mention the term "of another." Thus, it is theoretically possible (though no case has ever so held and hopefully none ever will) that a person who enters his own house to commit a felony (such as tax evasion) could be guilty of burglary.

None of the statutory changes considered individually are irrational. [Why should it matter whether or not a burglar opened something before entry (the common law rationale was that an open door or window was literally an open invitation to a burglar thereby rendering it inappropriate to provide such a negligent homeowner with the protection of the serious crime of burglary)? Don't stores or automobiles need as much protection as homes? Aren't daytime burglaries almost as bad as nighttime burglaries? How do you determine what the defendant's original intent was and is that really important?] Yet when all of these exceptions are taken together, it is apparent that many relatively nonserious offenses are treated as some form of burglary and punished more severely than they ought to be. To illustrate, in some states, it is a more serious offense to break into a car and steal a tape player from it than it would be to steal the entire car (shades of "breaking the bulk doctrine," § 7.03D *supra*).

California, which until recently has upheld burglary in some fairly bizarre cases has recently attempted to limit its scope by holding that entry of a forged check into tube attached to a bank does not constitute burglary of the bank. P. v. Davis, 958 P.2d 1083 (Cal.1998). However, if the forger had brought the check into the bank, he would have been guilty of burglary. Compare kidnapping § 5.05, supra.

The M.P.C. would deem one guilty of burglary "if he enters a building or occupied structure, or separately secured or occupied portion thereof, with purpose to commit a crime therein, unless the premises are at the time open to the public or the actor is licensed or privileged to enter." The crime is upgraded to a more serious felony if "it is perpetrated in the dwelling of another at night" or if the defendant "purposely, knowingly, or recklessly" injures another or attempts to do so or "is armed with explosives or a deadly weapon." M.P.C. § 221.1.

In addition to burglary's role as a crime against real property, it also functions as an inchoate crime, similar to attempt. This role will be discussed in § 14.06A, *infra*.

§ 7.12   Arson and Related Offenses

At common law, arson was defined as the malicious burning of the dwelling house of another. Like murder (ch. 2 *supra*), malice in arson need not mean ill will. An intentional or outrageously reckless burning of another's house is sufficient malice for arson. See R. v. Harris, 15 Cox Crim.Cas. 75 (C.Crim.1882).

Arson, like burglary (§ 7.11 *supra*), developed to protect the security of the home. And, like burglary (as well as many other common law crimes), arson is replete with hairline distinctions. For example, neither discoloration nor scorching will suffice for arson, but the slightest charring of wood (even if flames do not appear) will. *E.g.,* S. v. Pisano, 141 A. 660 (Conn.1928). Somewhat anomalously, blowing up a house is not arson, unless in the course thereof it catches on fire. Even here, the fire must occur while the house is still a house. If the explosion burns merely fragments of what prior to the explosion was a house, the crime is not arson. See Landers v. S., 47 S.W. 1008 (Tex.Cr.App.1898).

As in the case of burglary, much legislative modification has transpired. Buildings other than dwelling houses frequently are protected from burning by some degree of arson or lesser offense. Even personal property is protected under some statutes. Another common statutory innovation is to punish a person for burning his own property to defraud the insurance company (at common law it was not a crime to burn one's house unless it was located in such proximity to other homes as to create a substantial risk to them, in which case the crime was called houseburning).

The M.P.C. (M.P.C. § 220.1) punishes as an arsonist anybody who starts a fire or causes an explosion for the purpose of destroying another's building or occupied structure. It also includes a person who destroys his own property unless he can establish that he did not recklessly endanger another's person or property.

In addition to arson, most states punish the malicious destruction of real or personal property.

PART III
INGREDIENTS OF A CRIME

CHAPTER VIII
MENS REA (INTENT)

§ 8.01 In General

Part II dealt with particular crimes or with problems usually associated with those crimes. The remainder of the book (like Part I) applies to criminal law generally.

The concept of mens rea or intent certainly meets the test of general applicability. It is as basic in principle as a child's familiar exculpatory: "But, I didn't mean to do it." Its rationale is simply that criminal sanctions are not necessary for those who innocently cause harm. As Justice Holmes once pithily put it: "even a dog distinguishes between being stumbled over and being kicked." O. Holmes, *The Common Law,* p. 3.

Although the concept of mens rea is generally accepted, many problems arise in applying the concept to particular cases. Some crimes require a very high degree of intent, whereas others require sub-

129

stantially less. Larceny, for example, requires that the defendant *intentionally* take property to which he *knows* he is not entitled, *intending* to deprive the rightful owner of possession *permanently*. (See § 7.02 *supra*). Negligent homicide, on the other hand, requires only that the defendant *negligently* cause another's death. (See § 2.07 *supra*).

In addition, substantial problems are caused by imprecise terminology. Terms like "specific intent" and "general intent", for example, contribute far more to confusion than to clarity. "Specific intent" is the less difficult of these concepts. It usually refers to a particular state of mind necessary to satisfy an element of an offense. For example, courts frequently say that the intent necessary for first degree (premeditated) murder includes "a specific intent to kill." (See § 2.02 *supra*). Sometimes it means an intent to do something beyond that which is done (*e.g.* assault with intent to commit rape.)

General intent is an extraordinarily esoteric concept. It is usually employed by courts to explain criminal liability when a defendant did not intend to bring about a particular result. When employed in this manner, it is not an analytical tool, but simply an epithet applied to justify a result reached on other grounds. For example, in most jurisdictions, a defendant who kills another with a gun while voluntarily intoxicated to the extent that he is unaware that he even has a gun will be guilty of second degree murder (see § 11.02A *infra*). The real reason for this rule is that the courts deem intoxication so dangerous that one who causes death while voluntarily in that condition ought to be deemed a murderer. The articulated reason for such a result, however, is that second degree murder requires only a "general intent" thereby rendering a killing by a hopelessly intoxicated person second degree murder.

§ 8.02 Model Penal Code Terminology

The M.P.C. rejects traditional terminology, such as "specific intent" and "general intent," contending that there are four separately recognizable states of mind: purposeful, knowing, reckless, and negligent. Paraphrased and simplified, a defendant acts purposely when he consciously desires his conduct to cause a particular result, knowingly when he is aware that his conduct is practically certain to cause a particular result, recklessly when he is aware of a risk that his conduct might cause a particular result, and negligently when he should be aware of a risk that his conduct might cause a particular result. In regard to recklessness and negligence, the M.P.C. also demands that the risk be substantial and unjustifiable. M.P.C. § 2.02. See §§ 2.06–2.08, *supra*.

The M.P.C. also eschews categorizing an entire crime as requiring a particular state of mind. Rather, it prefers to ascribe a state of mind to each element of the crime. It uses the example of rape, for which purpose to effectuate sexual intercourse is generally required, whereas negligence or even less may suffice as to the element of non-consent.

M.P.C. Tent. Draft 4, pp. 123–129. (See §§ 4.01, *supra*, 8.06, *infra*).

In addition to the states of mind recognized by the M.P.C., there is a category of intent sometimes called "willful blindness," which does not quite fit in any of the four classic categories. A willfully blind defendant is one who is aware that there is a high probability that he is committing a crime, but intentionally avoids ascertaining the facts. A classic example is an individual who accepts a large sum of money to transport a package from Mexico to the United States. The transporter is not practically certain that the package contains drugs, but she is aware of the possibility and chooses not to find out. The better view seems to be that this state of mind will be treated as the equivalent of knowledge unless the transporter really believes that she is not transporting drugs. Failure to look, by itself, is not sufficient to constitute willful blindness unless the transporter has reason to believe that she may be carrying drugs. See U.S. v. Jewell, 532 F.2d 697 (9th Cir.1976) (dissenting opinion of Kennedy, J.). One reason this state of mind is treated as the equivalent of knowledge is that D would have transported the package even if she had known it contained drugs. See Alan C. Michaels, *Acceptance: The Missing Mental State*, 71 S. Cal. L. Rev. 953 (1998).

§ 8.03 Transferred Intent

Transferred intent is a convenient legal device which courts employ to justify convicting those who intend to harm one victim, but in fact harm another. To illustrate, assume that A throws a rock at B, but misses her and hits C. Because A intended no harm to C, he is not guilty of a battery against C (at least where criminal negligence will not suffice for a battery, see § 5.01, *supra*) unless his intent to strike B can be transferred to his actual striking of C. Courts have accomplished this by borrowing the tort doctrine of transferred intent and employing it in the criminal context.

Under the criminal doctrine of transferred intent, the intent is deemed to follow the criminal act regardless of who turns out to be the victim. This explanation obviously indulges the fiction that A's criminal animus toward B is transferred to C, resulting in A's guilt of a battery of C. Despite its fictitious nature, the doctrine of transferred intent has been accepted by the courts.

Transferred intent cases are often referred to as "bad aim" cases because of the disproportionate number of firearm and thrown projectile cases decided under the doctrine. Transferred intent also applies, however, when A poisons B's drink which is subsequently imbibed by C. Indeed, the doctrine is applicable to property damage cases as well. For example, if A attempts to set fire to B's dwelling house, but in fact burns only C's adjoining dwelling house, A is guilty of arson.

When the defendant's bad aim kills C instead of B, most jurisdictions hold that the degree of homicide is the same as it would have been if A had been on target. *E.g.,* S. v. Gardner, 203 A.2d 77 (Del. 1964).

An analogous unintended victim situation which arrives at the same result for different reasons arises when A kills C in the darkness believing C to be B. In this situation, A is guilty of murdering C because he actually intended to murder the person he killed, although he did so under a mistaken belief that C was someone else. The fiction of transferred intent is not necessary to bring A to justice in this situation. *E.g.,* R. v. Stopford, 11 Cox Crim. Cas. 643 (N.Cir.1870).

Courts have traditionally confined the doctrine of transferred intent to situations in which the resultant harm is similar to the intended harm. For example, when A, intending personal harm to B, threw a rock which accidentally broke C's window, he was found to be not guilty of malicious injury to property because his actual intent to do personal harm to B was different in kind from an intent to injure C's property [See R. v. Pembliton, 12 Cox Crim.Cas. 607 (Cr.App.1874)].

In an effort to avoid the fictional character of transferred intent, the M.P.C. approaches the problem of the unintended victim as one of causation, concluding that the requirement of purposely or knowingly causing a particular result is satisfied even when it is inflicted upon an unintended victim (M.P.C. § 2.03).

§ 8.04 Liability Without Fault

There are two kinds of liability without fault—strict and vicarious. Strict liability occurs when a conviction can be obtained merely upon proof that defendant perpetrated an act forbidden by statute and when proof by defendant that she exercised the utmost of care to prevent the act would be no defense. In other words, strict liability is where defendant's "I didn't mean it" will not help her. Vicarious liability is when a defendant's criminal liability is predicated upon the actions of another, usually an employee. When a defendant ordered the particular activity, her being held criminally responsible is not predicated on lack of fault nor is it unusual. (See § 15.01 *infra*). Vicarious liability, however, is sometimes extended to situations in which the principal violator deliberately disobeys the orders of the defendant employer (*e.g.,* bartender sells liquor to minors notwithstanding order of defendant bar owner not to do so).

The justification for strict or vicarious liability is a combination of several factors. First, the crime is usually a minor one involving no moral turpitude or social stigma and is generally punished by a fine. Second, a defendant who has violated such a statute normally does have some degree of culpability. Third, culpability, though normally present, is difficult to prove. For example, a defendant who sells adulterated food is usually careless, but to prove negligence in a particular case is difficult. Similarly, most bartenders who sell liquor to minors do so with their employers' approval. But proving approval in any particular case is difficult if not impossible. When these justifications are present, it is sometimes thought that the usual maxim that it is better to acquit a guilty person than convict an innocent one is inapplicable because of the relative lack of harm done by an erroneous conviction, as contrasted with the good done by encouraging an extremely high standard of care. See generally Morissette v. U.S., 342 U.S. 246 (1952).

Support of criminal liability without fault is far from unanimous. Apart from the obvious injustice to the individual, many contend that making criminals out of nonculpable people tends to cheapen respect for the criminal law ("if that respectable person down the street has committed a crime, why shouldn't I?"). Compare § 18.04 *infra*. The M.P.C. accepts liability without fault so long as the penalty is limited to a fine or civil penalty but rejects it when imprisonment is possible. M.P.C. § 2.05 and M.P.C. Tent. Draft 4, p. 140.

§ 8.05 Limitations on Liability Without Fault

A. CONSTITUTIONAL LIMITATIONS

Strict and vicarious liability crimes have generally been upheld when challenged on constitutional grounds. One notable exception is Smith v. California, 361 U.S. 147 (1959), in which the United States Supreme Court reversed a conviction for possessing an obscene book in a place where books are sold. The California courts had upheld Smith's conviction, holding that his claimed lack of knowledge of the book's character was irrelevant. The Supreme

Court, however, reversed on the ground that holding one strictly liable for possessing obscene material tends to inhibit the sale of nonobscene books as well as obscene ones. This is so because a book seller knows that unless he has inspected each book in his store and knows its character, he runs the risk of criminal prosecution. Therefore, the Court held that this kind of strict liability in the sensitive area of free speech violates the First Amendment.

Apart from *Smith* and cases like it, the United States Supreme Court has been reluctant to impose constitutional limitations upon liability without fault crimes [*But cf.* Lambert v. California, 355 U.S. 225 (1957), § 8.07, *infra*]. State courts have generally shared this reluctance, although they are not bound to do so inasmuch as they could interpret their own constitutions to forbid such crimes. One interesting illustration is C. v. Koczwara, 155 A.2d 825 (Pa.1959), wherein the Supreme Court of Pennsylvania held that imprisonment could not be imposed consistent with due process when liability is predicated upon another's conduct (in this case, a prosecution of a tavern owner for the conduct of his bartender in serving liquor to minors). However, the court expressed no difficulty with upholding a substantial fine, nor did it doubt that defendant could lose his liquor license. Furthermore, it did not purport to cast doubt on those cases upholding imprisonment for one who personally sold liquor to a minor whom he honestly and reasonably believed to be an adult. Minnesota has gone even farther, completely rejecting criminal liability for the absent owner. See S. v. Guminga, 395 N.W.2d 344 (Minn. 1986).

Another illustration is S. v. Campbell, 691 N.E.2d 711 (Ohio App.1997), where an Ohio court invalidated a strict liability misdemeanor manslaughter conviction on cruel and unusual punishment grounds. (See §§ 1.07 and 2.10). *Campbell*, however, proved to be extremely short-lived. Two years later, the Ohio Supreme Court rejected *Campbell* and upheld the statute, thereby reinstating the manslaughter indictment of a woman whose car drifted across the centerline, after she was rendered unconscious by a heart attack, thereby killing three people. S. v. Weitbrecht, 715 N.E.2d 167 (Ohio 1999).

B. NON–CONSTITUTIONAL LIMITATIONS

Courts tend to reject liability without fault when the usual reasons for such liability are absent. Thus, when the crime involves moral turpitude or carries the possibility of substantial imprisonment, the likelihood of finding that fault has been abrogated as a requirement is significantly diminished.

Occasionally, a court will hold that there is a presumption against liability without fault unless fault is explicitly abrogated by the legislature. Sweet v. Parsley, [1969] 1 All E.R. 347 (H.L.). Since legislation almost never explicitly requires strict liability and rarely requires vicarious liability, such an approach substantially reduces the incidence of such crimes. At the same time, it does not preclude liability without fault crimes, but merely requires that they be explicitly adopted by the legislature. Australian courts have adopted a modified version of this approach by allowing the defendant to prove due care as an affirmative defense whenever he is accused of what would otherwise be a strict liability offense, unless such a defense is specifically negated by the legislature. Proudman v. Dayman, 67 C.L.R. 536 (1941). (Compare § 12.01, *infra*).

Of course, the most obvious instance for rejecting strict liability is when the legislature indicates that mens rea is required by use of a term such as "knowingly" or "willfully." For example, in Flores–Figueroa v. U.S., 129 S.Ct. 1886 (2009), the United States Supreme Court held that one who uses a false social security number could not be convicted of knowingly using the number of another without proof that he knew that the number belonged to another person. Even with terms like "knowingly" or "wilfully", in a multi-element offense, there may be some question as to which of the elements the term applies (see discussion in §§ 8.06, 8.07 *infra*).

§ 8.06 Mistake of Fact

In a real sense, mistake of fact does not present a separate analytical problem. It is relevant only in that it serves to negate a particular state of mind which may be necessary to commit a given crime.

As a general proposition, an honest and reasonable mistake of fact will negate criminal liability. The following illustration which has already been presented in another context is worth reexamining at this juncture: A person who kills another pursuant to the honest and reasonable, albeit mistaken, belief that such action is necessary to preserve his life is not guilty of any homicidal offense (§ 6.02 *supra*). Here, the defendant's honest and reasonable mistake negates the mens rea necessary for murder.

There are instances, however, in which an honest and reasonable mistake will not be available as a defense. The most obvious are strict liability crimes. Since no intent is required in the first place (*e.g.*, for selling adulterated goods, § 8.04 *supra*), obviously an honest and reasonable mistake will not negate mens rea.

In addition, when the mistake merely changes the degree of the crime, and the character of the defendant's actual conduct is not significantly different from his intended conduct, his honest and reasonable mistake will not normally be a defense. To illustrate, if A steals B's merchandise which he honestly and reasonably believes is worth $195, but which in fact is worth $205, A is guilty of grand larceny rather than petit larceny (assuming of course that $200 is the dividing line). See § 7.02D *supra*. Similarly a burglar who burgles at nighttime, honestly and reasonably believing it is daytime is guilty of burglary (or if the state has degrees of burglary, nighttime burglary). (See § 7.11 *supra*).

One theory that explains this rule is akin to the assumption of risk doctrine in torts. That is, when a person steals property or breaks and enters another's dwelling with the intent to commit a felony, he assumes the risk that the property might be worth more than $200 or that he may have guessed wrong in regard to the exact beginning of nighttime. A more plausible explanation for the rule is that the mistake merely goes to a circumstance of the crime for which strict liability is sufficient. That is, the basic elements of larceny are the trespassory taking and carrying away of property with the intent to steal. This the defendant clearly did. The additional fact that the property is worth more than $200 is a circumstantial element of the offense rather than one requiring mens rea. Consequently, the defendant is strictly liable insofar as this element is concerned and a reasonable mistake of fact will not exculpate him. A similar analysis can be repeated for the "nighttime circumstance" in burglary.

The above rule does not apply to all cases in which the aggravating circumstance turns a general offense into one of a specialized character. For example, the crime of assault and battery upon a police officer in the performance of his duties is sometimes, but not always, inapplicable to a person who honestly and reasonably thinks he is beating a private citizen but in fact is beating an on duty police officer. See, *e.g.,* P. v. Prante, 493 P.2d 1083 (Colo.1972). This can be justified in that the aggravated nature of this crime (contempt for the law as well as the person being beaten) is not present in a person who does not know that he is beating a police officer. Jurisdictions reaching the opposite result focus on the presence of the harm (injury to police officers) which inspired the legislatures to adopt the statute. See U.S. v. Feola, 420 U.S. 671 (1975).

Perhaps the hardest kind of case in this area is where the defendant honestly and reasonably believes that he is committing an arguably immoral, but not criminal (or at most marginally criminal) act. One such illustration that we have already considered is statutory rape when the defendant honestly and reasonably believes that the girl is over the age of consent (§ 4.05 *supra*). There we noted that most, though not all, courts treat rape as a strict liability offense, thereby rendering an honest and reasonable mistake of age immaterial.

The question was thoroughly debated in the well known English case of R. v. Prince, 13 Cox Crim. Cas. 138 (Cr.App.1875), in which the availability of the defense of an honest and reasonable mistake of age to the crime of taking a girl under 16 from her father was in issue. The court ruled that the defense was unavailable, effectively holding age to be a circumstance to this crime, much like the value of property in grand larceny or the time of day in burglary. The court emphasized that it was not abandoning mens rea. Indeed, a majority of the judges indicated that an honest and reasonable mistake as to paternal consent would have been a good defense. When, however, the only mistake, age, went to the degree of the wrong (legal v. moral), the court found sufficient culpability to justify a conviction. The M.P.C. rejects *Prince* and holds (with some exceptions) that when a person honestly and reasonably thought he was committing a less serious offense, his punishment must be in conformity with the offense he thought he was committing (of course, in the *Prince* fact pattern, the defendant would have been completely exonerated). M.P.C. § 2.04(1), (2). Of course, the fact that today sex outside of marriage may well be a constitutional right (see 4.05, *supra*) may render the *Prince* reasoning inapplicable to statutory rape.

One type of case which almost defies explanation by sometimes rejecting the honest and reasonable mistake of fact defense is bigamy. Bigamy, being a serious felony, hardly fits into the classic strict liability mold (see §§ 8.04, 8.05(B) *supra*). Yet, some courts hold that an honest and reasonable but mistaken belief as to the death of a spouse or the dissolution of the marriage is no defense to a subsequent marriage which is in fact bigamous. *E.g.,* Turner v. S., 55 So.2d 228 (Miss.1951). The best explanation for this view (and it's none too good) is that integrity of the marriage institution is such an integral part of our society that anybody choosing to marry a second time must do so at his peril. Fortunately not all courts accept this view. See, *e.g.,* S. v. Smith, 697 So.2d 39 (La.Ct.App.1997).

Although an honest, but *unreasonable* mistake of fact is not normally a valid defense, there is an important exception—that being when the mistake negates a requisite state of mind. One obvious illustration is a larceny defendant who honestly but unreasonably believed that she was entitled to the property that she took. This honest but unreasonable "claim of right" negates the requisite mens rea for larceny (see § 7.02F *supra*).

A good contrast as to when unreasonable mistake of fact is rejected on the one hand and accepted on the other as a defense can be seen in the crimes of rape and assault with intent to commit rape. If a rape defendant had forcible sexual intercourse with a woman whom he honestly but unreasonably and mistakenly thought had consented, most jurisdictions would convict him of rape inasmuch as his mistake would not negate any element requisite to the crime of rape. Most jurisdictions require a mistake to at least be reasonable to be a defense to rape [*e.g.,* S. v. Smith, 554 A.2d 713 (Conn.1989)] and in some it may be doubtful that even a reasonable mistake will suffice. *Cf.* C. v. Ascolillo, 541 N.E.2d 570 (Mass.1989). But see D.P.P. v. Morgan, 2 All E.R. 365 (1975) (representing the English view that even an unreasonable mistake, if honest, will suffice). If, however, the same defendant had failed in his efforts to effectuate sexual intercourse, he would not be guilty of assault with intent to commit rape (at least under the better and prevailing view) because his honest and unreasonable mistake would negate his intent to have intercourse with someone who was not consenting, an intent necessary for assault with intent to commit rape, but not for rape. See P. v. Guillett, 69 N.W.2d 140 (Mich.1955). But see U.S. v. Short, 4 U.S.C.M.A. 437 (1954).

Sometimes an honest and unreasonable mistake will not exculpate the defendant entirely, but will reduce the severity of his crime. To use an example that has been presented earlier, in many states, one who honestly, but unreasonably, kills in self-defense is not guilty of murder because his honest belief negates malice aforethought, but is guilty of manslaughter because his unreasonableness precludes the killing from being excused entirely (see § 6.05 *supra*).

§ 8.07 Mistake of Law

It is doubtful that any maxim in the criminal law is better known than "ignorance of the law is no excuse." This maxim has on occasions been justified by the proposition that no person is to be superior to the law (sometimes called the principle of legality). That is, if ignorance of the law were recognized as a defense, the defendant's knowledge rather than the law of the land would determine what he could or could not do.

A sounder justification for rejecting the defense is the ease with which it can be fabricated. One can envision thousands of criminal defendants plaintively pleading, "But I didn't know it was against the law." Of course, one could discount this fear because although the defense can be raised frequently, it will not succeed very often. Nevertheless, the presence of such a defense could encourage one to violate the law, thinking (albeit incorrectly) that he could always say that he didn't know he was violating the law.

One important exception to the "ignorance of the law is no excuse" maxim is when the ignorance negates a specific state of mind. To repeat an oft-used illustration (at least in this book), ignorance or mistake of law (even of the unreasonable variety) may create a "claim of right" thereby negating the requisite intent for larceny. For example, a person may honestly and reasonably or unreasonably believe that he is entitled to take another's property to satisfy a debt. In most jurisdictions, this "mistake of law" creates a valid "claim of right" thereby precluding a larceny conviction (§ 7.02F *supra*). Another illustration is kidnapping when a defendant whose "mistake of law" causes him to think he has lawful authority to detain and transport his victim. Such a defendant would not be guilty of kidnapping (see § 5.05 *supra*).

Problems of statutory interpretation can arise as to the meaning of terms like "willfully" or "knowingly," and they have sharply divided the United States Supreme Court. For example, in Cheek v. U.S., 498 U.S. 192 (1991), the Court dealt with a tax resister accused of willfully failing to file an income tax return. Cheek claimed that a lawyer had told him that personal income was not subject to income tax, and that if the statute were construed otherwise, it would be unconstitutional. The Court held that his mistake of law, if bona fide, would negate the element of willfulness. It also held that his mistaken belief in the unconstitutionality of the tax code would *not* negate willfulness because a person who knows the law must take his chances as to its constitutionality. One dissent thought that Cheek's belief in the law's unconstitutionality did negate willfulness. Another dissenting opinion thought that Cheek's mistake of the tax law should not suffice because it was in regard to a non esoteric section of the code (the provision saying that it applies to income).

In Bryan v. U.S., 524 U.S. 184 (1998), a similar argument was made by an interstate gun runner accused of the federal offense of willfully transporting unregistered guns across state lines. Bryan knew that he was transporting unregistered guns across state lines (indeed, he had personally filed off the serial numbers), but he did not know that it was against *Federal* law. The Supreme Court, by a six to three vote, affirmed his conviction on the ground that the "willful" requirement was met by his knowledge that his conduct violated some law, even if he didn't know it was a Federal law.

Of course, these decisions, being nonconstitutional, are not binding on state courts. Thus, one must expect considerable disparity among states in construing words like "willfully" or "knowingly" insofar as they relate to mistake of law.

Another exception to the ignorance of the law is no excuse rule occurs when the defendant relies on a statute, judicial decision, or administrative ruling later held to be invalid. Indeed, there is good reason to believe that this rule is constitutionally required. [See Bouie v. Columbia, 378 U.S. 347 (1964), and discussion § 18.02 *infra*]. In addition, when erroneous advice is obtained from one charged with administering a regulatory statute, a "mistake of law" so occasioned is generally held to be a valid defense.

Thus, under some circumstances, it is possible to have a strict liability regulatory offense in which mistake of fact would not be a defense, but mistake of law would be. One must be careful not to read too much into this limited exception. It applies only when the erroneous advice is given by one charged with administering the statute. It is not usually applicable when some other state official, even the state's attorney, gives the erroneous advice. *E.g.,* Hopkins v. S., 69 A.2d 456 (Md.1949). [But *cf.* Cox v. Louisiana, 379 U.S. 559 (1965), in which the United States Supreme Court reversed a conviction for picketing in front of a court house on the ground that a policeman had intimated that picketing at the spot in question was lawful.]

Erroneous advice by one's own attorney is almost universally rejected as a defense. See P. v. Marrero, 507 N.E.2d 1068 (N.Y.1987). One case in which such a defense was recognized, Long v. S., 65 A.2d 489 (Del.1949), involved a Delaware resident who moved to Arkansas where he obtained a divorce. Upon returning to Delaware, he desired to remarry, whereupon he consulted a reputable Delaware attorney who advised him that his contemplated marriage would not be unlawful. Unfortunately, neither the prosecutor nor the trial court agreed with this advice. Consequently, he was convicted of bigamy. On appeal, the court held that when a defendant who is not totally ignorant of the law (but is aware of its existence, yet uncertain of its applicability to him) makes a good faith effort through reputable counsel to ascertain the effect of the law on him, his mistake of law defense is valid.

Perhaps the most interesting aspect of *Long* is its overwhelming rejection by other courts and the M.P.C. [M.P.C. § 2.04(3)]. Part of this rejection is the desire to prevent attorney shopping (which of course is difficult to prove) and to prevent attorneys from feeling pressured to give "good" advice to their clients. It should be noted, however, that these dangers were relatively insignificant in *Long*. It was to Long's advantage (even absent criminal prosecution) to have a valid divorce from his first wife. Indeed, upon learning that his original divorce was unlawful, he must discontinue living with his second wife or face a second bigamy prosecution (even in Delaware, mistake of law can only be raised once). Thus apart from the ever present danger of opening Pandora's box, *Long* seems like a soundly premised decision. New Jersey, by statute, substantially adheres to *Long*. N.J.Stat.Ann. 2C:2–4.

One important United States Supreme Court case that potentially could have torn the "ignorance of the law is no excuse" maxim to shreds is Lambert v. California, 355 U.S. 225 (1957), wherein the Court held that the due process clause of the United States Constitution rendered it constitutionally impermissible to punish a former felon for unlawfully failing to register as such with the local police, unless the State could prove actual or probable knowledge of the law on behalf of the defendant. To say the least, this potential tearing has not materialized. The opinion itself noted that the statute concerned passive nonfeasance, simply being present in a city and not registering (a fact which standing alone raises no problems, compare § 9.06 *infra*). Additionally, it emphasized that the defendant had done nothing which would cause her to be aware that there might be legislation affecting her in this way. This fact served to distinguish the case from strict liability convictions under regulatory statutes when the defendants should have been aware of the law governing their conduct (*e.g.,* pure food and drug cases).

Lambert has been given an extremely narrow reading by some lower federal courts. For example in Reyes v. U.S., 258 F.2d 774 (9th Cir.1958), the 9th Circuit held that *Lambert* was not applicable to a drug addict who left the country without registering with the border authorities. One of the court's distinctions seems to be that Reyes' leaving the country constituted a positive act whereas Lambert's living in the city was simply a non-act. Obviously, however, in both cases the essential breach was failure to register when mandated by the law. A second and more plausible distinction proffered was that a drug addict leaving the country is more likely to be aware of a duty to register than a felon living in Los Angeles. Even so, this seems like a strange place to draw a constitutional line.

While accepting no distinctions such as those drawn in *Reyes,* the Supreme Court has been reluctant to extend *Lambert.* No case has built directly upon it and its limitations were apparent in *U.S. v. International Minerals & Chemical Corp.,* 402 U.S.

558 (1971), where the Court refused even to construe the words "knowingly violates any regulation" (much less the Constitution) to require knowledge of the regulation (incidentally, Mr. Justice Douglas wrote both *Lambert* and *International Minerals*). Of course, *International Minerals* was justified on the likelihood of a shipper of corrosive liquids (unlike a former felon) being aware of the regulation. And, decisions such as *Cheek* seem to insure that sometimes ignorance of the law does matter. Nevertheless, Justice Frankfurter's dissenting observation in *Lambert* ["I feel confident that the present decision will turn out to be an isolated deviation from the strong current of precedent—a derelict on the waters of the law," 355 U.S. at 232] has so far proven to be true.

CHAPTER IX

ACTUS REUS

§ 9.01 Introduction

Actus reus, like mens rea, is normally a requisite for criminal liability. Literally, the term "actus reus" means guilty act. This has caused legal theoreticians to attempt to define what is meant by the term "act." Some theoreticians contend that an act is simply a voluntary muscular contraction (*e.g.*, crooking one's finger) whereas others contend that it also requires a set of circumstances (*e.g.* finger on the trigger of a loaded gun with the victim's heart at the end of the barrel) and a consequence (*e.g.* death of the victim). It seems unwise to dwell too long on this somewhat metaphysical debate in that it is clear that both criminal circumstances and consequences are requisite to criminal responsibility. Inasmuch as actus reus means guilty act and not simply act, it is probably easier to conceptualize actus reus as including circumstances and consequences as well as muscular contractions.

The classic justification for the actus reus requirement is the undesirability of punishing one merely for her thoughts. Until a person actually does something, we have no objective proof of the firmness of her criminal thoughts (after all, who among us hasn't at one time or another had a criminal thought, such as murdering her criminal law teacher). Nevertheless, the requirement should not be overstated. In attempt, for example, the actus reus requirement is satisfied by muscular contractions that merely come close to causing social harm (§ 14.03 *infra*). And in conspiracy, the mere act of agreeing (at least in some jurisdictions) is sufficient (see § 16.05 *infra*). Indeed, in some cases a failure to act will suffice (see § 9.06 *infra*).

§ 9.02 Voluntariness

For an act to suffice for actus reus, it must be voluntary. As employed at this juncture, the term voluntary simply means that the muscular contraction is willed. To illustrate, if A volitionally swings his arm in such a manner that it hits B's nose, A has acted voluntarily even if he did not know that B was anywhere near him. (Of course, in this situation A might have a defense of lack of mens rea, but not lack of actus reus.) On the other hand, if the wind blows A's arm into B's nose, A does have a good defense of no actus reus. Similarly, if A threatens to shoot B unless B shoots C, B's subsequent shooting of C is voluntary in the sense that we are now using the term. (For a discussion of the potential defense of duress in this situation, see § 11.03 *infra*). But if A pushes B against C, B has not committed a voluntary battery.

Because an act must be voluntary, a person who is acting as an automaton cannot be guilty of crime. A classic illustration is the epileptic who strikes another during a seizure. This rationale can be applied to a sleepwalker also. See Fain v. C., 78 Ky. 183 (1879). A more difficult problem is the person under hypnosis. In a sense his actions are not totally voluntary and for this reason the M.P.C. [M.P.C. § 2.01(2)(c)] would exclude conduct performed under hypnotic suggestion (there are very few cases in point). On the other hand, there is psychiatric opinion suggesting that a hypnotist can exert only limited control over a subject and cannot make the subject do something which the subject finds morally repugnant. Of course, a subject who deliberately gets hypnotized in order to commit an offense would not have a valid defense. Very likely, this would apply to a subject who allows himself to be hypnotized by a cult leader known to cause his subjects to commit crimes while hypnotized.

Two important exceptions to the automatism defense should be noted. First, when the automatism results from a disease or defect of the mind, some courts require that the defense be considered under insanity strictures. The interrelationship between automatism and insanity will be explored in § 10.08 *infra*.

A second limitation on automatism is that a defendant who is aware of his tendency to suffer blackouts can be guilty of a crime for recklessly creating a situation in which this tendency is likely to cause great danger if it should materialize. For example, in P. v. Decina, 138 N.E.2d 799 (N.Y. 1956), the court held that an epileptic could be convicted of negligent homicide for deaths that oc-

curred when his car jumped out of control following
a seizure to which the defendant knew he was
subject. *Decina* was a debatable decision in view of
the fact that Decina's only negligent act was driving
alone, precisely what his driver's license entitled
him to do. The principle, however, is eminently
sound. A less debatable application would be to a
driver who continued to drive while knowing he was
barely able to refrain from falling asleep.

§ 9.03 Actus Reus as a Constitutional Minimum

As we have seen, the Eighth Amendment's prohibition against cruel and unusual punishment prohibits punishment which is cruelly disproportionate
to the crime (§ 1.07 *supra*) and outlaws some types
of punishment entirely (see § 1.08 *supra*). In addition, this clause precludes punishing certain types
of legislatively declared "crimes" at all on the
ground that any punishment for that which should
not be criminal is cruel and unusual. The leading
case is Robinson v. California, 370 U.S. 660 (1962),
which held unconstitutional a ninety day sentence
for the crime of "be[ing] addicted to the use of
narcotics."

Robinson reasoned that this statute did not pro-
scribe any anti-social conduct within the state, but
merely the status or disease of being an addict.
Thus it was punishing the bare propensity to commit a crime rather than criminal conduct itself.
Furthermore, the disease was one which could be
contracted involuntarily, indeed involuntarily at

birth. Therefore if this "crime" were upheld, it would be possible, at least theoretically, to station a policeman at the hospital nursery and arrest each new addict as he is born into the world (but for the defense of infancy discussed in § 11.01 *supra*).

The exact scope of *Robinson* is uncertain. It might preclude such status crimes as being a vagrant, common prostitute, or common drunkard, at least to the extent that these crimes are based on what the defendant is rather than what he has done (although this type of crime is probably more easily attacked as unconstitutionally vague, see § 18.01 *infra*). Certainly *Robinson* forbids punishing a person for being afflicted with any disease or predisposition, be it homosexuality, alcoholism, leprosy, venereal disease, or the common cold. It might be argued, however, that the decision does not forbid punishing the intentional or reckless contracting of a disease such as narcotic addition or syphilis, provided, of course, that the intentional or reckless act occurred within the prosecuting State. Research, however, has discovered no such statutes.

Powell v. Texas, 392 U.S. 514 (1968), placed significant limitations on *Robinson,* the exact scope of which are unclear because of the Court's 4–4–1 division. Powell was a chronic alcoholic who claimed that his prosecution for public drunkenness constituted cruel and unusual punishment. No issue was raised as to the constitutionality of punishing a non-alcoholic for public drunkenness. On that question, it was assumed that being publicly drunk was an offensive condition, unlike being an alcoholic or drug addict, which was merely a status or a term descriptive of a propensity to commit certain crimes. Powell did argue, however, that it was cruel and unusual to punish a chronic alcoholic for this crime.

Mr. Justice Marshall (speaking for Warren, C.J., Black and Harlan, JJ.) rejected this argument principally on the ground that unless *Robinson* is limited to status or propensity type crimes, its impact on the criminal law would be excessive. For example, he observed that "[i]f Leroy Powell cannot be convicted of public intoxication, it is difficult to see how a State can convict an individual for murder, if that individual, while exhibiting normal behavior in all other respects, suffers from a 'compulsion' to kill, which is an 'exceedingly strong influence' but 'not completely overpowering.' " *Id.* at 534. In addition to his concern about constitutionalizing "irresistible impulse" (see § 10.03 *infra*), Marshall worried about the alcoholic or addict who needed to rob or kill in order to feed his habit, a situation which he perceived as not significantly different from *Powell* in principle. In his view, all of these questions were better left to the states to explore through their own conceptions of the proper function of the criminal law rather than to be adjudicated permanently by a Supreme Court mandate.

Mr. Justice Fortas (speaking for Douglas, Brennan and Stewart, JJ.) would have allowed the defense, drawing a distinction between symptoms which are a direct result of a disease (drinking and being drunk directly result from alcoholism) and indirect effects such as robbery and/or murder to obtain alcohol or drugs or money to buy them.

Mr. Justice White agreed with Fortas' conclusion that it would be cruel and unusual to punish someone for doing that which he was physically compelled to do. In White's view, however, it was possible for Powell to get drunk at home. Thus, he was not compelled to be drunk in public. Therefore, punishing him for being drunk in public was not cruel and unusual. *Cf.* Martin v. S., 17 So.2d 427 (Ala.App.1944) (where the defendant while drunk was taken by the police from his home to the highway where he was arrested for being drunk in public. The court reversed his conviction on actus reus grounds.)

Of course, the fact that Powell's conviction was upheld does not preclude a state from making chronic alcoholism a defense to public drunkenness. Indeed, one of the reasons for Marshall's opinion was that he was not persuaded that eliminating the "drunk tank" would improve the plight of the alcoholic. States can, however, improve his plight by allowing chronic alcoholism as a defense to public drunkenness and providing treatment for those who successfully raise this defense. This approach has been adopted in some states. (See, *e.g.,* N.C.Gen. Stat. § 14–445(a).)

§ 9.04 Concurrence of Actus Reus and Mens Rea

As a general proposition, it is not enough that both actus reus and mens rea occur, they must occur concurrently. For example, if A intentionally shoots to kill B but misses and later accidentally kills B, A is not guilty of murder. In one spectacular case along this line, Jackson v. C., 38 S.W. 422 (Ky.1896), the defendant incorrectly thought he had murdered his victim in Ohio, brought what he thought was her corpse to Kentucky whereupon he decapitated it, an act which turned out to be the actual cause of death. The court rejected the non-concurrence argument, apparently though not clearly, on the ground that the mere intent to mutilate a corpse was conditioned on the victim's actually being a corpse, and that had the defendant been aware of the victim's being alive, he would have intended to kill her.

§ 9.05 Actus Reus and Strict Liability

Although strict liability crimes dispense with mens rea (§ 8.04 *supra*), they do not eliminate actus reus. To illustrate, a person driving an automobile suffers an epileptic seizure (at least for the first time). If, while under the throes of such seizure, the driver involuntarily drives through a red light (a strict liability offense), he is not guilty of any traffic offense. *Cf.* Hill v. Baxter, [1958] 1 All E.R. 193 (Q.B.1957).

Sometimes it is difficult to ascertain whether a defendant committed a forbidden act (actus reus) without evil intent (mens rea) or didn't even commit the act (a point of considerable significance when a strict liability offense is charged). For example, in Kilbride v. Lake, [1962] N.Z.L.R. 590, the

defendant was charged with permitting a motor
vehicle to be on the highway without a warrant of
fitness sticker on the windshield. It was conceded
that when the defendant parked his car on the
street ("highway"), the sticker was present, but
when he returned, it had been removed by some
mysterious source. Defense counsel argued that the
offense required mens rea which his client obviously
did not have. The court, however, reversed his
conviction on the ground of no actus reus. It reasoned that the offense called for two acts (or more
accurately an act and an omission, see § 9.06 *infra*):
(1) placing the car on the highway, and (2) not
having the warrant of fitness sticker on the windshield. Since the second act (omission) was not
attributable to the defendant, he lacked the necessary actus reus for the crime.

In S. v. Baker, 571 P.2d 65 (Kan.App.1977), the
Court held that a defective cruise control did not
constitute an actus reus defense to speeding. The
court suggested that defective brakes or throttle
might be a defense, but, apparently because the
court thought the speed control device to be an
unnecessary appendage to the car, refused to accord
the same defense to that kind of defect. Even cases
of defective brakes tend to split the courts on the
actus reus issue. Compare S. v. Kremer, 114 N.W.2d
88 (Minn.1962) (defense) with Kettering v. Greene,
222 N.E.2d 638 (Ohio 1966) (no defense). States in
the latter category functionally eliminate actus reus
by holding the driver strictly liable for whatever
happens as a result of his voluntary act of driving.

§ 9.06 Omissions

As a general proposition, an omission or failure to act is not a basis for criminal liability. One classic illustration of no liability is a six foot tall expert swimmer who deliberately sits by the side of a five foot pool thoroughly enjoying watching a four foot tall child drown. One reason commonly given for this rule is the difficulty of ascertaining at what point the danger to the rescuer becomes too great to hold him criminally responsible. Another reason is that the law ought to direct its energies towards punishing those whose existence has added to human misery rather than those who have merely been neutral towards it. In our hypothetical, for example, the expert swimmer did not worsen the child's plight, he simply failed to improve it.

There are several exceptions to the no duty to act rule. The most obvious is when a statute specifically requires a person to act, such as a statute requiring a person to fill out an income tax return. It is of course no defense for one accused of such a crime to say "but I didn't do anything." States vary considerably as to their statutory requirements. A legislature could, of course, require any person to save another where he could do so with no risk to himself. Only a few legislatures have done so, however. (*See e.g.*, 12 Vt.Gen.Stat. § 519.)

Sometimes a duty to act can be predicated upon a status relationship. Common illustrations are a parent's duty to his child or a husband's duty to his wife. Thus, a father who fails to save his child from drowning (assuming that he can do so in safety) or summon medical attention to cure his seriously ill child may be guilty of a homicidal offense when the child drowns or dies of the illness. In the drowning illustration, the crime would most likely be murder if the father were aware of the near certainty of death, and first degree murder if death was the result which he premeditatedly desired (compare §§ 2.01, 2.02, 2.08 *supra*). In the medical aid illustration, the crime would probably be involuntary manslaughter (see § 2.06 *supra*) since the father's inaction does not create a certainty of death, but merely increases the probability thereof. Of course, a father can be guilty of murder for failing to administer medicine to his child if he knows that such failure will cause death. Causation problems are also present in this type of case. For instance, a father who fails to summon a physician for his dying daughter will not be criminally liable for her death if a physician's aid would not have made any difference. Jurisdictions are split over the degree of difference the physician's presence must make. To illustrate, one court held that a man could be convicted of involuntary manslaughter even though his wife would have died whether or not a doctor had been summoned, merely because the defendant's conduct "hastened" his wife's death. S. v. Mally, 366 P.2d 868 (Mont.1961). Another court, however, exculpated the parents of a girl because the State failed to prove that medical aid would have saved her. Craig v. S., 155 A.2d 684 (Md.1959). (Compare the causation problem when the defendant has acted affirmatively, Ch. III *supra*.)

Contractual obligation as well as status relationship can be the ground upon which a duty to act is predicated. Hence, a babysitter or nurse hired to protect a child is under a legal duty similar to that of the child's father. This rule is not limited to a person hired by the child's parent. A public hireling is under the same obligation. Thus, in our drowning child hypothetical, if the six foot tall expert swimmer is a lifeguard who has been hired by the pool to protect people, he will be criminally liable (probably for murder) for allowing the child to drown.

Even if there is no contractual obligation, a duty to act can be predicated upon a voluntary assumption of such a duty. Thus, in the drowning child case, if the expert swimmer had told the child's parents that he would watch her, the swimmer would be criminally liable for allowing the child to drown. The fact that he was not being paid for his services is immaterial. Similarly, a person who gratuitously swims half way out to a drowning person, thereby discouraging others from attempting a rescue, and then willfully decides to abandon the rescue at a point when it is too late for others to help, may be guilty of a homicidal offense. *Cf.* Jones v. U.S., 308 F.2d 307 (D.C.Cir.1962).

The principle of voluntarily agreeing to aid can probably be extended to one who agrees to go with another to a place where they will be isolated from all other aid, such as two mountain climbers or fishermen. Each might be liable if he should fail to make an effort to save the other from an unanticipated hazard (assuming no serious risk to his own life). Similarly, a person who invites another to his premises might be said to be under a duty to protect that person from harm while that person is visiting him. One well known case which seems to reject this proposition is P. v. Beardsley, 113 N.W. 1128 (Mich.1907), in which the defendant and his mistress engaged in a weekend of illicit sexual activity whereupon she took several morphine tablets which turned out to be fatal due to his failure to summon medical aid. The court reversed Beardsley's manslaughter conviction concluding that it "would be very repugnant to our moral sense" to hold that a man owes the same duty to a woman who is visiting his home for casual sexual activity as a husband owes his wife. Although probably wrongly decided, *Beardsley* is explicable on the ground that the victim's difficulties were principally of her own making rather than the result of an accident.

Sometimes the basis upon which a duty to act is predicated is not clear. For example in Davis v. C., 335 S.E.2d 375 (Va.1985), Davis lived with her elderly mother, who was too ill to care for herself. Pursuant to an agreement with her mother, Davis received her mother's social security and food stamp allotment. The agreement also provided for Davis to care for her mother. Unfortunately she provided inadequate food, heat, and medical care. Upon her mother's death, the court upheld a manslaughter conviction indicating that defendant had breached a legal duty. The court appeared to predicate liability on Davis' contractual obligation, but presumably it could have been predicated upon a voluntary assumption of care, or possibly even on a status relationship, although the duty of adult children to parents under circumstances like *Davis* is not clear.

A duty to act is sometimes imposed because of the defendant's criminal or negligent act in creating the need for rescue. For example, if a man rapes a girl who because of grief jumps or falls into a river and drowns, he may be criminally responsible for her death if he could have saved her, but refrained from doing so. Jones v. S., 43 N.E.2d 1017 (Ind.1942). In such a case, if her jumping or falling into the river were fairly attributable to the rape, the defendant might have been guilty of murder even if he couldn't save her on the theory that his affirmative act (rape), rather than his failure to save her, caused her death (compare § 2.09 and Ch. III *supra*). Nevertheless, it is possible to conclude that the jumping or falling into the river was not so related to the rape as to hold the defendant liable for that alone, but was sufficiently related to it to justify imposing liability for his failure to rescue her.

Perhaps a better illustration is the duty to act based on negligence. In the swimmer and child at the pool hypothetical, let us assume that the swimmer negligently (but not grossly negligently) pushed the child in the water. If he were unable to rescue her without substantial risk to himself, he would probably be guilty of no crime, or at most negligent homicide (see § 2.07 *supra*). If, however, he were easily able to save her and refrained from doing so because of his perverse desire to see her drown, he would probably be guilty of murder (although there do not appear to be any cases in point).

A harder problem is the person who non-negligently creates a danger for another and then intentionally refrains from saving her. To again invoke the swimmer hypothetical, assume the child runs into the swimmer along the side of the pool (through no negligence on his part) and bounces off of him into the five foot pool. Is the expert swimmer liable if he deliberately watches the child drown? What little authority can be gleaned from relevant cases seems to be split. Probably the better view in this situation is to hold the swimmer liable in that his presence was not simply a neutral fact, but served to put the child in a significantly worse position than that in which she would have been had he not been there.

PART IV
SPECIAL DEFENSES

CHAPTER X
INSANITY

§ 10.01 Introduction

When an especially brutal or senseless killing transpires, it is not uncommon for the average citizen to conclude that "he must have been insane, because sane people don't do this." In a sense this may be correct. Such a person probably is insane in the sense that his mental processes have permitted him to deviate so far from societal norms that psychiatric treatment may be required prior to his becoming fit to return to society. This, however, is not the sense in which the term "insanity" is used in the criminal law. Rather, the insanity defense is limited to separating those otherwise guilty criminal defendants for whom criminal sanctions are inappropriate from those for whom criminal sanctions are appropriate. The necessity of this limitation is manifest. Were it otherwise, a murderer could assert insanity as a defense successfully simply by acting in a brutal or senseless manner.

Despite the manifest necessity of this limitation, there are those who have criticized one test or another as being deficient because of its failure to conform to a psychiatric conception of insanity. The short, but I believe complete, answer to this criticism is that the defense is not supposed to focus on who is or is not insane in the sense of being mentally ill, but rather who is or is not insane in the sense of not being fairly subject to the strictures of the criminal law. In analyzing the various insanity tests, it is imperative to keep this limited purpose in mind.

§ 10.02 M'Naghten Right–Wrong Test

The test most frequently employed to ascertain the sanity of a defendant is denominated the "M'Naghten right-wrong test." The test was first enunciated in M'Naghten's Case, 8 Eng.Rep. 718 (H.L.1843). (M'Naghten had an insane delusion that the Prime Minister was seeking to kill him. Thinking that the Prime Minister's private secretary was in fact the Prime Minister, M'Naghten killed the secretary.) The case required that "at the time of the committing of the act, the party accused was laboring under such a defect of reason, from disease of the mind, as not to know the nature and quality of the act he was doing, or if he did know it that he did not know he was doing what was wrong." *Id.* at 722.

Courts have not been particularly concerned with the nature of the "disease of the mind" so long as it in fact produced the requisite "defect of reason."

Indeed, there is authority suggesting that low intelligence will suffice. S. v. Johnson, 290 N.W. 159 (Wis.1940).

A more significant problem is the meaning of "know." It is susceptible of meaning either "being intellectually aware" or "having a moral appreciation." One may "know" it is wrong to kill in the sense that he can articulate these words, but lack the capacity to really feel or appreciate the wrongfulness of killing. Most states that follow *M'Naghten* have not addressed themselves to this ambiguity, preferring simply to say "know" to the jury and let its members impose whatever construction upon the word they may deem appropriate. Of those jurisdictions that have wrestled with this dichotomy, most have chosen to adopt the broader or "appreciation" concept. *E.g.,* 18 U.S.C.A. § 17.

The term "nature and quality of the act" has seldom been the topic of extensive judicial discourse. It usually has been assumed to mean physical consequences of the act. To take the M.P.C.'s now classic illustration, a man who squeezes his wife's neck thinking he is squeezing lemons does not know the nature and quality of his act. M.P.C. Tent. Draft 4, p. 156. Although an occasional court has suggested that ability to appreciate the moral as well as physical quality of the act is necessary [see S. v. Esser, 115 N.W.2d 505 (Wis.1962)], this seems to go more to the question of appreciation of wrongfulness rather than to appreciation of the nature and quality of the act.

The word "wrong" is also susceptible of differing definitions. It could mean legally wrong or morally wrong. If the defendant knows that his conduct is morally wrong but does not know that it is illegal, he will of course have no defense inasmuch as ignorance of the law is no excuse. See § 8.07 *supra*. The converse, however, is not necessarily true. One may know that an act is illegal, but because of an insane delusion believe that the act is morally right. There is a split of opinion as to whether inability to know that an act is morally wrong will suffice under *M'Naghten*. Those who would allow this defense contend that one who believes that an act is morally right (*e.g.,* God commanded me to kill) is substantially undeterrable. On the other side, it can be argued that a person who knows he is about to violate a law and is not deterred by the immorality of what he is doing, needs to be subject to the criminal law if he is to be deterred at all.

M'Naghten has been criticized for not conforming to modern psychiatric notions of insanity. This criticism, however, ignores the fact that the insanity defense is not designed to define psychiatric illness, but to ascertain who is or is not an appropriate subject for the criminal law. See § 10.01 *supra*.

A criticism with more force suggests that focusing on ability to distinguish right from wrong (the cognitive element) misdirects emphasis. This argument suggests that the real question should be one's capacity to control her behavior rather than merely understand its wrongfulness. Defenders of *M'Naghten,* however, contend that if one knows that her conduct is wrong and does it anyway, she is at least to some degree blameworthy, whereas she who does not even know that her conduct is wrong is not blameworthy at all.

Congress substantially codified *M'Naghten* in response to a public outcry over the *Hinckley* (a case remarkably similar to *M'Naghten*, in which John Hinckley was found not guilty by reason of insanity on the charge of attempted murder of President Reagan) verdict:

> "It is an affirmative defense to a prosecution under any federal statute that, at the time of the commission of the acts constituting the offense, the defendant, as a result of a severe mental disease or defect, was unable to appreciate the nature and quality or the wrongfulness of his acts. Mental disease or defect does not otherwise constitute a defense." 18 U.S.C.A. § 17.

§ 10.03 Irresistible Impulse

Some of the states that follow *M'Naghten* have supplemented it by allowing a defendant who knew he was doing wrong to successfully plead insanity where his disease of the mind prevented him from controlling his conduct. There is some dispute as to how "irresistible" the impulse must be. One extreme definition suggests that the defense is unavailable unless the defendant would have committed the crime even if there had been a "policeman at [his] elbow." U.S. v. Kunak, 5 U.S.C.M.A. 346 (1954). Other courts simply ask whether the defendant had the capacity to control his conduct. See S. v. White, 270 P.2d 727 (N.M.1954).

The criticism of "irresistible impulse" depends on its definition. Where it is defined in "policeman at the elbow" terms, it has been criticized as too restrictive. A person may lack substantial capacity to control his conduct under normal circumstances yet be able to muster the capacity in the hypothetical situation. Furthermore, when the term "impulse" is stressed, no defense is available to an insane person who has brooded over a contemplated course of criminal conduct, but because of his mental disease has ultimately engaged in it.

Where "irresistible impulse" has been defined more broadly, it has been criticized for allowing a defense when a prospective criminal might be deterred. Indeed, it has been suggested that when the compulsion towards the crime is strong but not totally overpowering, the threat of criminal sanctions is especially important. Furthermore, psychiatrists often find it difficult to distinguish an impulse which was not resisted from one which could not have been resisted.

In summation, "irresistible impulse" is not really one test, but many. At its strictest, it is not significantly different from *M'Naghten*. See § 10.02 *supra*. At its most expansive levels, it approximates *Durham*. See § 10.04 *infra*.

§ 10.04 The Durham Test

In 1954, the Circuit Court of Appeals for the District of Columbia adopted a test for insanity which provided "that an accused is not criminally responsible if his unlawful act was the product of mental disease or mental defect." Durham v. U.S., 214 F.2d 862, 874–75 (D.C.Cir.1954). This test, which was first applied in New Hampshire in 1869 (S. v. Pike, 49 N.H. 399), was calculated to maximize the contributions of psychiatrically trained people to the law as well as increase the number of mentally ill who could take advantage of the insanity defense. Although an understanding of the test is essential to understanding evolving concepts of insanity, it has to be described as an experiment that failed.

The word "product" was defined in Carter v. U.S., 252 F.2d 608 (D.C.Cir.1957), to require "but for" causation. That is but for the mental disease or mental defect the defendant would not have committed the crime. This has been criticized as requiring a mental gymnastic that quite simply cannot be accomplished. How can one say what one would have done had his mental condition not been what it was? We just do not know.

Another problem with *Durham* was the definition of "mental disease or mental defect." To be sure, *M'Naghten* employs similar terminology. There, however, a particular effect has to be discernible (inability to distinguish right from wrong). Consequently, the courts have not been particularly concerned as to what constitutes a disease of the mind sufficient to progress to the next step § 10.02 *supra*. Under *Durham*, on the other hand, there was nothing the mental disease or mental defect had to be except a factor causing the crime. Thus, what did or did not constitute a mental disease or defect was especially important under *Durham*.

Durham did not define these terms except in relation to each other. It defined a disease as a condition which is capable of improving or deteriorating and a defect as a condition which lacks these capabilities. Five years after *Durham*, in Blocker v. U.S., 274 F.2d 572 (D.C.Cir.1959), the court held that a defendant with a sociopathic personality was entitled to a new trial when subsequent to his conviction, it appeared that the psychiatric profession (or a portion thereof) had changed its view about sociopathy and were now labelling it a mental disease.

In McDonald v. U.S., 312 F.2d 847 (D.C.Cir.1962), the court recognized the injustice of predicating a defense on a temporary psychiatric classification of a particular condition as well as the fact that classification of a condition as a disease for psychiatric purposes is not necessarily an accurate classification for purposes of the criminal law. Thus it redefined mental disease or defect to include "any abnormal condition of the mind which substantially affects mental or emotional processes and substantially impairs behavior controls." *Id.* at 851.

In Washington v. U.S., 390 F.2d 444 (D.C.Cir. 1967), the court limited the role of psychiatric testimony to a description of the defendant's mental condition, leaving it to the jury to decide whether the condition was "a mental disease or defect" and/or whether the crime was a "product" of it.

Finally, in U.S. v. Brawner, 471 F.2d 969 (D.C.Cir.1972), the court overruled *Durham* in favor of a modified version of the M.P.C. test. See § 10.05 *infra*. Which, of course, was itself superseded by the Federal statute 18 U.S.C.A. 17. See § 10.05, *infra*. Thus *Durham* is no longer the law in any jurisdiction. Nevertheless, its advent (as evidenced by the criticism it engendered) was probably the most important single factor in creating a modern rethinking of the entire insanity question.

§ 10.05 M.P.C. Test

The test of insanity under the M.P.C. is as follows: "(1) A person is not responsible for criminal conduct if at the time of such conduct as a result of mental disease or defect he lacks substantial capacity either to appreciate the criminality (wrongfulness) of his conduct or to conform his conduct to the requirements of law. (2) As used in this Article, the terms 'mental disease or defect' do not include an abnormality manifested only by repeated criminal or otherwise antisocial conduct." M.P.C. § 4.01.

The framers of the M.P.C. deemed *M'Naghten* and "irresistible impulse" sound insofar as they formed a basis for exculpation, but questioned whether, at least in some of their forms, they went far enough. Thus, it adopted a test very similar to the more liberal versions of "irresistible impulse." It uses the word "appreciate" rather than "know" and is neutral as to the word "criminality" or "wrongfulness." (See § 10.02 *supra*.)

Its use of the phrase "lacks substantial capacity" modifies *M'Naghten* and "irresistible impulse" which generally have been thought to require a total lack of capacity. *Durham* on the other hand could be read as requiring only a slight impairment of capacity. Thus, the M.P.C. rule could be regarded as a compromise between these extremes. Its framers justify the phrase on the ground that it comports with psychiatric realities in that a person is rarely totally lacking in capacity or totally in control of himself.

The M.P.C. test differs from *Durham* principally in its rejection of the amorphous "product" test. Rather than ask whether the crime was the product of a disease or defect it asks what impact the disease or defect had on the defendant's cognitive or behavioral capacities. Like *Durham,* the M.P.C. does not define "mental disease or defect" except that, unlike *Durham,* it excludes those diseases "manifested only by repeated criminal or otherwise anti-social conduct."

The M.P.C. test has already had a significant impact in the law, having been adopted in one form or another by most Federal Circuit Courts of Appeal and some states. Furthermore, it is likely to be considered by other states when they revise their criminal law. It is not realistic to think that it will be adopted in toto by each of these states, but rather that portions of it might be adopted. Indeed, it has been supplanted by *M'Naghten* in Federal cases. See 18 U.S.C.A. § 17, § 10.02, *supra*.

Some of the courts that adopted the basics of the M.P.C. test had rejected the exclusion of diseases manifested only by repeated criminal behavior. See, *e.g.,* U.S. v. Smith, 404 F.2d 720 (6th Cir.1968). In U.S. v. Currens, 290 F.2d 751 (3d Cir.1961) the court used only that portion of the test that referred to substantial capacity to conform one's conduct to the criminal law, reasoning that focusing on the capacity to appreciate the criminality of one's conduct puts too much weight on the cognitive element. In U.S. v. Brawner, 471 F.2d 969 (1972) (where the D.C. Circuit overruled *Durham*) the court superimposed the *McDonald* definition of mental disease or defect upon the M.P.C. test. (See § 10.04 *supra*). Thus, this version of the test provided that the defendant is not criminally responsible for his acts if, because of an abnormal condition of the mind which substantially affects mental or emotional processes and substantially impairs behavior controls, he lacks substantial capacity either to appreciate the wrongfulness of his conduct or to conform his conduct to the requirements of the law.

In its latest statutory revision, New York rejected much of the M.P.C. test, preferring to continue with *M'Naghten*. Nevertheless, it did choose to adopt the M.P.C.'s concept of substantiality. Specifically, it provides that "[i]n any prosecution for an offense, it is an affirmative defense that when the defendant engaged in the proscribed conduct, he lacked criminal responsibility by reason of mental disease or defect. Such lack of criminal responsibility means that at the time of such conduct, as a result of mental disease or defect, he lacked substantial capacity to know or appreciate either: (1) the nature and consequence of such conduct; or (2) that such conduct was wrong." N.Y.—McKinney's Penal Law § 40.15.

§ 10.06 Abolition of the Insanity Defense

Occasionally it has been suggested that the insanity defense should be abolished. Two sharply contrasting arguments have been advanced in support of such an abolition. One argument is that the insanity defense is in fact used to allow society to incarcerate an innocent but dangerous person; that is, a person who has committed a dangerous act, but who lacked sufficient capacity to be held criminally responsible. This is accomplished by civilly committing a person who is found not guilty by reason of insanity. (This procedure will be explored more thoroughly in § 10.07 *infra*). The argument contends that this is an illegitimate purpose and should be eliminated by allowing the defendant to argue that he lacked mens rea rather than that he is not guilty by reason of insanity.

A second argument for abolishing the insanity defense is that it seeks to draw a line which is essentially undrawable. Many criminals are mentally unbalanced to some degree and the concept of a mental disease is not nearly so clear as that of a physical disease. Thus, the real question is how mentally unbalanced must a person be in order to have a defense. This presents a certain degree of unfairness in that it gives a complete defense to a person who is barely on one side of an imprecise line and no defense at all to one just on the other side (at least in the absence of the kind of partial insanity that might negate a specific element of a crime, such as premeditation, see § 10.09 *infra*). Furthermore, this inexactitude magnifies the possibility of jury errors. Finally, there is respectable psychiatric opinion which suggests that telling a person who has committed a crime that he is not responsible for his actions can be seriously detrimental to his recovery.

It is doubtful that a total withdrawal of the question of sanity from a trial would be acceptable to a legislature or a court today. For example, a law which precluded a defendant from showing that he thought he was squeezing lemons rather than his wife's neck would, to say the least, be constitutionally suspect. See S. v. Strasburg, 110 P. 1020 (Wash. 1910).

On the other hand, a law which withdrew questions of sanity except when relevant to particular states of mind might be sustained. For example, the person who thought he was squeezing lemons could introduce that fact to prove he lacked the intent to kill. Similarly, a person who because of an insane delusion believed she was empress of the world and owned all of the property therein could not be guilty of larceny when she took another's property because of her "claim of right" to the property. (See § 7.02F *supra*). P. v. Wetmore, 583 P.2d 1308 (Cal.

1978) Utah, Idaho, and Montana have enacted such statutes, and they have been held constitutional. See S. v. Herrera, 895 P.2d 359 (Utah 1995).

A State enacting such a statute could provide that all those who have the requisite mental state for a particular crime, but are nevertheless insane, should be sentenced to a center for the criminally insane rather than a prison for all or part of their sentence. In addition, the court could treat their insanity as a mitigating factor when imposing its sentence. Of course, like any other mitigating circumstance, it may not necessarily be determinative.

The United States Supreme Court has indicated that the States have a great deal of latitude on the question. While intentionally leaving open the question of whether a State could abolish the insanity defense, the Court indicated that any version of the insanity defense would be constitutionally permissible. See Clark v. Arizona, 548 U.S. 735 (2006)

Some states which have not totally abolished the insanity defense have added a verdict of guilty but mentally ill. Under such a verdict, the defendant's mental incompetence becomes relevant, but again not necessarily determinative, at sentencing.

§ 10.07 Disposition of Insane Defendants

In most jurisdictions, the jury can return a verdict of guilty, not guilty, or not guilty by reason of insanity. A few jurisdictions, most notably California, bifurcate the trial by having a jury first determine guilt or innocence, and then, if the defendant is found guilty, having a second jury determine whether or not the defendant was insane when the crime was committed. See Cal. Penal Code § 1026(a) (West 1985).

Upon a finding of not guilty by reason of insanity, some jurisdictions and the M.P.C. (M.P.C. § 4.08) provide for automatic commitment. Other jurisdictions provide for discretionary commitment by the judge or jury or at a separate hearing to determine the need for commitment.

Although the constitutionality of compulsory commitment was once questioned on both due process (fundamental fairness requires a hearing) and equal protection (criminal defendants who are found not guilty by reason of insanity are treated less favorably than non-criminals who are believed to be insane and/or dangerous, in that the latter are entitled to a hearing before commitment) grounds, it is now clear that such commitment is constitutional. See Jones v. U.S., 463 U.S. 354 (1983).

In one sense, compulsory commitment is to the defendant's advantage in that a jury, knowing that the defendant will not be free to walk the streets, is more apt to find in favor of his insanity plea. Furthermore, a legislature or court may be more willing to adopt a liberal insanity defense if it knows that those acquitted by reason of insanity will be automatically civilly committed. Of course, this does not justify a procedure which in fact denies a defendant his constitutional rights.

Once a defendant has been committed, he is theoretically entitled to be treated and to be released when cured. The burden of establishing the right to be released, however, is generally placed upon the defendant. In Foucha v. Louisiana, 504 U.S. 71 (1992), the Supreme Court held that one must be *both* mentally ill and dangerous to remain committed. If the detainee is still dangerous, but no longer mentally ill, he must be released.

§ 10.08   Interrelationship Between Automatism and Insanity

In recent years there has been considerable literature on the interrelationship between automatism (involuntary act, see § 9.02 *supra*) and insanity. From the defendant's perspective, automatism is the more complete defense inasmuch as a successful insanity defense subjects him to either mandatory or discretionary commitment or at least a hearing on the question of commitment. See § 10.07 *supra*. A successful automatism defense does not subject the defendant to a similar risk of commitment although it may alert the authorities to commence civil commitment proceedings against him.

When the defendant's automatism results from a disease of the mind, there is authority that it must be treated as insanity. In view of the fact that such things as somnambulism (sleepwalking), Tibbs v. C., 128 S.W. 871 (Ky.1910), and epilepsy, P. v. Higgins, 159 N.E.2d 179 (N.Y.1959), have been held to constitute mental diseases, it is easy to see how, at least in some jurisdictions, insanity can virtually swallow automatism as a defense.

Analytically, this rejection of automatism seems unsound. A person who lacks the physical power to control his act for whatever reason has not committed a crime at all and should not have to rely on special defenses. See S. v. Hinkle, 489 S.E.2d 257 (W.Va.1996) (See § 9.02 *supra*). On the other hand an automatist defendant may be just as dangerous as an insane one. For example, in R. v. Charlson, [1955] 1 All E.R. 859 (Ches. Assizes), the defendant, who until the incident in question had been a model father, struck his ten year old son in the head with a heavy mallet and threw him out of the window. Because this behavior was caused by a cerebral tumor and therefore was automatist, he was found not guilty and returned to his family. *Charlson* has been criticized for allowing a person with potentially dangerous propensities to be returned to a situation where those propensities might once again manifest themselves. Arguably this danger outweighs any theoretical inaccuracy created by treating certain automatist cases as cases of insanity.

Perhaps the ultimate answer is to provide for civil commitment hearings after a finding of not guilty by reason of automatism as well as not guilty by reason of insanity.

§ 10.09 The Effect of Insanity on the Specific Elements of a Crime

In addition to allowing insanity as a defense by whatever standard (*M'Naghten,* irresistible impulse,

Durham, or M.P.C.), most, but not all, jurisdictions admit evidence of insanity to establish that the defendant lacked a particular state of mind required for the crime with which he is accused. To take the illustration from § 10.06 *supra,* a defendant might wish to introduce psychiatric evidence that she believed herself to be empress of the world and owner of all of the property therein and therefore lacked an intent to steal when she took another's property which she believed she owned. Some jurisdictions do not allow this type of evidence to be introduced because of their belief that insanity is an all or nothing defense. *E.g.,* Foster v. S., 52 N.E.2d 358 (Ind.1944). This approach has been rightly criticized, however, for allowing an insane person to be convicted upon proof of fewer elements than it would take to convict a sane person. See P. v. Wetmore, 583 P.2d 1308 (Cal.1978)

The significance of the question was highlighted in Clark v. Arizona, 548 U.S. 735 (2006), where the defendant, who all agreed was afflicted with paranoid schizophrenia, claimed to believe that space aliens were inhabiting, among other things, the bodies of Flagstaff police officers. He claimed that he was operating under that belief when he killed a Flagstaff policeman. Arizona precluded the defendant from introducing psychiatric evidence to prove that he lacked the intent to kill a policeman. Thus Clark was required to prove his delusion by clear and convincing evidence as part of his insanity defense. Clark failed to do so, and was convicted.

The Supreme Court upheld Clark's conviction, thus constitutionalizing a State's right to convict an insane person without proving beyond a reasonable doubt that he had the mens rea which would be required of a sane person. This inverts the usual role of insanity which is to acquit a person who might actually have the mens rea necessary to commit a crime (e.g. one who, knowing that the law forbids his conduct, intentionally kills another human being because he perceived God to be ordering the killing.) See Loewy, *The Two Faces of Insanity,* 42 Texas Tech. L. Rev. ___ (2009).

As a practical matter, the situation suggested in the hypothetical is not of great import. The defendant in that situation probably does not know the nature and quality of her act and certainly does not know that it is wrong. Consequently, she would have a defense under any of the insanity tests anyway. Of course, for the reasons suggested in §§ 10.07 and 10.08, most defendants would prefer an outright acquittal to a finding of not guilty by reason of insanity.

Evidence of insanity in regard to a particular state of mind is especially important in first degree murder cases, however, when the defendant seeks to introduce psychiatric testimony that he lacked the capacity to premeditate or deliberate. See § 2.02 *supra.* Here it is entirely possible that a defendant can tell the nature and quality of his act, know that it is wrong, not have an irresistible impulse, nor meet the *Durham* or M.P.C. tests, yet be sufficiently insane so as not to be able to premeditate. Once again, most, but not all courts, would allow evidence of his mental defect to be introduced in this situation. See, *e.g.,* U.S. v. Brawner, 471 F.2d 969 (D.C.Cir.1972), overruling Fisher v. U.S., 149 F.2d 28 (D.C.Cir.1945).

Those jurisdictions that have abolished the insanity defense still allow evidence of insanity to be introduced to disprove an element of the offense charged. See S. v. Herrera, 895 P.2d 359 (Utah 1995).

§ 10.10 Insanity After the Crime

A defendant who is insane at the time his trial is scheduled cannot be tried until he regains his sanity. As a practical matter this rule eliminates most of the more severely insane defendants from ever being tried, thereby precluding the court from ascertaining whether or not they were insane at the time of the crime.

The standards for determining sanity for purposes of standing trial are quite different from those employed to determine criminal responsibility. In the oft-quoted case of Dusky v. U.S., 362 U.S. 402 (1960), the Supreme Court held "that the 'test [for standing trial] must be whether he has sufficient present ability to consult with his lawyer with a reasonable degree of rational understanding—and whether he has a rational as well as factual understanding of the proceedings against him.' "

Many state statutes provide for compulsory commitment of one who is insufficiently sane to stand trial. These statutes are constitutionally suspect in light of Jackson v. Indiana, 406 U.S. 715 (1972), which required a civil commitment hearing as a condition of continued detention for an extreme mental defective who would very likely never be sufficiently sane to stand trial. The Court reasoned that if it were to allow Indiana to detain Jackson until he were mentally fit for trial, it would effectively be sanctioning lifetime incarceration without proof that he ever committed an anti-social act. If Jackson is construed narrowly, it would not apply to a potential defendant for whom there is a reasonable possibility of his regaining his sanity. On the other hand, Jackson can and probably should be read as forbidding any lengthy detention pending fitness for trial without at least some determination of dangerousness. *See e.g.* U.S. v. Juarez, 540 F.Supp. 1288 (W.D.Tex.1982).

Occasionally a person who is unfit to stand trial contends that he ought to be able to raise those defenses for which his fitness is irrelevant. For example, in U.S. v. Barnes, 175 F.Supp. 60 (S.D.Cal. 1959), an incompetent defendant sought to have his indictment dismissed on the ground that he was denied a speedy trial. His claim was buttressed by the fact that his three co-defendants successfully raised this defense. Nevertheless, the court held that he was not entitled to raise even this issue until he regained his sanity. *Barnes* has been rejected by the M.P.C. which provides: "The fact that the defendant is unfit to proceed does not preclude any legal objection to the prosecution which is susceptible of fair determination prior to trial and without the personal participation of the defendant." M.P.C. § 4.06.

A defendant who becomes insane during the trial may have the proceedings terminated at any time prior to sentencing. If he becomes insane after sentencing, some state statutes provide for his transfer to a psychiatric ward for the duration of his sentence or until cured, whichever comes first, *e.g.,* West's Ann.Cal. Penal Code § 2684. Of course for this purpose, the test for insanity is whether this person needs psychiatric treatment.

Finally, a person who has become insane after having been sentenced to death is entitled to a stay of execution until he recovers his sanity. This rule is sometimes rationalized on the ground that no legitimate punitive purpose (see Ch. I *supra*) can be served by executing a person who is so insane that he is not aware that he is about to be executed. It can also be defended as necessary to afford the condemned person one last opportunity to explain why he should not be executed. The Supreme Court has held that this rule is constitutionally required under the Eighth Amendment's cruel and unusual punishment clause. Ford v. Wainwright, 477 U.S. 399 (1986).

CHAPTER XI

OTHER DEFENSES

§ 11.01 Infancy

At common law a child under seven was conclusively presumed to be incapable of committing a crime. From seven to fourteen a rebuttable presumption of incapacity was created. This presumption, which progressively weakened as the child approached fourteen, could be rebutted by proof of actual criminal capacity such as hiding evidence of the crime or bribing witnesses. See S. v. Milholland, 56 N.W. 403 (Iowa 1893). A boy under fourteen was conclusively presumed to be incapable of rape. Foster v. C., 31 S.E. 503 (Va.1898).

Although these common law rules remain the law in most states today (subject to statutory age changes in some), they are not as important as they once were because of the advent of the juvenile court system. Most juveniles under fourteen (or for that matter under eighteen) are tried in juvenile courts as delinquents rather than criminal defendants, thereby rendering the defense of infancy irrelevant. See, *e.g.,* Borders v. U.S., 256 F.2d 458 (5th Cir.1958). There are a few decisions, however, that because of the quasi-criminal nature of a delinquency proceeding, allow infancy to be raised as a defense in such proceedings. In re Gladys R., 464 P.2d 127 (Cal.1970).

In recent years, juvenile crime has reached a level of violence sufficiently great to cause some rethinking of the juvenile justice system. Some recent decisions have indicated a greater willingness to try juveniles as adults. Typical of this trend is Alabama's statute § 12–15–34(d) which lists six factors to consider in assessing transferability to adult court. These include: (1) The nature of the present offense. (2) The extent and nature of the prior delinquency record of the child. (3) The nature of past treatment efforts and the nature of the response of the child to the effort. (4) Demeanor. (5) The extent and nature of the physical and mental maturity of the child. (6) the interest of the community and of the child requiring that the child be placed under legal restraint or discipline.

Applying these factors to a fifteen year old accused of murder and robbery, who had previously threatened school and law enforcement personnel, the Alabama Court of Appeals affirmed a transfer to an adult court. J.F.B. v. S., 729 So.2d 355 (Ala.Cr. App.1998). Age sometimes seems to be a factor also. The closer one is to eighteen, the more likely she is to be tried as an adult. See Maddox v. S., 931 S.W.2d 438 (Ark.1996). Although, in one extreme case, a majority of the Pennsylvania Supreme Court implied that it might be possible to try a nine year old for the premeditated murder of a playmate. However, the court reversed the determination because the lower court had employed the wrong standard. C. v. Kocher, 602 A.2d 1308 (Pa.1992).

§ 11.02 Intoxication

A. VOLUNTARY INTOXICATION

The classic rule in regard to voluntary intoxication (either from alcohol or drugs) is that it cannot negate general intent but can negate specific intent. Because of the ambiguity inherent in these terms (see § 8.01 *supra*), it is helpful to focus on what courts do rather than what they say.

When the intoxicating substance merely reduces or eliminates inhibitions, courts are unanimous in holding that no defense is created. This rule has been criticized in that punishing a man for doing while drunk what he would not have done while sober is in effect punishing him for getting drunk. In defense of the rule, however, it can be argued persuasively that excessive drinking or pill-popping is not significantly different from and is less justifiable than any other source of lost moral inhibitions such as an over-reaction of grief to the death of a loved one or anger over a fight with one's spouse.

There is a split of authority as to whether intoxication can serve as a defense to rape. Some courts hold that because rape is a "general intent" crime, no amount of intoxication can negate the crime. *E.g.,* Walden v. S., 156 S.W.2d 385 (Tenn.1941). Others hold that when the intoxication is so extreme that the defendant can't even form the intent to have intercourse, he would not be guilty. *E.g.,* S. v. Evenson, 24 N.W.2d 762 (Iowa 1946). Even here, however, the defense would rarely be successful unless the defendant were unconscious. Neither an inability to remember the event nor a drunken belief that the victim had consented would constitute a defense. See § 8.06, *supra.*

Assault with intent to commit rape (or for that matter assault with intent to commit murder or any other crime) is a different situation. The very name of the crime implies that there must be an intent to commit another crime. Thus, under the better reasoned view, a defendant whose drunkenness causes him to believe that his intended sex partner has consented is not guilty of assault with intent to commit rape. See U.S. v. Short, 4 U.S.C.M.A. 437 (1954) (dissenting opinion of Brosman, J.). There are a few cases, however, that will not allow evidence of intoxication to negate even specific intent. See Chittum v. C., 174 S.E.2d 779 (Va.1970). *Cf.* U.S. v. Short, *supra.*

Montana forbids the introduction of evidence of intoxication to negate any state of mind. It also requires proof that the defendant acted purposely or knowingly in order to be guilty of murder. In Montana v. Egelhoff, 518 U.S. 37 (1996), the defendant argued that due process required that he be allowed to introduce evidence of intoxication to disprove the State's theory that he acted purposely or knowingly when he killed his victims. Although badly fractured, the Court upheld Egelhoff's conviction. Four of the justices saw no problem with Montana limiting the evidence that could rebut specific states of minds. Four other Justices thought that was unconstitutional. The case was ultimately decided by Justice Ginsburg, who contended that the effect of Montana's law was to treat intoxicated persons as though they acted purposely or knowingly, whether or not they in fact so acted. In her view, that was constitutionally permissible. Thus, she cast the fifth vote to uphold Egelhoff's conviction.

The upshot of *Egelhoff* is, at least, that states are free to treat intoxicated defendants as if they had a state of mind that they in fact do not have. Unless, of course, the state itself has a constitutional provision precluding such treatment . . .

Evidence of intoxication usually is held to be inadmissible in a simple assault or an assault with a deadly weapon case. The rationale is either that assault is a "general intent" crime or that even a drunk can formulate the simple intent to strike another person. See P. v. Hood, 462 P.2d 370 (Cal. 1969).

The hardest cases in this area seem to be those in which intoxication is interposed as a defense to homicide. Usually it is relevant to negate premeditation and/or deliberation (see § 2.02, *supra*) and thereby reduce what would otherwise be first degree murder to second degree murder. *E.g.*, S. v. Propst, 161 S.E.2d 560 (N.C.1968). On the other hand, when the defendant's intoxication renders him unaware that he was killing a human being, most courts will not allow it to reduce murder to manslaughter, and, of course, that is constitutional under *Egelhoff*.

Theoretically, this seems unsound since a person could be so intoxicated that (to again use the classic hypothetical) he thinks he's squeezing lemons rather than his wife's neck. The framers of the M.P.C. recognized this theoretical unsoundness, but suggested that when intoxication is involved, a "special rule" is appropriate. Thus it provides that "[w]hen recklessness establishes an element of the offense, if the actor, due to self-induced intoxication, is unaware of a risk of which he would have been aware had he been sober, such unawareness is immaterial." M.P.C. § 2.08. *Cf.* Montana v. Egelhoff, 518 U.S. 37 (1996) (Ginsburg, J., concurring in the judgement).

Under this theory, the drunk who squeezed his wife's neck thinking it was a lemon would be so outrageously reckless for not perceiving that it was his wife's neck (a risk of which he would have been aware had he been sober) that his conduct would be said to evince an "abandoned and malignant heart," thereby rendering him guilty of second degree murder (see § 2.05 *supra*). See P. v. Register, 457 N.E.2d 704 (N.Y.1983).

Several factors prompted the framers of the M.P.C. to adopt this rule. It is the unusual case in which a person is so intoxicated that he really is unaware of the risk as opposed to merely imprudent enough to take it. Furthermore, ascertaining whether a defendant (who probably can't remember anyway) really was so intoxicated that he did not perceive the risk is a difficult, if not impossible, task. When this difficulty is superimposed upon the social disutility of one's achieving such a high degree of intoxication in the first place, the scales are balanced in favor of this special rule for intoxication. See M.P.C. Tent. Draft 9, p. 9.

B.　INVOLUNTARY INTOXICATION

Most jurisdictions treat an involuntarily intoxicated defendant the same as one who is insane. Thus an involuntarily intoxicated defendant who because of her intoxication can't distinguish right from wrong, or has an "irresistible impulse" to adhere to the wrong, or lacks substantial capacity to appreciate the criminality of her conduct or conform her conduct to the requirements of the law, depending on the jurisdiction (see Ch. XIII *supra*), would have a valid defense.

One is involuntarily intoxicated when forced to take an intoxicating substance against her will (see § 11.03 *infra*), or takes it without knowledge or reason to know of its intoxicating character. The M.P.C. holds that pathological intoxication, that is intoxication which is grossly disproportionate to the amount of the substance ingested, is involuntary when the defendant was unaware of her unusual susceptibility. M.P.C. § 2.08(5)(c). Compare P. v. Low, 732 P.2d 622 (Colo.1987).

§ 11.03 Duress (Coercion)

When a defendant raises a defense of duress, he is usually contending that he should be treated as a victim rather than a criminal. To illustrate, suppose A, a bank robber, draws his gun and says to B, a teller, "Your money or your life." B is not guilty of larceny when he trespassorily takes the money from the bank's cash drawer and turns it over to A, knowing that there is a substantial risk that A will deprive the bank of possession permanently, even though but for the threat upon his life B would be guilty (see §§ 7.02, 7.03 *supra* for the elements of larceny). Similarly, if C threatens to stab Mrs. D unless she engages in sexual intercourse with him, Mrs. D is not guilty of adultery, even if an isolated act of extra-marital intercourse would normally suffice for this crime.

Because cases of this nature are seldom prosecuted, the case law development of this defense is rather sparse. Most courts that have considered the question, however, have indicated that the threat must be of death or serious bodily harm, usually to the defendant himself, *e.g.,* S. v. St. Clair, 262 S.W.2d 25 (Mo.1953), although some jurisdictions have allowed a threat to another, particularly, a close relative, to suffice, *e.g.,* S. v. Milum, 516 P.2d 984 (Kan.1973). Undoubtedly, this death or serious bodily harm requirement is sound where the defendant's crime is serious. When, however, his crime is more trivial, a lesser threat should suffice, *e.g.,* "park here illegally or I'll break your windshield."

Of course, the courts are not generally confronted with illegal parking cases.

Most courts require that the threat be immediate to suffice as a defense. This is to prevent defendants from relying on duress when there is time to do something about it. However, this is not universally true. For example, in S. v. Toscano, 378 A.2d 755 (N.J.1977), a doctor participated in a medical fraud on an insurance company, allegedly because of future threats to himself and his family. The court held that the lack of temporal immediacy was relevant to the resolution of the case, but that it should not have precluded the defendant from going to the jury. Obviously, he would not only have to establish the threats, but also that he reasonably believed that the police could not protect him.

Duress cases frequently present problems of weighing individual fairness against utilitarian concerns. For example, in P. v. Carradine, 287 N.E.2d 670 (Ill.1972), the defendant feared giving testimony against a local street gang. From her perspective, the law's requiring her testimony placed her in an unconscionable dilemma. But from the State's perspective, the alternative was to allow street gang members to go unpunished. The court refused to allow her defense, perhaps, in part, because she couldn't (or wouldn't) identify any specific threat from a specific gang member.

Of course, a defendant who is not substantially free from guilt cannot raise the defense. For example, one who joins a gang of robbers cannot claim duress when the leader says "rob Mr. X or I'll kill you."

Most jurisdictions do not recognize duress as a defense to murder. *E.g.,* Official Code Georgia Ann. § 16–3–26. The framers of the M.P.C. believe that this rule is too harsh and would make duress an affirmative defense whenever the defendant "was coerced to (commit any crime) by the use of, or a threat to use, unlawful force against his person or the person of another, which a person of reasonable firmness in his situation would have been unable to resist." M.P.C. § 2.09.

It goes without saying that in any of these cases, the person applying the duress is guilty, frequently as a first degree principal. See § 15.01 *infra.*

§ 11.04 Necessity

Necessity differs from duress in that the defendant's conduct is usually precipitated by natural rather than human forces. On occasions, however, the defense of necessity may arise from a reaction different from that anticipated in a duress producing situation. For example, in the § 11.03 *supra* hypothetical where C threatens to stab Mrs. D if she does not engage in sexual intercourse with him, Mrs. D would have the defense of necessity (not duress) to a criminal trespass charge if she runs into a stranger's house and telephones the police.

In some cases, the statute defining the crime (or the clear common law development) recognizes certain types of necessity as a defense. Indeed, self-defense (Ch. VI *supra*) probably can be categorized as a species of this defense. Another illustration [now obsolete because of Roe v. Wade, 410 U.S. 113 (1973), discussed in § 18.04B *infra*] was the necessity of preserving a pregnant woman's life as a defense to abortion.

Absent statute (or specific common law recognition such as self-defense), the scope of the defense is limited. Some courts have rejected it entirely [see, *e.g.,* R. v. Dudley and Stephens, 15 Cox Crim.Cas. 624 (Q.B.1884), discussed in § 1.03B *supra*], but this view has been rejected in the United States, sometimes on constitutional grounds [see *e.g.,* Cross v. S., 370 P.2d 371 (Wyo.1962), in which the court found the defendant not guilty of illegally shooting game animals in defense of his property due to the constitutional guarantee that one cannot be deprived of property without due process of law].

Most courts do require the necessity to be great, however, and the harm actually done to be less than the harm avoided. S. v. Green, 470 S.W.2d 565 (Mo.1971), is a good illustration of the reluctance of some courts to accept this defense. Green, a frail prison inmate, had been subjected to repeated homosexual rapes. To avoid a future attack which was threatened for that evening, he escaped. The court held this escape to be unjustifiable as a matter of law because the "[d]efendant had several hours in which to consider and report these threats." *Id.* at 568. The court was unimpressed with defendant's argument (presented in the dissenting opinion) that a "prison official told defendant that the alternatives were to defend himself, submit, or 'go over the fence.' " *Id.* at 570. Unlike *Green,* most courts allow necessity as a defense in prison safety cases, but only if the defendant turns himself in immediately upon reaching the safety of the outside world. This certainly limits the potential for abuse (and arguably any real utility) of the defense. See U.S. v. Bailey, 444 U.S. 394 (1980).

The M.P.C. limits the necessity defense to those situations in which "the harm or evil sought to be avoided by such conduct is greater than that sought to be prevented by the law defining the offense charged; and . . . a legislative purpose to exclude the justification claimed does not plainly appear." M.P.C. § 3.02.

The last part of the M.P.C.'s test is especially important. Most courts will not allow necessity where the defendant's conduct is designed to thwart some right or policy protected by the government. Thus blockades of facilities such as nuclear plants or abortion clinics because of the defendant's belief that she is doing more harm than good usually will not qualify for the necessity defense. Similarly, medically-necessary marijuana use will not be a defense to possession of marijuana if it appears that the legislature considered the problem and opted to not allow the defense. See S. v. Tate, 505 A.2d 941 (N.J.1986).

A type of case in which necessity might be expected to prevail is speeding to get a heart attack victim to the hospital. fortunately, most such cases do not reach the appellate court reporters.

§ 11.05   Entrapment

The purpose of the entrapment defense is to prevent the government from manufacturing crime. The government's role in any given crime can range from trivial to overpowering. At one extreme, an undercover police officer may do nothing more than offer to purchase narcotics at the going price from one whom he believes to be a pusher. At the other extreme, the government agent, to persuade the suspect to sell him narcotics, may apply immense pressure such as establishing a friendship for that purpose and playing on his "friend's" sympathies to overcome his "friend's" unwillingness to sell.

It is occasionally argued that entrapment should apply even in the first situation since the crime would not have occurred but for the policeman's request. Conversely, it can be contended that even in the second situation entrapment should not apply since the defendant did intentionally commit a crime. Neither of these extreme contentions have prevailed. Rather, the general rule would disallow entrapment in the first case and allow it in the second. "To determine whether entrapment has been established, a line must be drawn between the trap for the unwary innocent [entrapment] and the trap for the unwary criminal [no entrapment]." Sherman v. U.S., 356 U.S. 369 (1958).

The most significant area of disagreement in entrapment is the relevance of the defendant's predisposition towards the crime with which he is charged. Under one view, such evidence is highly relevant since it tends to establish that the defendant is not an unwary innocent. Consequently, under this view, evidence of the defendant's past criminal record is relevant to establish predisposition. Many courts that have considered the question, including the United States Supreme Court, have adopted this position. See Sherman v. U.S., *supra.*

Even under this view, it is necessary that the defendant have the predisposition *before* the government seeks to entrap him. If the government's conduct created the predisposition, the defendant is treated as though he were not predisposed, and is entitled to the defense. See Jacobson v. U.S., 503 U.S. 540 (1992).

Other courts, however, contend that the entrapper's conduct is the only relevant issue. According to this position, the question is whether inducements were sufficient to induce a hypothetical non-predisposed person to commit a crime and not whether this particular defendant was or wasn't predisposed. California [P. v. Barraza, 591 P.2d 947 (Cal.1979)] and the M.P.C. (M.P.C. § 2.13) have taken this position.

The difference can be illustrated with the following hypothetical dialogue:

Policeman: "Will you have sex with me for a million dollars?"

Woman: "Sure thing, I'd do it for two dollars."

Where predisposition is relevant, the woman would not have a defense to prostitution, since she obviously is predisposed to commit the crime. Where only the nature of the inducement is relevant, however, the court might allow the defense since the amount of the inducement arguably is such as to encourage a woman who is not particularly disposed towards prostitution to commit this crime.

The entrapment defense is aimed strictly at governmental misconduct. Thus, if a private person, unassociated with the government, entraps another into committing an offense, the defense is not available. See Henderson v. U.S., 237 F.2d 169 (5th Cir.1956).

The M.P.C. rejects entrapment when causing or threatening bodily harm (to one other than the entrapper) is an element of the offense [M.P.C. § 2.13(3)]. There is no reported litigation on this question, which hopefully means that police or other governmental agents are not encouraging this sort of activity.

The entrapment defense is not predicated on the Constitution. Consequently, states are free to adopt any test they desire or to reject the defense entirely. Currently, however, all states recognize some form of the defense.

§ 11.06　Excessive Government Involvement

In recent years, it has been argued that there are some types of government involvement in crime that are so excessive that due process forbids conviction of the government's "partner in crime," *i.e.* the real criminal. A majority of the Supreme Court appeared to endorse this proposition in Hampton v. U.S., 425 U.S. 484 (1976), a case in which one Federal agent supplied narcotics to Hampton so that he could sell them to another Federal agent. As Justice Brennan put it: "The Government is doing nothing less than buying contraband from itself through an intermediary and jailing the intermediary."

For the most part, excessive government involvement has remained a theoretical defense. In *Hampton,* only Justices Brennan, Marshall, and Stewart would have reversed the conviction. Two other justices, Powell and Blackmun, suggested that in extreme cases of outrageous governmental overinvolvement (of which *Hampton* was not an example) it might be appropriate to overturn a conviction. The remainder of the Court would never reverse a conviction on this ground. Thus far, there have been very few convictions of this kind overturned. Various F.B.I. scams involving predisposed defendants and substantial government involvement have resulted in conviction. See *e.g.* U.S. v. Gamble, 737 F.2d 853 (10th Cir.1984).

One of the post-*Hampton* cases to uphold the excessive involvement defense was U.S. v. Twigg, 588 F.2d 373 (3d Cir.1978), in which the Government agents helped set up a drug manufacturing lab providing an essential ingredient that was difficult to obtain (phenyl–2–propanone), finding an isolated farmhouse at which to set up the lab, providing a portion of the glassware, and most importantly, providing the expertise to run the laboratory, which neither of the defendants possessed. The court distinguished a pre-*Hampton* Supreme Court case, U.S. v. Russell, 411 U.S. 423 (1973), which had affirmed a drug manufacturing conviction of defendants whose phenyl–2–propanone had been provided by the government, but who personally provided the lab and the expertise to manufacture the controlled substance.

PART V
PROOF OF FACTS

CHAPTER XII
BURDEN OF PROOF

§ 12.01 Relevance to Substantive Criminal Law

At first glance, burden of proof would appear to be a procedural issue with no direct relevance to substantive criminal law. Deeper analysis, however, reveals such a close relationship between the two that burden of proof ought to be included in a comprehensive study of the criminal law.

Most issues relevant to criminal liability have to be established by the State beyond a reasonable doubt (see § 12.02, *infra*.) For example, in a murder case, the State must establish beyond a reasonable doubt that the defendant proximately caused the victim's death (see Ch. III, *supra*). Put differently, the issue of proximate causation is so important to criminal liability that we refuse to convict somebody when there is merely a reasonable possibility that he did not proximately cause the death.

At the other extreme, some potential substantive issues are simply immaterial. For example, in strict liability crimes, it is immaterial whether or not the defendant intended the harmful result. It is enough that she sold adulterated food or served liquor to a minor. For the reasons discussed in § 8.04, *supra,* we consider it better to convict a few morally innocent people than to risk the escape of several guilty ones.

In between these extremes are a category of cases in which the defendant's state of mind is relevant, but not critical. In these cases, we allow the defendant to try to prove a set of facts which if true warrant acquittal, but if not proven will result in conviction. For example, a State may wish to mollify the harshness of a statutory rape law that regards mistake of victim's age as immaterial. (See §§ 4.04, 8.06, *supra*) That same State, however, might be reluctant to require its prosecutors to prove knowledge of the victim's youth beyond a reasonable doubt. One possible compromise is to allow the defendant to prove that he made a reasonable mistake.

States which adopt this approach have effectively concluded that awareness of youth is less important than other aspects of the crime (such as intent to engage in sexual intercourse), but is not altogether immaterial.

§ 12.02 The General Rule

In general, the State is required to prove every element of a crime beyond a reasonable doubt.

Because this burden is so high, it necessarily maximizes errors. The jurors are effectively told to acquit many of those whom they believe are probably guilty (*i.e.* those whom they believe are more likely than not guilty, but about whom they have a reasonable belief of a possibility of innocence).

The reason for this seemingly abnormal approach is the belief that we do more harm by convicting an innocent person than we do by acquitting one who is guilty. In In re Winship, 397 U.S. 358 (1970), the United States Supreme Court emphasized three factors in holding that the Due Process clause precludes criminal conviction unless the State proves beyond a reasonable doubt every fact necessary to constitute the crime. First, from the perspective of the criminal defendant, an erroneous conviction results in a substantial and largely irreparable loss of liberty and standing in the community. Second, from the perspective of the criminal law, much of its moral force would be lost if large numbers of innocent people were thought to be languishing in prisons because they couldn't prove their innocence. Finally, from the perspective of the ordinary citizen going about his business, it is important to know that if he is ever accused of crime, a conviction will be impossible to obtain unless the State can prove every element of the crime beyond a reasonable doubt.

§ 12.03 What Is a Reasonable Doubt

The term "reasonable doubt" is almost never quantified. That is, it cannot be defined in percentage terms such as 72%, 87%, or even 99% certain. The test is whether the doubt, whatever its percentage, is reasonable.

The difficulty with some reasonable doubt instructions is that they can be confusing, inaccurate, or both. For example, in Cage v. Louisiana, 498 U.S. 39 (1990), the United States Supreme Court invalidated an instruction that, among other things, defined reasonable doubt as a doubt that "would give rise to a grave uncertainty," and "is an actual substantial doubt." It added: "What is required is not an absolute or mathematical certainty, but a moral certainty."

The first quoted phrase is, of course, inaccurate because a reasonable doubt does not have to give rise to a "grave" uncertainty. The second phrase is confusing. If substantial means of substance, it is correct. If it means large, it is not correct. And, given the "grave" language, it is likely that the jury understood it to mean large. Finally, the phrase "moral certainty," an archaic relic of the nineteenth century was confusing at best and wrong at worst when juxtaposed with the other instructions.

In Victor v. Nebraska, 511 U.S. 1 (1994), the Court was faced with two instructions that had some, but not all, of the *Cage* problems. In one of the *Victor* cases (*Sandoval v. California*), the Court confronted the following instruction: "It is not a mere possible doubt; because everything relating to human affairs is open to some possible or imaginary doubt. It is that state of the case which after the entire comparison and consideration of all the evidence, leaves the minds of the jurors in the condition that they cannot say that they feel an abiding conviction to a moral certainty of the truth of the charge."

The Court unanimously upheld the *Sandoval* charge. While critical of the term "moral certainty," the Court rightly concluded that, in context, the term described nothing less than reasonable doubt and therefore was not constitutionally flawed. As to the exclusion of "mere possible doubt," the court, again rightly, concluded a mere possible doubt was not a reasonable doubt.

In the other *Victor* case (Victor v. Nebraska), the charge was somewhere between *Cage* and *Sandoval*. The charge did not contend the offending "grave uncertainty" language of *Cage*. it did, however, have the offending "substantial doubt" language from *Cage* in it as well as the "moral certainty" language. Additionally, it had other questionable language equating reasonable doubt with that doubt that a reasonable person would have "in one of the graver and more important transactions of life to pause and hesitate before taking the represented facts as true." Despite the fact that people frequently marry, change jobs, and buy houses without being convinced beyond a reasonable doubt that they are doing the right thing, the Court, dividing 7–2. concluded that the instruction passed constitutional muster. It noted that, in context, the phrase "substantial" meant not imaginary. Once more, it critiqued, but did not condemn, the "moral certainty language."

The bottom line of all this is that the overall instruction must make clear that the benefit of any doubt based on reason and common sense must be given to the defendant, and that any instruction that implies otherwise will be unconstitutional.

Forty years ago, as a draftsman for the North Carolina Superior Court Judges' Pattern Jury Committee, I drafted the following reasonable doubt instruction that I still believe is a more accurate than most in explaining the law: "A reasonable doubt is not a vain, imaginary, or fanciful doubt. It is a doubt based on reason or common sense arising out of the evidence or lack of evidence as the case may be. It means that in order to convict the defendant, you must be fully satisfied and entirely convinced of his/her guilt."

Upon reflection, however, with special regard for the number of innocent people that we now know are convicted, I would embellish the charge to emphasize the distinction between clear and convincing evidence (which is insufficient) and reasonable doubt. See Loewy, *Taking Reasonable Doubt Seriously,* ___ Chicago Kent L. Rev. ___ (2009).

§ 12.04 Expansion of Winship (Mullaney v. Wilbur)

Before *Winship,* prosecutors in all states were required to prove each element of a crime beyond a reasonable doubt. (*Winship* itself arose in the quasi-criminal context of a juvenile proceeding, where the reasonable doubt principle was not so firmly entrenched.) Consequently, the *Winship* rule appeared destined to change very few, if any, procedures. In Mullaney v. Wilbur, 421 U.S. 684 (1975), however, the Supreme Court indicated a willingness to apply the concept of facts necessary to constitute a crime more seriously than some of the states.

Mullaney involved a Maine murder conviction. At that time, Maine law defined felonious homicide as a single offense divided into two categories: murder and manslaughter. The distinguishing criterion was malice aforethought. Maine presumed malice aforethought upon proof of an intentional and unlawful killing, thereby requiring the defendant to prove adequate provocation as a defense (see § 2.04, *supra*). Thus, under Maine law if the jury was uncertain as to whether or not the defendant killed in a justifiable heat of passion, it was required to return a verdict of guilty of murder.

Maine argued that inasmuch as provocation did not affect the defendant's liability for "the crime" of criminal homicide, imposing the burden on the defendant to prove mitigation did not remove the State's obligation to prove every fact necessary to constitute the crime. The Court rejected this argument, holding that the difference in lost liberty between a murder and manslaughter conviction is sufficiently great that the State cannot allow a murder conviction to be upheld unless it proves malice aforethought (*i.e.* absence of provocation) beyond a reasonable doubt.

§ 12.05 Contraction of the Rule (Patterson v. New York)

After *Mullaney* there was some doubt as to whether a defendant could ever be required to prove an affirmative defense. In Patterson v. New York, 432 U.S. 197 (1977), however, the Supreme Court held that Mullaney did not absolutely preclude such a requirement. Indeed, *Patterson* upheld the burden of proof shift in a case remarkably similar to *Mullaney*. Under the New York law at issue in *Patterson*, murder was defined as intending to cause and causing the death of another human being. The crime could be reduced to manslaughter only if the defendant proved that he acted under the influence of an extreme emotional disturbance for which there was a reasonable explanation or excuse.

The Court perceived two significant differences between *Patterson* and *Mullaney*. First, in New York, unlike Maine, malice aforethought is not an element of murder. Consequently, the absence of provocation is not necessary to establish an element of the crime. Second, by adopting the M.P.C.'s standard of "extreme emotional disturbance," New York significantly expanded a defendant's opportunity to reduce his crime to manslaughter (see § 2.04, *supra*). The Court found that saddling the defendant with the burden of proof was a reasonable quid pro quo for this substantive statutory gain.

Because *Patterson* did not overrule *Mullaney,* we know that the burden of proving exculpatory matter can sometimes be imposed on the defendant, but other times cannot be. The exact dividing line is unclear at best and wavering at worst. The Court, viewing insanity as a defense rather than the negation of mens rea (see Ch. X, *supra*), has allowed states to impose the burden of proving insanity on the defendant. See Rivera v. Delaware, 429 U.S. 877 (1976). The same result would probably apply to entrapment (§ 11.05, *supra*) or duress (§ 11.03, *supra*) which are excuses that a State is not required to recognize.

A defense like self-defense (ch. VI, *supra*) would seem to be more difficult. The defense has been universally recognized to such an extent that our collective conscience would be shocked if any State were to convict a person who killed in order to save his life from a would-be assassin. Nevertheless, where the absence of self-defense is not listed as an element of murder or assault, the Supreme Court has held that the burden of proof may be shifted to the defendant. Martin v. Ohio, 480 U.S. 228 (1987). Most jurisdictions, however, require the State to disprove self-defense beyond a reasonable doubt.

Another difficult defense is automatism (see § 9.02, *supra*). In one sense, automatism clearly negates the most basic ingredient of a crime: a voluntary act. On the other hand, the defense is closely related to insanity (see § 10.08, *supra*) in that the key to each lies in the head of the defendant. Consequently, there has been some tendency to impose the burden of proving automatism on the defendant. See Fulcher v. S., 633 P.2d 142 (Wyo. 1981). Whether the Supreme Court will uphold this burden shifting remains to be seen.

When the burden of proof is shifted to the defendant, the standard of proof is usually by a preponderance of the evidence. In Leland v. Oregon, 343 U.S. 790 (1952), however, the Supreme Court upheld a requirement that the defendant prove insanity beyond a reasonable doubt. Although such an onerous requirement on a defendant is unusual, the latest Congressional statute, 18 U.S.C.A. § 17 (see § 10.02, *supra*), requires defendants in Federal courts to prove insanity by clear and convincing evidence. (See also Ariz.Rev.Stat. § 13–502).

Sometimes an issue can arise as to whether the burden of proof really was shifted. In *Montana v. Egelhoff* (§ 11.02, *supra*), for example, where the Court held that precluding evidence of intoxication to negate purpose or knowledge in a murder case did not violate Due Process, the defendant argued that his inability to introduce evidence negating his state of mind effectively reduced the state's burden of proof. The Court (or at least **a** plurality) disagreed, holding that the State still had to prove purpose or knowledge beyond a reasonable doubt, and that an evidentiary rule designed to make it easier for the prosecutor to carry his burden was not the functional equivalent of reducing the quantum of that burden.

§ 12.06 Burden of Proof and Sentencing

In recent years, the Supreme Court has confronted the question of whether sentencing factors can be regarded as something different from elements of the crime in regard to burden of proof. For example, if a statute provides for one sentence for robbery and another if a firearm was brandished during the robbery must the state prove beyond a reasonable doubt that a firearm was brandished? Or, if the statute provides one penalty for assault and another for racially-motivated assault, must the State prove racial motivation beyond a reasonable doubt?

In general, the decisions seem to hold that if the sentence enhancing factor is merely something for the court to take into account, it need not be proven beyond a reasonable doubt. Similarly, if the sentence enhancing factor requires a mandatory minimum, but that minimum is within the statutory maximum for the crime, due process does *not* require proof of the sentencing factor beyond a reasonable doubt. However, if the sentence enhancing factor authorizes or requires a sentence *beyond* the statutory maximum, the State must prove that factor beyond a reasonable doubt.

The Supreme Court has established these propositions in four significant cases. In the first, McMillan v. Pennsylvania, 477 U.S. 79 (1986), the Court was faced with a statute that required a minimum sentence of five years for certain crimes committed with the visible possession of a firearm. However, in order to impose the sentence, the judge was only required to find the visible possession of the firearm by a preponderance of the evidence. In four companion cases, the respective trial judges all found the sentencing requirements unconstitutional and sentenced the defendants to less than the minimum five years. The United States Supreme Court disagreed, emphasizing that the maximum penalty for the relevant crimes had already been established and that judges traditionally had both the power and duty to consider certain sentencing factors. See 1.06, *supra*.

The next case, Apprendi v. New Jersey, 530 U.S. 466 (2000), involved a statute that increased the maximum penalty for certain crimes that were committed with a racial bias. Apprendi pled guilty to a crime that normally would be subject to a ten year maximum sentence. Because the trial judge found by a preponderance of the evidence that Apprendi acted with a racial bias the maximum was upped to twenty years. Acting within the latter maximum, the trial judge sentenced Apprendi to twelve years in prison. The Supreme Court reversed, largely on the ground that any factor which raises the maximum sentence must be determined by a jury and beyond a reasonable doubt.

Apprendi was followed by Ring v. Arizona, 536 U.S. 584 (2002), which involved the constitutionality of an Arizona statute that allowed a judge to find the aggravating circumstances necessary to justify capital punishment (see 1.08, *supra*) after a jury determination that the defendant was guilty of first degree murder. Following *Apprendi*, *Ring* held that absent aggravating circumstances there would be no basis for execution. In the Court's view, the aggravating circumstances in *Ring* were analogous to the racial animus in *Apprendi*. Therefore unless the jury found the aggravating circumstances beyond a reasonable doubt, capital punishment was unconstitutional.

Finally, in Harris v. U.S., 536 U.S. 545 (2002), the Supreme Court confronted the question of whether in light of *Apprendi* and *Ring* (which relied on *Apprendi* to overruled a prior contrary decision), *McMillan* should be overruled. Four of the Justices on the Court thought that *McMillan* and *Apprendi* were consistent because *Apprendi* involved expanding the maximum sentence without a jury determining the existence of supporting facts beyond a reasonable doubt, whereas *McMillan* merely involved an adjustment of sentencing within the already prescribed maximum. Four other Justices thought that the cases were not consistent and that *McMillan* should be overruled. The case was ultimately decided by Justice Breyer who agreed that *McMillan* and *Apprendi* were irreconcilable, but, adhering to his *Apprendi* dissent would have overruled *Apprendi*, and retained *McMillan*. Thus, by a 5–4 vote, *McMillan* survived.

CHAPTER XIII

PRESUMPTIONS AND INFERENCES

§ 13.01 Definitions

It is important to understand the differences among the following concepts:

(1) inference (permissive presumption);

(2) mandatory presumption requiring some evidence in rebuttal (burden of production);

(3) mandatory presumption shifting the burden of proof; and

(4) conclusive presumption.

An inference (permissive presumption) is a fact which a jury may but need not infer. A common illustration is the inference of intent from conduct. When A shoots B in the heart, killing him instantly, a jury is permitted to infer that A intended to kill B. The jury is not, however, required to reach that conclusion. If the jury were so required, it would be a mandatory presumption and not an inference.

A mandatory presumption requiring some evidence in rebuttal does not shift the burden of proof. Rather it requires a jury to accept certain facts as true unless some evidence has been introduced in rebuttal. To illustrate, in most jurisdictions when a jury finds beyond a reasonable doubt that the defendant intentionally killed the victim, the jury is under a duty to find the defendant guilty of murder unless some evidence of justification, excuse, or mitigation is introduced. For example, until some evidence of self-defense is introduced, a jury is required to find that the killing was not in self-defense. Once the defendant introduces some evidence of self-defense (*e.g.* his testimony that the victim was trying to kill him), the presumption is rebutted. At that point, the burden of disproving self-defense shifts to the State (at least in most jurisdictions; but see Martin v. Ohio. § 12.05, *supra*). Courts sometimes categorize the defendant's burden as the burden of production to distinguish it from the burden of proof (or persuasion) which remains with the State.

A mandatory presumption shifting the burden of proof differs from a mandatory presumption creating a burden of production in that the burden of proof remains with the party against whom the presumption operates. The Maine procedure invalidated in Mullaney v. Wilbur (§ 12.04, *supra*) is a good example. Once the State proved an unlawful intentional killing, malice aforethought was presumed until the defendant proved that it was more likely than not that he acted in a justifiable heat of passion. Merely introducing some evidence of heat of passion would not have rebutted that presumption.

Finally, a conclusive presumption is simply a rule of law. It requires a jury to find fact B if it has found fact A. For example, suppose a statute provides that: "It is unlawful for any person to knowingly fail to file an income tax return. Anybody who owns a copy of the Internal Revenue Code shall be deemed to know of his duty to file a tax return." Assume that the Government proves beyond a reasonable doubt that the defendant owns a copy of the Internal Revenue Code and that he failed to file his income tax. Assume further that the defendant proves that he never read the Code and had no knowledge of his duty to file the return. Under these circumstances, the defendant should be found guilty because the conclusive presumption effectively creates a rule of law which provides that: "It is unlawful for any person who owns a copy of the Internal Revenue Code to fail to file an income tax return, whether or not he knows of his obligation to do so."

§ 13.02 Constitutionality

An inference (permissive presumption) is constitutionally permissible if there is a rational connection between the proven fact and the presumed fact and the presumed fact is more likely than not to follow from the proven fact. [See County Court of Ulster County v. Allen, 442 U.S. 140 (1979)] Consequently the inference posited in § 13.01, *supra* that a jury may infer that A intended to kill B if it believes that A shot B in the heart should be a permissible one. It is certainly more likely than not that one who shoots another in the heart intends to bring about that person's death.

A prudent judge, however, should be careful not to say anything which a jury or an appellate judge could construe as a mandatory or conclusive presumption. For example, in the above hypothetical, the jury should be told that if it finds that A shot B through the heart, it may, but need not find that A intended to kill B. In any event, with or without the inference, the jury may not return a verdict of guilty unless it is convinced beyond a reasonable doubt that A in fact intended to kill B.

The Supreme Court has not explicitly dealt with mandatory presumptions requiring some evidence in rebuttal. When the presumption, as it usually does, deals with a special defense which would not normally be part and parcel of a crime (*e.g.* insanity, duress, self-defense, or provocation) it should be constitutional. The State cannot reasonably be expected to disprove a defense unless it has some idea of what the defense is. Consequently, the defendant is usually required to introduce some evidence of one of these defenses before the State is obliged to rebut it.

On the other hand, were the State to presume intent absent some evidence to the contrary, the presumption of innocence would arguably be compromised. Therefore, a better case can be made for the unconstitutionality of a presumption of intent. In Francis v. Franklin, 471 U.S. 307 (1985), the Supreme Court noted that the constitutionality of such a presumption was not before the Court, and expressly declined to resolve the issue.

A mandatory presumption which shifts the burden of proof is just another way of looking at the problems in § 12.04 and § 12.05, *supra.* To the extent that *Mullaney* precludes such a shift, the presumption is unconstitutional.

Arguably a conclusive presumption ought to be constitutional because the State is simply saying that the conclusively presumed element is immaterial. In Sandstrom v. Montana, 442 U.S. 510 (1979), however, the Supreme Court overturned a murder conviction because the jury was instructed that "the law presumes that a person intends the ordinary consequences of his voluntary acts." Montana argued that the instruction merely permitted the jury to infer intent from the defendant's conduct. The Court, however, concluded that a reasonable juror would believe either that the presumption was conclusive or rebuttable only by the defendant's proving it to be false in his case. According to the Court, either interpretation would have been unconstitutional.

Interestingly, Montana, if it so chose could have defined murder as a death resulting from a voluntary act, the ordinary consequences of which are the death of another human being (see § 2.08, *supra*). In such a case the defendant's intent to kill would have been immaterial. Because, however, Montana chose to make intent material, any presumption which allows the State to satisfy the element by less than proof beyond a reasonable doubt is unconstitutional.

PART VI

INCHOATE AND GROUP CRIMINALITY

CHAPTER XIV

ATTEMPT

§ 14.01 General Scope and Purpose

Although not recognized at very early common law, attempt is universally recognized as a part of the criminal law today (although there are jurisdictions in which it is not applicable to all offenses). In the sections which follow, the full scope and limitations of attempt will be developed. For now, however, it will suffice to conceptualize attempt as a substantial but unsuccessful effort to commit a particular crime. Because the effort must be unsuccessful, a person cannot be prosecuted for both an attempt and the completed crime. In such a case, the attempt could be said to merge with the completed crime, thereby abrogating itself.

The crime of attempt is necessary to punish those who have demonstrated that they are a manifest danger to society. The term "manifest" is employed in its literal sense and as such refers to somebody who has taken one or more affirmative steps towards the commission of a crime. Therefore, it is not inconsistent with the rule that a person cannot be punished merely for his evil thoughts (see § 9.01 *supra*).

The penalties for attempt vary, but in most jurisdictions, the attempted crime is punished less severely than the completed crime. Some have argued that this gradation scheme is explicable only if one accepts retribution as the principal justification for punishment (see § 1.02C *supra*). They contend that the need to reform the attemptor is no less than the need to reform the perpetrator of the completed crime (see § 1.02A *supra*), that the need to restrain the attemptor (§ 1.02B *supra*) may be even greater inasmuch as the attemptor has not yet completed the object of his crime and thus may be especially dangerous if unconfined, and finally that the need to deter an attempt (§ 1.02D *supra*) is virtually as important as deterring the completed crime. The M.P.C. believes that the dichotomy can be justified on the ground that a person contemplating a crime does not think he is going to be unsuccessful. M.P.C. Tent. Draft 10, p. 24. Hence, he is not going to concern himself with the penalty for an attempted crime. Therefore, that penalty has little, if any, value as a general deterrent [see § 1.02D(2) *supra*]. Consequently, from a deterrent standpoint, it makes sense to impose a relatively light penalty for attempt and reserve the more severe penalties for those crimes which a prospective defendant might reasonably contemplate committing. The M.P.C. accepts this dichotomy for the more serious offenses, such as murder, but rejects it for the less serious offenses (M.P.C. § 5.05).

Another reason for punishing attempt less seriously than the completed crime is that the attemptor has caused less harm. Inflicting harm has always been an aggravating factor in both intentional and unintentional crimes. Consequently, it is not surprising that one who commits a robbery would be punished more severely than one who merely attempts one.

§ 14.02 Mens Rea

In classic judicial language, a criminal attempt requires specific intent (see § 8.01 *supra*). To illustrate, let us examine the crime of attempted murder (note: we have already considered the closely related offense of assault with intent to commit murder which in some jurisdictions supplements and in others supplants attempted murder, § 5.03 *supra*). As indicated in § 2.01 *supra,* there are four states of mind which will generally suffice for "malice aforethought", thereby rendering a killing murder. They are (1) intent to kill, (2) intent to cause serious bodily injury, (3) outrageous recklessness and (4) perpetration of a felony. Of these, only intent to kill will suffice for attempted murder. A person who intends to inflict serious injury does not have the specific intent to kill and thus cannot be guilty of an attempted murder. See P. v. Harris, 377 N.E.2d 28 (Ill.1978). Similarly, a rapist, who knows that he is HIV positive, but does not intend to kill his victim (at least in the absence of other evidence) and, under the prevailing view, cannot be guilty of attempted murder. See Smallwood v. S., 680 A.2d 512 (Md.1996).

In M.P.C. language, it is difficult to say whether an attempt must be done "purposely," or whether "knowingly" will suffice (see § 8.01 *supra*). As a practical matter, it will not normally make much difference. One type of case in which it might make a difference is when a person, in order to collect insurance money, attaches a bomb to the ignition of her two month old Lemon V–8 automobile, hoping and expecting that it will explode when the repair shop employee drives it to the repair shop and expecting that the employee will be killed but hoping that he will not be. Of course, if the bomb explodes and the employee is killed, the car owner is guilty of at least second degree murder (§ 2.08 *supra*). But, if the bomb fails to explode, does she have a defense to attempted murder on the ground that her purpose was not to kill? Obviously, the answer depends on one's precise definition of "specific intent," and the courts have not been terribly explicit on this point. The M.P.C. opts for liability in this type of situation believing "that the manifestation of dangerousness is as great—or very nearly as great—as in the case of purposive conduct." (M.P.C. Tent. Draft 10, p. 29)

Because attempt requires a specific intent, it is impossible to attempt a crime which by definition cannot be committed intentionally. For example, involuntary manslaughter cannot be attempted because definitionally it requires its perpetrator to cause death unintentionally. (§§ 2.06, 2.10 *supra*). Thus, if one caused death intentionally his crime would not be involuntary manslaughter. Therefore, if he attempted to cause death, his crime would not be attempted involuntary manslaughter (but would be attempted murder or perhaps attempted voluntary manslaughter).

There are a few jurisdictions that reject this view, holding that an attempt need only be committed with the same state of mind necessary to commit the underlying crime. Thus attempted involuntary manslaughter can be committed by reckless conduct that comes close to causing another's death. See P. v. Thomas, 729 P.2d 972 (Colo.1986). Obviously there are problems with this view because, taken to its logical conclusion, it would hold every robber guilty of attempted felony/murder. See § 2.09, *supra*. The better view for punishing extremely reckless behavior that causes no physical harm is the M.P.C.'s reckless endangerment concept, which makes reckless endangerment a felony. See M.P.C. § 210.4. Some states have followed that approach. See N.J.S.A. 2C: 12.2.

§ 14.03 Proximity to Completion

Probably the most significant and very nearly the most difficult (except for impossibility § 14.08 *infra*) aspect of attempt is the proximity to completion one must achieve before he can be deemed to have attempted a crime. One very unenlightening re-

sponse sometimes given is that mere preparation
will not suffice. This of course does not resolve the
problem; it simply restates it. An early case, R. v.
Eagleton, 6 Cox Crim.Cas. 559 (Cr.App.1855), intimated that to be guilty of an attempt, one must
perform the last act necessary for the offense which
he is accused of attempting. This view, however, has
never taken hold—it was rejected by the *Eagleton*
court in the very year it was announced, R. v.
Roberts, 7 Cox Crim.Cas. 39 (Cr.App. 1855)—and it
is doubtful that any jurisdiction would follow it
literally today because it would virtually abolish the
offense. If D hasn't completed his crime yet (*i.e.* his
shot missed), there is still more to do (*i.e.* fire
another shot that doesn't miss).

One test employed in some jurisdictions is the
unequivocal or res ipsa loquitur test, *i.e.,* that the
defendant's act, standing alone, is unequivocally
consistent only with his intent to commit the allegedly attempted crime. In one application of the test,
Campbell and Bradley v. Ward [1955] N.Z.L.R. 471,
the defendants entered a parked car, were spotted
by police officers, fled the scene, were subsequently
apprehended and confessed that their purpose in
entering the car was to steal a battery and radio.
The court reversed an attempted larceny conviction
on the ground that their acts alone (exclusive of the
confession) were too equivocal to establish intent.

The "unequivocal" test is not without its detractors. One criticism is that it reduces the value of
confessions in attempt cases. While there may be
some dispute as to the value of police obtained

confessions as in *Campbell*, the unequivocal test would also limit the value of extra-official confessions. Thus, if Campbell and Bradley had told an innocent third party that they planned to steal a battery and radio from the car, and the third party had reported this to the police, conviction still would have been impossible.

Perhaps a more serious indictment of the "unequivocal" test is that virtually no act is truly res ipsa loquitur. Even a person who empties a six-shooter into another can argue that he was only trying to injure the victim and that it was his skilled shooting and not luck that prevented the victim's death. It is unlikely, however, that any jurisdiction would refuse to submit such a case to the jury on the ground that no unequivocal intent had been shown. Thus, in the strong sense of the term, the whole concept of unequivocality is a myth.

Even accepting the test as one of relative unequivocality, it seems inherently incapable of properly separating those who should be punished from those who should not be. Presumably, a person who makes a careful diagram of a home he is planning to burglarize, including the manner in which he intends to enter, has performed a relatively unequivocal act (what reason other than burglary could he have?). Yet, this person is so much farther from his ultimate objective than the defendants in *Campbell* that it seems unjust to adopt a test which would convict him and acquit them.

Another test frequently employed asks whether the defendant is dangerously close to completion. Of the modern rules, this one comes closest to the *Eagleton* last act test. Under it, a would-be robber who had not yet located his victim was acquitted of attempted robbery, P. v. Rizzo, 158 N.E. 888 (N.Y. 1927), and a prospective building burner who had arranged combustibles in the building and driven to within a quarter of a mile thereof to burn it before changing his mind was found to be not guilty of an attempt, C. v. Peaslee, 59 N.E. 55 (Mass.1901).

Some jurisdictions permit an attempt conviction when a defendant with the requisite criminal intent performs a substantial act towards the commission of a crime. Under this test, a prospective burglar was convicted of attempted burglary upon being apprehended in an alley with burglar tools, even though he hadn't yet determined which of the buildings he was going to burglarize, P. v. Gibson, 210 P.2d 747 (Cal.App.1949). The M.P.C. opts for this approach inculpating he who "purposely does or omits to do anything which, under the circumstances as he believes them to be, is an act or omission constituting a substantial step in a course of conduct planned to culminate in his commission of the crime." The M.P.C. adds the caveat that the conduct must be "strongly corroborative of the actor's criminal purpose." It lists several seemingly preparatory activities, however, which it would not deem insufficient per se. Among these are "searching for ... the contemplated victim" (compare *Rizzo, supra*), "reconnoitering the place contemplated for the commission of the crime" and "soliciting an innocent agent to engage in conduct constituting an element of the crime." M.P.C. §§ 5.01(1)(c), 5.02(2)(a), (c), (g).

The principal advantage of the "substantial act" test is that it permits the criminal law to reach farther back into preparatory conduct, thereby facilitating the police in their efforts to "nip crime in the bud." Of course, this creates a concomitant disadvantage in that it significantly increases the risk that people who have not firmly determined to commit a crime will be convicted. This problem can be exacerbated where a dubiously obtained confession induces a court to minimize, if not ignore, the "substantiality" requirement. See, *e.g.,* McQuirter v. S., 63 So.2d 388 (Ala.App.1953).

Sometimes a court will purport to apply the M.P.C. substantial act test, but reverse a conviction by emphasizing what has not been done, rather than what has been done. See U.S. v. Still, 850 F.2d 607 (9th Cir.1988). Obviously, that is not what the M.P.C. had in mind by drafting its test. But, one must always be careful to analyze what a court is in fact doing, not simply what it says it is doing.

A final test for attempt, sometimes called the "probable desistance" test, asks whether the defendant had gone so far along the road of crime that it is unlikely that he would have voluntarily desisted from completing the crime. When this test is employed objectively (*i.e.,* would the average person who had done this be likely to voluntarily desist?), it seems fair as well as reasonably aimed at what ought to be the most relevant question in deciding whether to punish inchoate criminality (although, perhaps unavoidably, a bit vague). When, however, it is employed subjectively (*i.e.*, would this person be likely to voluntarily desist?), it is susceptible of unfair application. For example, two people might be caught doing precisely the same thing (*e.g.*, carrying burglar tools in a courtyard, see *Gibson supra*), one of whom may be convicted because of his past propensity for going through with such criminal designs, while the other may be acquitted because of his propensity in the other direction. Thus, the result might depend more on what he had done in the past than on what he is doing today (compare entrapment § 11.05 *supra*). Not all of the "probable desistance" cases are clear as to whether they are applying an objective or subjective test.

It would be inappropriate to close this section without noting that a large number of jurisdictions have not really defined the boundaries of attempt beyond the unilluminating observation that mere preparation will not suffice.

§ 14.04   Abandonment

Regardless of how a jurisdiction separates preparation from attempt, a defendant who crosses the line, but then abandons his criminal scheme, may argue that he should not be convicted. When the alleged crime is assault or battery with the intent to commit a more serious crime such as murder or rape (see § 5.03 *supra*), rather than merely attempted murder or rape, courts rarely if ever accept abandonment as a defense. This is because the assault or battery is a completed crime in itself (see §§ 5.01, 5.02 *supra*) as well as an attempt to commit the more serious crime (rape or murder). And, of course, a crime already completed cannot be abandoned. [Technically an assault which is defined as an attempted battery might be deemed an incomplete or inchoate crime. Nevertheless, it is a very special kind of attempt, requiring the last possible act short of completion (see § 5.02 *supra*). Therefore, it is more like a completed crime than most attempts.]

Even when the attempt has not reached the level of an assault, there is one instance where no court would accept abandonment as a defense. This is when the abandonment is involuntary. While courts are not totally uniform as to what constitutes involuntariness, it is clear that such things as the arrival of a policeman when the robbery is about to be completed, Stewart v. S., 455 P.2d 914 (Nev.1969), or a well-placed kick by a prospective rape victim will render the abandonment precipitated thereby involuntary. Even in more marginal cases, when the reason for abandonment does not totally negate culpability [such as a would be rapist's achieving emission prior to penetration, Roundtree v. S., 43 So.2d 12 (Fla.1949), or learning that his intended victim is pregnant, Le Barron v. S., 145 N.W.2d 79 (Wis.1966)], courts tend to treat the abandonment as involuntary. Sometimes this result is justified by the extraneous nature of the causative factor. More

realistically, it is because given the original manifestation of dangerousness, the defendant's qualified
abandonment does not dispel the danger.

When the abandonment is truly voluntary, *i.e.,*
prompted by no extraneous circumstances, courts
are divided as to whether it constitutes a defense.
Those rejecting the defense analogize attempt to a
completed crime, noting that a thief cannot avoid a
larceny conviction by returning the property and
apologizing. Similarly, they contend that a prospective thief who goes so far as to attempt larceny
should not be exculpated by his decision to abandon
the project. Furthermore, it can be argued that
denying the abandonment defense buttresses the
deterrent attributes of attempt in that it warns a
prospective criminal that once he gets in too deep,
he will not be able to extricate himself.

Those jurisdictions recognizing voluntary abandonment do so on the theory that an inchoate crime
is not analogous to a completed one and that a
person who is prepared to discontinue his criminal
endeavor prior to fruition should be encouraged to
do so. See S. v. Latraverse, 443 A.2d 890 (R.I.1982).
Indeed, it is hard to imagine a person whom we
would like to deter any more than one who has
crossed the line dividing preparation from attempt,
but has not yet completed the substantive crime.

To some extent, acceptance *vel non* of the voluntary abandonment defense may depend upon the
jurisdiction's definition of attempt. Jurisdictions requiring the defendant's act to be dangerously proxi-

mate to completion might be loathe to exculpate a defendant who has gone this far, regardless of his change of heart. For example, in S. v. Gartlan, 512 S.E.2d 74 (N.C.Ct.App.1999), a depressed minister tried to kill himself and his children by allowing carbon monoxide to come from his car into his home. (His motive for killing the children was apparently that he did not want them to have to live without him after his suicide.) After one of his children awoke him to tell him another one was ill, he realized the error of his ways, turned off the car, summoned help, and all of the children were saved. Nonetheless, his conviction for attempted murder was upheld largely because North Carolina requires that an attempt be dangerously proximate, and, having gone that far, it is too late to abandon the project.

On the other hand, a jurisdiction requiring merely a substantial act towards the completion of a crime might be expected to view the voluntary abandonment defense more favorably. Thus, it is not surprising that the M.P.C. accepts the defense. M.P.C. § 5.01(4). Similarly, one would expect the defense to be honored in probable desistance jurisdictions (especially subjective probable desistance jurisdictions) since the defendant has demonstrated the certainty and not merely the probability of desistance. Unfortunately, there do not appear to be enough decisions on abandonment to ascertain the accuracy of these expectations.

Even where voluntary abandonment is not recognized as a defense as such, its presence may be sufficient to induce a court to find that the defendant never crossed the preparation attempt line in the first place [see C. v. Peaslee, 59 N.E. 55 (Mass. 1901) and § 14.03 *supra*] or that he never harbored the requisite intent for attempt [see Oakley v. S., 125 N.W.2d 657 (Wis.1964) and § 14.02 *supra*].

§ 14.05   Solicitation Vis–A–Vis Attempt

Although late in developing, the common law ultimately recognized solicitation as a crime, at least when felonies and serious misdemeanors were solicited. R. v. Higgins, 102 Eng.Rep. 269 (K.B. 1801). This continues to be the law in some jurisdictions. Others are more selective, punishing only selected solicitations, such as riot or bribery. Even those jurisdictions that punish all or most solicitations rarely punish them as severely as the crime being solicited. The M.P.C. rejects this position, believing the solicitor to be as dangerous as the perpetrator of the completed crime, and punishes him with equal severity except when the crime is extremely serious, such as murder (M.P.C. § 5.05). Compare § 14.01 *supra*.

Because solicitations are almost always communicated by speech (or writing) and frequently involve political objectives (*e.g.,* violent overthrow of the government), the First Amendment is often a factor in solicitation cases. Both common law solicitation and the First Amendment require that the solicitor specifically intend that the solicitee(s) engage in a particular kind of criminal conduct. Further, the First Amendment prohibits punishment unless the solicitor incites as opposed to merely advocates criminal action. Brandenburg v. Ohio, 395 U.S. 444 (1969); *cf.* Yates v. U.S., 354 U.S. 298 (1957). Thus, a person who tells his audience that they ought to burn down city hall is not likely to be convicted (even if much to the delight of the speaker, some of his audience in fact burn down city hall) whereas one who tells his audience that they must burn it down now most likely will be convicted. Two additional factors must be considered, however. First, a seemingly uninciting exhortation may be known by both the speaker and the audience to be a call to immediate action, in which case, conviction may be appropriate. Second, a statement which on the record may look inciting, may have in fact been intended as mere political hyperbole, thereby rendering a conviction improper. See Watts v. U.S., 394 U.S. 705 (1969).

Regardless of whether soliciting a particular crime is itself an offense, it is possible to argue that such conduct constitutes an attempt. When the solicitee is an innocent agent (*e.g.,* defendant asks a teenager to bring him what he claims is his car, but which in fact belongs to another), this argument is especially persuasive. However some courts (those requiring a dangerous proximity to completion, see § 14.03 *supra*) would not impose attempt liability unless the solicitee accepted. S. v. Bowles, 79 P. 726 (Kan.1905).

When the solicitee is aware of the criminal enterprise (*e.g.,* a hired killer), many courts require the solicitee to do sufficient acts to constitute an attempt before the solicitor can be convicted of attempt. S. v. Davis, 6 S.W.2d 609 (Mo.1928). Indeed, a few courts would never permit such a solicitor to be guilty of an attempt on the ground that he, the solicitor, never personally intended to commit the offense. See S. v. Schleifer, 121 A. 805 (Conn.1923). Under this view, a solicitor is guilty of solicitation (or nothing) until such time as the crime is completed at which time he becomes an accessory before the fact (see § 15.01 *infra*) to the substantive offense. There are some jurisdictions, however, that treat solicitation, Rudolph v. S., 107 N.W. 466 (Wis. 1906), or solicitation plus, such as paying money or aiding with plans to perpetrate the crime, S. v. Mandel, 278 P.2d 413 (Ariz.1954), as being sufficient to impose attempt liability. More commonly, however, solicitation is treated as an attempt when the crime would be complete or nearly complete upon the solicitee's acceptance (*e.g.*, bribery). S. v. Bunch, 177 S.W. 932 (Ark.1915).

§ 14.06 Other Preparatory Offenses

A. BURGLARY

We have already examined burglary as a crime against property (§ 7.11 *supra*). At this juncture it is appropriate to examine it as a preparatory inchoate offense. Both attempt and burglary require a specific intent to commit a crime. Both require a substantial overt act. The nature of the act and its proximity to completion vary for attempt (§ 14.03

supra) whereas for burglary, a breaking and entry are normally required (§ 7.11 *supra*). At this point, however, the similarity ends.

Attempt is at most punished as severely and usually is punished less severely than the completed crime (§ 14.01 *supra*). Burglary, on the other hand, is usually a more severe offense than that which is contemplated. For example, larceny (even from a home) which is usually the object of burglary, is rarely punishable by more than five years imprisonment. Yet burglary, which is merely breaking and entering with intent to commit the larceny, is sometimes punishable by life imprisonment. Furthermore, unlike attempt, which merges with the substantive crime, burglary usually does not merge, thus rendering a person liable to be convicted of both burglary and larceny upon his pilfering property after a break-in. *E.g.,* Mead v. S., 489 P.2d 738 (Alaska 1971).

B.　POSSESSION

In an effort to nip crime in the bud, legislation has been enacted punishing possession of certain items. Sometimes the crime requires an intent to misuse the item (*e.g.,* possession of obscene books with intent to distribute them). Other possession crimes require no more than possession, but are aggravated by a wrongful intent (*e.g.,* possession of marijuana frequently is treated as a misdemeanor, but is aggravated to a felony when the defendant intends to distribute it). In either of the above two cases, juries are sometimes permitted to infer wrongful intent from the quantity of the item possessed. When, however, such an inference does not logically follow from the fact of possession, it would violate due process to let the case go to the jury. Barnes v. U.S., 412 U.S. 837 (1973), Turner v. U.S., 396 U.S. 398 (1970). See § 13.02, *supra*. Finally, there are some possessory offenses in which mere possession is sufficient. In some states, possession of burglar tools is in this category.

C. VAGRANCY

Until fairly recently, it was not uncommon for the police to charge someone with vagrancy whom they suspected was up to criminal activity, but whose actions had not gone far enough to constitute an attempt. In those instances, in which the defendant had almost (but evidently not quite) gone far enough for an attempt, this was not a serious abuse. For example, in S. v. Grenz, 175 P.2d 633 (Wash. 1946), the defendant, equipped with chicken-stealing equipment, had almost, but not quite broken into a chicken fence. While conceding (arguably incorrectly) that the defendant had not proceeded far enough for an attempt, the court sustained his vagrancy conviction. Unfortunately, vagrancy convictions could be sustained on a lot less, such as being Black in a predominantly White area. After Papachristou v. Jacksonville, 405 U.S. 156 (1972), however, it is doubtful that the typical vagrancy statute can be sustained even in the *Grenz* situation, much less in a case in which the crime is seriously abused. (See § 18.01 *infra*).

§ 14.07 Attempt to Attempt

It is nothing short of black letter law to say that "there is no such thing as an attempt to attempt a crime." While undoubtedly accurate as an abstract proposition of law, the simplicity in which the maxim is couched belies the number of instances that the law has reached beyond the attempt stage and punished what would otherwise be preparation. Two such instances, possession of certain items and vagrancy, were discussed in the immediately preceding section.

Some jurisdictions recognize attempted solicitation. This can occur where the solicitor mails an inciting letter to a prospective solicitee which is never received by him. R. v. Banks, 12 Cox Crim. Cas. 393 (Wor.Sp.Assizes 1873).

Burglary, which has its inchoate aspects (§ 14.06A *supra*) can also be attempted. Thus, in a sense, a person planning to break into another's home to steal, but caught before reaching the premises, can be guilty of "attempted attempted larceny." Indeed, this progression can go back even further since possession of burglar tools is frequently a criminal offense (§ 14.06B *supra*).

By far the most interesting cases in this area are the attempted assault cases. Where assault is defined as intentionally putting another in fear of a battery (see § 5.02 *supra*) there is of course no basis for denying the possibility of an attempt. Where, however, assault is defined as an attempted battery, attempted assault looks very much like the forbidden "attempt to attempt" a battery. For this reason some courts have held that there is no such crime as attempted assault. *E.g.,* Allen v. P., 485 P.2d 886 (Colo.1971). Other courts, however, have held that an attempted assault can exist, defining it as an attempted battery which has not progressed far enough to be an assault. An excellent illustration upholding such a theory is S. v. Wilson, 346 P.2d 115 (Ore.1959), in which the defendant was captured after trying to locate his wife in her place of employment with the intent to shoot her.

§ 14.08 Impossibility

Perhaps the most difficult aspect of attempt (if not all of criminal law) is the appropriately named defense of "impossibility." "Impossibility" is particularly difficult to capsulize in a nutshell because as soon as one appears to have developed an all encompassing theory, somebody will think of a case which doesn't quite fit, thereby requiring either an anomalous result or reformulation of the theory. Furthermore, various fact situations tend to differ ever so slightly from one another, gradually shading from one category to another, but often not clearly in any. Thus, one cannot always say for certain whether a particular case is determined by one principle or another. The best that can be done is to apply one's overall understanding of the subject area to a particular case and thereby attempt to resolve it. It is absolutely imperative that the reader recognize this limitation if he is to have any hope of understanding the "impossibility" defense.

One type of "impossibility" which is universally recognized as a defense is true "legal" or "juridical" impossibility, *i.e.*, when that which the defendant thinks she is doing as well as that which she is in fact doing is not forbidden by the law. To illustrate, in some jurisdictions, a person who lies under oath by making a false, but immaterial statement, cannot be convicted of perjury. Neither can she be convicted of attempted perjury even if she believes that a false immaterial statement is perjurious. *Cf.* P. v. Teal, 89 N.E. 1086 (N.Y.1909). Similarly, in a jurisdiction adopting the common law rule which renders a boy under fourteen legally incapable of rape (see § 11.01 *infra*), such a boy cannot be guilty of attempted rape since that which he thinks he is doing (forcibly engaging in sexual relations) does not, because of his age, constitute rape. Foster v. C., 31 S.E. 503 (Va.1898).

There is another category of "impossibility" sometimes denominated "legal," but analytically very different from true "legal" or "juridical" impossibility. That is the situation in which that which the defendant thinks he is in fact doing is against the law, but that which he is doing is lawful. Classic examples include the professor who takes what she thinks is her colleague's umbrella, but which actually is her own, or the man who has forcible sexual relations with a woman he believes to be his sister-in-law, but who turns out to be his wife. By denominating this type of impossibility "legal," courts have reversed an attempted embracery (jury tampering) conviction of one who offered a bribe to a supposed juror who was in fact not a juror, S. v. Porter, 242 P.2d 984 (Mont.1952), and a conviction for attempt to take a deer out of season because the deer turned out to be stuffed, S. v. Guffey, 262 S.W.2d 152 (Mo.App.1953). In U.S. v. Thomas, 13 U.S.C.M.A. 278 (1962), however, the Uniform Court of Military Justice upheld an attempted rape conviction, notwithstanding that unbeknown to the defendants, the victim had died prior to the rape.

The difference between the categories is that in a case like *Thomas,* the only reason the defendant is not guilty of completed rape is a *fact* (she was dead) about which he was mistaken. On the other hand, in the "true legal impossibility" case, everything that the defendant intended (in any sense of the word) to do was permitted by law. Thus, he cannot be guilty. In a sense, this is the converse of the "ignorance of the law is no excuse" maxim (§ 8.07 *supra*). Just as one cannot normally be acquitted because he didn't know his conduct was unlawful, he cannot be convicted because he didn't know his conduct was lawful.

There is a third type of "impossibility" sometimes categorized as "legal" that occurs when a law requires a particular element or condition as a prerequisite to an attempt, and that condition is not met. The classic illustration is R. v. Carr, 168 Eng. Rep. 854 (Cr.Cas.Res.1819), in which the defendant, who attempted to shoot another with an unloaded gun which he thought was loaded, was acquitted of the statutory crime of attempting to discharge a loaded gun at another. To distinguish this type of impossibility from true "legal impossibility," it is helpful to think of it as "conditional impossibility" (although courts have not employed this phrase). When the condition is clearly required for the attempt (as in *Carr*), the result seems reasonable. There have been instances, however, in which courts have imposed totally unreasonable conditions on attempt liability. The oft-cited case of P. v. Jaffe, 78 N.E. 169 (N.Y.1906), is a good illustration. Jaffe appealed a conviction for attempting to receive stolen goods, knowing the same to be stolen. The goods had lost their character as stolen goods inasmuch as they had been returned to their rightful owner who was "playing along" to get Jaffe (the fence) convicted. The Court of Appeals reversed Jaffe's conviction on the ground that an attempt required knowledge of the stolen character of the goods which of course could not exist if the goods were not in fact stolen. The fallacy of this reasoning is that knowledge in this absolute sense is not a condition of the crime. Rather, all that is required is subjective belief. If the rule were otherwise, nobody could ever be convicted of receiving stolen goods. A fence could always say "I believed that the goods were stolen, but I didn't 'know' it to a certainty." See § 7.07 *supra*.

The framers of the M.P.C., citing *Jaffe* as an example of the misuse of the "impossibility" defense, reject legal as well as factual impossibility

except when it is "true legal impossibility." M.P.C.
§ 5.01(1)(a) and M.P.C. Tent. Draft 10, pp. 30–38.

Factual impossibility (that is where that which
the defendant is trying to do is unlawful, but his
means are incapable of achieving these ends) is
rarely recognized as a defense. Thus, an impotent
old man who tries to rape a girl can be guilty of
attempted rape, Preddy v. C., 36 S.E.2d 549 (Va.
1946) [although evidence of personal awareness of
his impotence is relevant to show that he really
lacked the specific intent to rape necessary for an
attempt, S. v. Ballamah, 210 P. 391 (N.M.1922)].
Similarly, a prospective pickpocket who picks an
empty pocket and a would-be con man who tells an
unbelieved lie are guilty of attempted larceny, R. v.
Ring, 17 Cox Crim.Cas. 491 (Cr.Cas.Res.1892), and
attempted false pretenses, C. v. Johnson, 167 A. 344
(Pa.1933), respectively.

Even when the impossibility is factual, there is a
reluctance to impose liability where the chance of
success is so remote that the defendant has not
manifested himself as dangerous. The classic example of this is the voodoo doctor who fervently ex-
pects his malediction to cause another's death. The
M.P.C., while not per se exculpating this type of
attempt, does provide that "(i)f the particular conduct charged to constitute a criminal attempt . . . is
so inherently unlikely to result or culminate in the
commission of a crime that neither such conduct
nor the actor presents a public danger warranting
the grading of such offense under this Section, the
Court shall exercise its power . . . to enter judgment

and impose sentence for a crime of lower grade or degree, or in extreme cases, may dismiss the prosecution." M.P.C. § 5.05(2).

Of course, the cases are seldom this easy. The defendant who feeds a harmless substance to his intended victim, thinking it is poison, is no closer to murder than the voodoo doctor. Yet, the defendant himself is more dangerous since he probably will use greater care in his next effort. When he actually does administer poison, but not enough to cause death, courts have little difficulty in imposing liability for attempted murder. C. v. Kennedy, 48 N.E. 770 (Mass.1897).

A final factor in the impossibility cases is the objective certainty of a defendant's intent. When, for example, a defendant administers water to his intended victim, it is hard to be objectively certain that he really intended to poison her. (Compare the "unequivocality" test, § 14.03 *supra*). Of course, much of the difficulty might disappear if the defendant asks a store clerk for a bottle of arsenic and immediately serves the contents of the bottle (which turned out to be water) to his intended victim. The concept of objective certainty probably justifies the "no liability" result which courts tend to reach in cases which they wrongly categorize as cases of "legal impossibility." For example, the professor who takes her own umbrella believing it belongs to her colleague should be acquitted of attempt not because it was legally impossible (nor, as is sometimes argued, because one can't be punished for her thoughts alone), but because objectively speaking, she has done nothing to manifest herself as a thief.

In recent years, the problems of objective certainty and legal impossibility have been raised in cases involving sting operations by adult police officers pretending to be juveniles interested in sex. The adult who actually answers an email to meet a person posing as a child has usually, but not always, been convicted. The issues, of course, are how sure are we of the defendant's actual intent (as opposed to fantasy) and whether the jurisdiction views this type of impossibility as "legal."

CHAPTER XV

ACCOUNTABILITY FOR THE ACTS OF OTHERS

§ 15.01 Parties to Crime

If every crime were the work of a single criminal, there would be no need for this section. Unfortunately for both society and the criminal law student, such is not the case. A typical crime might have many parties. For example, the big boss may dispatch A, B, and C to rob a bank. A to perform the actual robbery, B to stand by as a lookout and to aid if necessary, and C to drive the getaway car. The plans might further call for A, B, and C to hide out at the boss' mountain cabin with the boss and his girlfriend providing the shelter.

In the above fact pattern, the big boss is an accessory before the fact. He is not a principal because he was not present at the time the crime was being committed. Nevertheless, he did counsel, procure and/or encourage the commission of the crime. Thus, he is an accessory before the fact. At common law an accessory before the fact could not be punished unless the principal was first convicted and even then was generally subject to less severe penalties. Most jurisdictions reject both of these rules today, subjecting the accessory before the fact to the same punishment as the principal and allowing him to be convicted regardless of whether or not the principal is convicted (although it must, of course, be proven that somebody actually committed the crime). Inasmuch as the accessory before the fact is frequently (as in the hypothetical) the "brains" of the operation, the rejection of these common law rules seems sound.

A, who actually robbed the victim, is a first degree principal. B and C are second degree principals. B is a second degree principal (or aider and abettor) because he was present at the time of the robbery giving aid and comfort to A, the first degree principal. C is also a second degree principal because though not actually present in the bank, he was "constructively present," that is, aiding the commission of the crime inside the bank by his very presence outside of the bank. The terms first degree principal and second degree principal are descriptive terms designed to aid analysis. Even at common law, there never was any difference in penalty between them nor was it necessary that one be convicted before the other, and this lack of differentiation continues today.

An accessory after the fact is one who, though not present at the commission of the crime, renders aid, comfort, and/or shelter to the criminal. In the hypothetical, both the big boss and his girlfriend are accessories after the fact, assuming of course that the girlfriend knew about the crime. It is possible for the same person to be both an accessory before the fact and an accessory after the fact to the same crime (although research has disclosed no case sustaining a total punishment in excess of that authorized for the principal criminal). Thus, the big boss can be liable in a dual capacity. It is not possible, however, to be both a principal and an accessory before or after the fact. Thus, neither A, B nor C are accessories after the fact no matter how much they shield each other. Both at common law and today, accessories after the fact are punished less severely than principals and their liability is dependent upon the principal's guilt.

Two other types of post-crime aid are misprision of a felony and compounding a felony. The ancient crime of misprision of a felony was said to be complete upon mere failure to report a known felony. There is little evidence, however, that it was ever more than a textbook crime, and though an occasional court has accepted it [*e.g.,* S. v. Flynn, 217 A.2d 432 (R.I.1966)], there have been very few prosecutions therefor in the United States.

Compounding a felony, that is accepting money or other consideration in exchange for not prosecuting or reporting a felony was recognized at common law and is still recognized today. It is seldom enforced (although it could be) when a victim accepts compensation from the criminal in exchange for his agreement not to prosecute. It is normally used to punish a bribed witness whose failure to report the crime he witnessed may be thought to obstruct justice.

§ 15.02 Actus Reus (How Far Must One Go)

An aider and abettor or accessory before the fact must aid or encourage the commission of a crime. The easiest kind of case is one in which the defendant actually performs some physical act in support of the crime. Hence, one who furnishes a gun to a murderer or a room to a prostitute, acts as a lookout for a robber, or aids a murderer by preventing another from delivering a warning to the victim, have all committed a sufficient act to be aiders and abettors or accessories before the fact. (*Note*: some of the above may not be convicted because of insufficient mens rea, § 15.03 *infra*, in spite of the sufficiency of their act.) Indeed, merely speaking words of encouragement has been held to suffice. Hicks v. U.S., 150 U.S. 442 (1893).

The more difficult cases are those in which the defendant is present at the time of the crime under circumstances suggesting approval. Usually, this is insufficient to impose liability, but there are exceptions. One obvious exception is when the defendant is under a duty to act (compare § 9.06, *supra*). Thus, it is arguable that a father may not stand idly by while his minor son attacks a third party. *Cf.* S. v. Miranda, 715 A.2d 680 (Conn.1998). Similarly, in some jurisdictions the owner of an automobile cannot sit back in the passenger seat while her friend drives it in a reckless manner. Story v. U.S., 16 F.2d 342 (D.C.Cir.1926).

Another basis for complicity is accompanying the principal to the scene of a contemplated crime pursuant to an agreement to render such aid as may be necessary. Even if the necessity never materializes, the defendant's being there for that purpose is sufficient. See Hicks v. U.S., *supra*.

The hardest cases (and the ones which most severely split the courts) are those raising the question of how much circumstantial evidence is sufficient to allow the jury to infer complicity from the non-manifestation of disapproval. Bailey v. U.S., 416 F.2d 1110 (D.C.Cir.1969) held that the defendant's brief discussion with the principal robber just prior to an armed robbery together with his joining the flight of the principal defendant upon their hearing a witness shout, "Look, they're robbing him," was insufficient to allow a jury to infer complicity. The court reasoned that his presence and discussion with the principal were not necessarily related to the robbery, and his flight was as consistent with innocent fear as it was with guilt. The dissent maintained that the defendant's prior association with the principal (they had earlier been participants in a dice game), coupled with his flight, warranted a jury concluding that Bailey was involved in the crime.

In addition to the question of sufficiency of evidence, cases of this type sometimes turn on clarity of the jury instruction. For example, in U.S. v. Garguilo, 310 F.2d 249 (2d Cir.1962), the court reversed the conviction of one about whom there was testimony that he personally carried counterfeit bills for the principal defendant. The court based its reversal on the instruction which implied that presence, coupled with knowledge and passive approval, was sufficient; a position which it rejected.

The difficulty facing the courts in cases like *Bailey* and *Garguilo* is that they must choose between branding the defendant a serious felon (robber or counterfeiter in these cases) or exculpating him entirely. Yet, in reality his conduct may be somewhere between these extremes. One alternative is to allow conviction on relatively flimsy evidence and expect the trial judge to accommodate his sentence accordingly.

Whatever evidence is required, courts do not insist upon "but for" causation. That is, they do not require the state to prove that but for the aid, the crime would not have been committed (a well nigh impossible requirement). There must, however, at least have been the possibility that the aid could have been effective. Thus, if A shouts at B telling him to kill C, but B kills C without hearing A, there is authority holding A not liable, Clem v. S., 33 Ind. 418 (1870), although even under these circumstances the M.P.C. would impose liability [M.P.C. § 2.06(3)(a)(ii)]. If, however, B does hear A, but claims he would have killed C anyway, A is liable for this added (though perhaps unnecessary) encouragement.

Any substantial affirmative cover-up aid will suffice for accessory after the fact liability. In addition to actually hiding the defendant, false statements of his whereabouts to police will suffice. P. v. Duty, 74 Cal.Rptr. 606 (Cal.App.1969). A refusal to cooperate with police or a withholding of known relevant information, however, is not normally sufficient. S. v. Clifford, 502 P.2d 1371 (Or.1972).

§ **15.03** Mens Rea (Intentional Crimes)

This section is limited to crimes that must be committed purposely or knowingly (also known as "specific intent" crimes, see § 8.01, *supra*). Accessorial liability for crimes which can be committed unintentionally will be discussed in § 15.05, *infra*.

In most jurisdictions, the defendant must act knowingly. That is he must know (1) that the principal is going to commit a crime; and (2) that his (the aider and abettor or accessory before the fact) conduct is likely to aid in that endeavor. See S. v. Daves, 144 N.W.2d 879 (Iowa 1966). Generally, a belief is tantamount to knowledge. Thus, a seller's belief that his product will be used to commit a crime may suffice for this element. R. v. Bainbridge, [1959] 3 All E.R. 200 (Cr.App.).

In addition to knowledge, most jurisdictions require an intent to aid. Thus a defendant who sees A killing B, tries to dissuade A, but winds up unintentionally encouraging him is not guilty of aiding and abetting murder. Hicks v. U.S., 150 U.S. 442 (1893).

The difficulty here, as elsewhere in the law (compare, *e.g.*, § 14.02 *supra*), is in ascertaining the meaning of intent. In one sense, of course, a person who knows that his conduct will facilitate a crime and engages in that conduct anyway "intends" to commit that crime. In another sense, however, one who has no desire that the crime occur, but merely wishes to make a sale of a particular item, regardless of how it is used, does not "intend" to commit a crime. Illustrations are as limitless as a law professor's imagination: *e.g.,* (1) A sells B a gun and bullets, knowing that B intends to assassinate the President of the United States; (2) C rents a motel room to D, knowing that she intends to use it for purposes of prostitution; and (3) E, a tailor, makes F a coat with special pockets, knowing that he intends to use it for smuggling. Neither A, C, nor E in the hypotheticals desire the results contemplated by B, D, and F—they merely wish to sell the armaments, rent a room and make a coat, respectively.

The two leading cases point in opposite directions. In one, Backun v. U.S., 112 F.2d 635, 637 (4th Cir.1940), Judge Parker said: "The seller may not ignore the purpose for which the purchase is made if he is advised of that purpose, or wash his hands of the aid that he has given the perpetrator of a felony by the plea that he has merely made a sale of merchandise." In the other, U.S. v. Peoni, 100 F.2d 401, 402 (2d Cir.1938), Judge Learned Hand opined: "All the words used—even the most colorless, 'abet'—carry an implication of purposive attitude towards [the crime]." Although the modern tendency is probably in favor of the *Peoni* rule [adopted by the M.P.C. § 2.06(3)(a)], there have not been that many decisions and sometimes other factors have been considered. Compare P. v. Beeman, 674 P.2d 1318 (Cal.1984), with U.S. v. Fountain, 768 F.2d 790 (7th Cir.1985).

Sometimes courts have predicated liability on the defendant's stake in the venture. See S. v. Gladstone, 474 P.2d 274 (Wash.1970). In a sense, all defendants who sell products have such a stake, since the principal would not purchase the item if he were not going to commit the crime. As the term is usually employed, however, it means something more. A portion of the proceeds from the crime will obviously suffice. Similarly an increased rate in the prostitution hypothetical could convict the motel owner of living off the earnings of a prostitute, R. v. Thomas, [1957] 2 All E.R. 181 (C.Cr.), whereas merely renting the room would not suffice (except in a jurisdiction strictly adhering to the *Backun* admonition).

When the item sold has no legitimate use, a court might predicate liability upon knowledge plus sale alone. A tailor-made coat with special pockets for smuggling provides a classic illustration. One difficulty with imposing liability in such a case is its potential magnitude. For example, would the tailor be liable for twenty counts of smuggling if the principal smuggler perpetrated that number of escapades prior to capture? Perhaps it is significant that research has disclosed no case imposing that magnitude of liability for this type of accessory.

The M.P.C. draftsmen tentatively proposed a test of knowing substantial facilitation. [M.P.C. § 2.04(3)(b) (Tent. Draft 1, 1953).] Under this test, a defendant who sold easily obtainable items to a criminal would not be guilty (absent purpose or stake in the venture) whereas one who provided hard to get items would be. Presumably, this test would exculpate the motel owner (the prostitute could always go to another motel) whereas the tailor might be convicted. Perhaps because of the uncertainty of this test, the M.P.C. ultimately rejected it.

The severity of the crime is another factor. One might be willing to tolerate the motel owner's "business is business" attitude without extending such toleration to the gun dealer. [For a helpful review case discussing these factors in the related context of conspiratorial liability, see P. v. Lauria, 59 Cal.Rptr. 628 (Cal.App.1967).] Compare § 16.07 *infra*.

It should be apparent that the problem here is similar to that suggested in § 15.02 *supra, i.e.*, no middle ground. Liability equal to a true aider and abettor or accessory seems excessive in most, if not all, of these cases. Yet, the conduct is not consistent with innocence either. Thus, a lesser offense would seem appropriate. New York has adopted a "criminal facilitation" statute for one who provides another with the means to commit a crime (which is in fact committed), believing that he is probably rendering such aid. Such facilitation is treated as a crime less serious than the crime being facilitated. N.Y.—McKinney's Penal Law § 115.00.

These problems do not usually arise in accessory after the fact cases, but they could. A person who rents a motel to one whom he knows is hiding from the law is a good illustration. Although the authority is limited, the motel clerk would probably not be guilty without more. Of course, if he gives false information to the police about his "guest" (even if it is motivated by a motel policy to aid all guests), he would be guilty. *Cf.* Maddox v. C., 349 S.W.2d 686 (Ky.1960).

§ 15.04 Scope of an Aider's Liability

To what extent is an aider liable for the unplanned crimes of his cohort? To illustrate, A and B agree to attack C with fists, but A shoots C dead instead. D and E, armed with pistols, plan to rob a bank, and during the robbery D shoots and kills both F, a cashier who refuses to turn over the money and G, an unobtrusive bystander against whom D had long carried a grudge. H and I agree to rob a store, but agree that no guns will be used. I waits in the car as the wheel man. I steals a gun from the store and shoots J, the store owner. On his way out, he also shoots K, a policeman attempting to thwart the robbery.

In these types of cases, many courts adopt a foreseeability test. That is, if the actual consequence was a reasonably foreseeable natural and probable consequence of the criminal enterprise, each participant is liable for the acts of the others.

In the first illustration, B would not be liable for the shooting if he neither knew nor should have known of A's gun. When he should have known but did not know, the question of liability is not clear. When he knew of the gun, but did not know of A's intent to use it, he would be guilty of manslaughter. And, if he knew of the gun and A's intent and went along to aid in the beating anyway, most courts would find him to be an aider and abettor of murder. See generally [1966] Crim.L.Rev. 385.

In the second illustration, E would be guilty of the murder of F since that shooting was a natural and probable consequence of the plan, but would not be guilty of the wholly extraneous killing of G. Cf. Mabry v. S., 110 So.2d 250 (Ala.App.1959).

The M.P.C. rejects the natural and probable test on the ground "that the liability of an accomplice ought not to extend beyond the criminal purposes that he shares or knows. Probabilities have an important evidential bearing on these issues; to make them independently sufficient is to predicate their liability on negligence when for good reason, more is normally required before liability is found." M.P.C. Tent. Draft 1, p. 26.

A few courts reject the natural and probable test from the other direction, holding that one is responsible for whatever acts are committed by his cohort in the course of the felony. Thus, in the third hypothetical, under this test, I would be liable for the shooting of both J and K. See P. v. Kessler, 315 N.E.2d 29 (Ill.1974).

§ 15.05 Mens Rea (Unintentional Crimes)

There is substantial disagreement among courts in regard to the degree of mens rea necessary to be an accessory before the fact or aider and abettor to an unintentional crime. Some courts have held that there can be no such thing as accessorial liability to a crime which by definition must be committed unintentionally, such as involuntary manslaughter (see §§ 2.06, 2.10 *supra*). They reason that to be an accessory or aider and abettor, one must intend the forbidden result which, of course, is impossible in such a crime. Thus, in S. v. Gartland, 263 S.W. 165 (Mo.1924), the court held that when two policemen were recklessly shooting bullets at a fleeing car, only the one who actually fired the fatal shot could be convicted of manslaughter.

At the other extreme, Jacobs v. S., 184 So.2d 711 (Fla.App.1966) upheld the conviction of a drag racer for involuntary manslaughter even though the victim's death was caused by a substantial and culpably negligent deviation from the original race plans by one of the other racers and the defendant was in a position where he not only could not prevent the deviation, but couldn't even see it.

A sounder approach to the problem is R. v. Creamer, [1965] 3 All E.R. 257 (Cr.App.) in which the court affirmed the manslaughter conviction of one who had procured what turned out to be a fatal illegal abortion by introducing the abortionist and the victim for purposes of the operation. The court explicitly rejected those cases which held that one cannot be an accessory before the fact to manslaughter, noting that one can intentionally procure a dangerous crime or reckless act. However, the court emphasized the importance of actually procuring the wrongful act, approving an earlier decision [R. v. Taylor, 13 Cox Crim.Cas. 68 (Cr.App.1875)] which had reversed a manslaughter conviction of a minor accessory before the fact to fighting (though not present at the fight, he held a pound from each of the principals with instructions to give the two pounds to the winner) on the ground that he had not procured the fight. *Creamer* also seemed to require that death result from the risk created. Thus, if the abortionist, unbeknown to the accessory, permitted an unqualified assistant to perform the operation, it would seem that the accessory would not be liable for manslaughter (although the opinion is not explicit on this point).

Occasionally, courts will be so beguiled by accessorial form that they ignore the substance of the state's case. A striking example is P. v. Marshall, 106 N.W.2d 842 (Mich.1961), in which the defendant in contravention of a state statute lent his car to a person who the defendant knew was drunk. While the defendant was home sleeping, the drunk operated the automobile in such a manner as to kill a third person. The court held that Marshall could not be guilty of aiding and abetting manslaughter since he wasn't present at the time of the killing and could not be an accessory before the fact since it was not counselled by him. Assuming the accuracy of the observation, it totally ignores the personal (first degree principal) basis of liability. Marshall, in violation of a statute and presumably recklessly, lent his car to a drunk. A natural consequence of this violation (indeed the likely reason for the statutory enactment) is that injury or death to an innocent person will occur, which is precisely what happened. Therefore, the court should have had no difficulty affirming the conviction. Fortunately, other courts have not experienced such difficulty. For example, in C. v. Feinberg, 253 A.2d 636 (Pa.1969), a store owner who sold industrial Sterno to "skid-row alcoholics", knowing that they intended to drink it, was held liable for involuntary manslaughter.

In regard to strict liability crimes, the rule seems to be (though authority is scant) that an aider or accessory (assuming he is not one upon whom vicarious liability is also placed, see § 8.04 *supra*) is not strictly liable for inadvertently helping another commit a strict liability offense. See Johnson v. Youden, [1950] 1 All E.R. 300 (K.B.).

§ 15.06   Relationship to Principal's Liability

Although accessorial liability is predicated upon the act of another, the degree of criminality is not necessarily identical. To illustrate, assume that A, B, and C are at a bar. A provokes B in such a manner as to render B's killing A manslaughter (see § 2.04 *supra*). However, before B can kill A, C (a stronger person) offers to kill A with B's knife if B will give it to him. Thus C kills A. C, the first degree principal, is guilty of murder, whereas B, the aider and abettor, is guilty only of voluntary manslaughter. Conversely, if cold-blooded C were to hand the knife to hot-blooded B, who did the killing, the principal (B) would be guilty of mere manslaughter whereas the aider and abettor (C) would be guilty of murder. *Cf.* Pendry v. S., 367 A.2d 627 (Del.1976).

It is even possible to have an innocent principal and a guilty aider. For example, in the hypothetical, if, unbeknownst to C, it were necessary for B to kill A in self defense and C gave B the knife, not out of a desire to save B, but out of a desire to have A killed, principal B would be innocent, but aider C would be a murderer. Arguably, however, this situation is better analyzed in terms of C's being the principal and B merely his instrumentality for perpetrating the crime.

Occasionally, a principal's innocence will eliminate an essential element of the offense, thereby negating a culpable cohort's guilt. In one case, the principal, a relative of the intended victim, purported to go along with the aider and abettor, who planned a burglary. The aider and abettor lifted the first degree principal into the window whereupon the principal removed the merchandise and they both fled. The court held that the aider could not be convicted of burglary on the ground that the principal, who broke and entered, did not intend to commit a felony, while the aider, who intended to commit a felony, did not break and enter. Thus, nobody broke and entered with the intent to commit a felony, a requisite for burglary (see § 7.11 *supra*). Of course, if the apparent aider had merely used the apparent principal as a dupe, the aider would have been a first degree principal himself and guilty. Such, however, was not the case. S. v. Hayes, 16 S.W. 514 (Mo.1891).

A procedural, as opposed to substantive, defense would not aid a defendant in a case like *Hayes*. If, for example, the first degree principal was given immunity in return for his testimony or had diplomatic immunity, the aider could still be prosecuted. *Cf.* Farnsworth v. Zerbst, 98 F.2d 541 (5th Cir. 1938).

§ **15.07**   **Special Personal Defenses**

Occasionally a crime will be so obviously intended to protect a class of individuals that a member of that class cannot commit it. For example, an under-aged girl cannot be guilty of aiding and abetting unlawful carnal knowledge of herself regardless of how much she encourages a man to have sexual intercourse with her. R. v. Tyrell, 17 Cox Crim. Cas. 716 (Cr. Cas. Res. 1893). In addition, when a crime necessarily requires two people, such as prostitution (prostitute and customer) or selling liquor without a permit (seller and buyer) and the legislature only provides punishment for one (the prostitute and seller in the hypotheticals), it is generally presumed that the other, although not really a victim, is not punishable under the statute. This is sometimes justified on the ground that the law is better served by preserving each individual customer (who is usually involved in only a small percentage of the prostitute or liquor seller's crimes) as an innocent witness rather than a potential criminal. See, *e.g.,* U.S. v. Farrar, 281 U.S. 624 (1930).

Certain crimes are defined in such a way as to render a particular class of persons incompetent to commit them. For example, in most states neither the victim's husband nor a woman meets the definition of a rapist (see § 4.03 *supra*). Nevertheless, it is possible for such a person to aid and abet a rape by helping the principal to have forcible sexual intercourse with the victim. Indeed, it is possible for a woman or husband of the victim to be a non-participating first degree principal. This could occur when such a person forces an unwilling man to have sexual relations with the unwilling victim. See S. v. Haines, 25 So. 372 (La.1899).

§ 15.08 Abandonment

It is generally held that one who has given sufficient aid to be an accessory to a crime can be exculpated if he effectively abandons the project prior to the crime's commission. S. v. Peterson, 4 N.W.2d 826 (Minn.1942). Of course, an uncommunicated subjective abandonment will not suffice. Karnes v. S., 252 S.W. 1 (Ark.1923). Effective abandonment will vary with the aid. If the defendant solicited or otherwise vocally encouraged the crime, his informing the principal of his new found disapproval should suffice. If he provided an instrumentality, such as a gun, for the crime, it may be necessary that he reacquire it, or so the M.P.C. suggests. M.P.C. § 2.06(6)(c) and M.P.C. Tent. Draft 1, p. 37. Of course, his denunciation of the scheme to the police in time to prevent the crime is sufficient. Compare withdrawal from conspiracy § 16.05 *infra*.

If the defendant properly withdraws, he will not be guilty simply because the crime is committed anyway. S. v. Allen, 47 Conn. 121 (1879).

CHAPTER XVI

CONSPIRACY

§ 16.01 Introduction

Conspiracy is an agreement between two or more persons to commit an unlawful act or a lawful act in an unlawful manner. The agreement is the actus reus and the intent to commit the unlawful act is the mens rea. Conspiracy's purposes are akin to both attempt and complicity.

As an inchoate (attempt-type) crime, it reaches further back into the planning stage than attempt by punishing mere agreement to commit a crime (although some jurisdictions require a slight overt act, see § 16.05 *infra*). This is justified on the theory that the agreement reduces the equivocal nature of the intent and renders it more likely that the contemplated crime ultimately will be committed.

The second basis for punishing conspiracy is the maxim "in union there is strength." When the union's purposes are criminal, it is understandable that the courts and legislatures would think it necessary to attack this added strength.

As one might suspect, this crime is especially popular among prosecutors; indeed, it has been dubbed "the prosecutor's darling." It is, however, an unusually amorphous crime, subject to what some would call considerable abuse. In the pages that follow, we shall explore some of conspiracy's more unusual attributes.

§ 16.02 Punishment

There is little uniformity among the states as to how conspiracies ought to be punished. The framers of the M.P.C. observed the following different types:

"(1) Statutes providing that conspiracy is a misdemeanor regardless of its object. . . .

(2) Statutes fixing the maximum sentence for conspiracy at a constant level regardless of the conspiratorial objective. . . .

(3) Statutes providing different maxima for conspiracies to commit different types of substantive crimes. . . .

(4) [Statutes] relat[ing] the general conspiracy sentence to that provided for the criminal objective." M.P.C. Tent. Draft 10, pp. 177–78.

More significant than these gradations, however, is the availability of cumulative punishment for conspiracy and the contemplated crime. For example, if A and B agree to rob C and in fact do rob him, they could receive the maximum sentence for robbery, plus a sentence for conspiracy. *Cf.* Callanan v. U.S., 364 U.S. 587 (1961). In this regard, conspiracy differs from other inchoate crimes. A person could not be convicted of attempted robbery as well as robbery of the same person. In such a case, the attempt would be said to merge with the completed crime. See § 14.01 *supra.*

The justification for not merging conspiracy with the completed crime is that in the "in union there is strength" type danger of a conspiracy has been thought to transcend the danger of any particular crime. The M.P.C. has adopted a compromise position, holding that when a conspiracy has only one objective (*e.g.,* A and B agreeing to rob C), the conspirators may be punished for either the conspiracy or the completed crime, but not for both [M.P.C. § 1.07(1)(b)]. When, however, the conspiracy is broader than one crime (*e.g.,* A and B conspire to rob C, D, and E on separate occasions), double punishment is permissible.

§ **16.03** **Basis for Complicity**

In Pinkerton v. U.S., 328 U.S. 640 (1946), the Supreme Court held that one co-conspirator could be held accountable for the acts of his fellow conspirator. At first glance, this does not seem too surprising since a co-conspirator normally is involved in the planning of the crime, thus rendering himself at least an accessory before the fact, if not a second degree principal, see § 15.01 *supra.* In *Pinkerton,* however, the Court concluded that involvement in the planning of a particular offense was not essential so long as the defendant agreed to the same general type of offenses that actually were committed. Indeed, some of the offenses for which Pinkerton was convicted were committed without his knowledge (so far as the record showed) and while he was in prison.

Pinkerton is not universally accepted. The M.P.C. rejected it on the ground that if mere membership in a conspiracy were sufficient for complicity, a conspirator who contributed very little to a large conspiracy could be convicted of many substantive offenses. M.P.C. § 2.06 and M.P.C. Tent. Draft 1, pp. 20–24. In view of the relative ease with which one can become a member of a large conspiracy (see § 16.06 *infra*), the M.P.C. position seems sound. In one egregious example, Anderson v. Superior Court, 177 P.2d 315 (Cal.Dist.Ct.App.1947), the court held that a woman who provided customers to a criminal abortionist could be liable for each abortion he performed, even if the particular woman upon whom a given abortion was performed was introduced to the abortionist, not by the defendant, but by a fellow conspirator whom the defendant had never met. As the framers of the M.P.C. said of a closely related situation: "Law would lose all sense of just proportion if in virtue of that one crime [conspiracy], each [conspirator] were held accountable for thousands of offenses that he did not influence at all." M.P.C. Tent. Draft 1, p. 21.

The M.P.C. rule would not necessarily have exculpated Pinkerton from accessorial liability. If, for example, it were clear that the conspiracy called for the crimes to continue even if one of the conspirators were to become incarcerated, Pinkerton would probably have been liable as a traditional accessory before the fact. Evidence that he continued to share in the proceeds of the unlawful operations would have been persuasive evidence of his continuing role in the substantive crimes. See § 15.03 *supra.* Such evidence, however, was unnecessary in *Pinkerton,* because the Court held that participation in the conspiracy alone was sufficient for complicity.

§ 16.04   The Object Which Renders a Conspiracy Criminal

One of the more unusual aspects of conspiracy law is that the object of the conspiracy need not always be criminal itself. Recall that in § 16.01, *supra,* conspiracy was defined as "an agreement to commit an unlawful [not necessarily criminal] act, or a lawful act in an unlawful [again, not necessarily criminal] manner." The term "unlawful" can include civil wrongs as well as criminal.

A possible illustration is obtaining property by false promises. We noted earlier that in many jurisdictions, a false promise will not suffice for the crime of obtaining property by false pretenses principally because of the difficulty of knowing for certain what the defendant's original intent was and the consequent danger of inadvertently convicting an innocent person (§ 7.05D *supra*). When, however, there is proof of agreement, much of this danger disappears. Concomitantly, the harm to society increases. It is one thing to tolerate an individual's false promise calculated to obtain property. It is quite another to tolerate such conduct as planned group behavior. Thus, the "in union there is strength" maxim may not only justify the concept of conspiracy, but may arguably justify the extension of conspiracy to conduct which would be non-criminal if committed by an isolated individual.

When the legislature chooses to criminalize a conspiracy notwithstanding the non-criminality of its objectives (as in the above example), no great unfairness is perpetrated upon the defendant since he has fair notice of what to avoid. Some legislatures, however, have passed catch-all statutes forbidding conspiracies "to commit any act injurious to the public health, to public morals, or to trade commerce or for the perversion or obstruction of justice or the due administration of the law." Further, some courts have held the common law to be broad enough to punish such conspiracies even without the aid of a statute.

In Musser v. Utah, 333 U.S. 95 (1948), the Supreme Court held such a statute to be unconstitutionally vague unless it could be narrowed by the State court. The Supreme Court reasoned that "[s]tanding by itself, it [the statutory provision] would seem to be warrant for conviction for agreement to do almost any act which a judge and jury might find at the moment contrary to his or its notions of what was good for health, morals, trade, commerce, justice or order." *Id.* at 97. On remand, the Utah Supreme Court was unable to narrow the statute and thus held it unconstitutionally vague. S. v. Musser, 223 P.2d 193 (Utah 1950). Compare § 18.01 *infra, cf.* § 18.03 *infra.*

One way to eliminate the vagueness of conspiracy would be to punish all those who conspire to commit any unlawful act (criminal or civil). Because of the obvious harshness of such an approach, it has never been considered seriously.

Other courts have tried to limit generally defined conspiracies to the most egregious sort of "non-criminal" conduct, *e.g.,* systematic gross usury to poor and necessitous wage earners, coupled with a scheme to prevent their (the wage earners') recovery of it, reasoning that "an enlightened conscience should have no difficulty in recognizing [such] a wrong as being embraced within its [conspiracy's] wide compass." C. v. Donoghue, 63 S.W.2d 3, 9 (Ky.1933).

Apart from *Musser,* the Supreme Court has shown no proclivity towards reversing such decisions. Thus, decisions like *Donoghue* are at least arguably constitutional. It is worth noting, however, that it was this type of conspiracy law which justified convicting early day unionists for conspiring to raise the wages of workers. See, *e.g.,* P. v. Fisher, 14 Wend. 9, 28 Am.Dec. 501 (N.Y.Sup.Ct.1835).

§ **16.05** **Agreement—The Actus Reus of Conspiracy**

In some jurisdictions, an agreement is all the actus reus that the prosecutor must prove in order to establish conspiracy. *E.g.,* S. v. Moritz, 293 N.W.2d 235 (Iowa 1980). In others, he must establish an overt act in furtherance of the conspiracy as well. Even in the latter type of jurisdiction, however, the overt act requirement is more procedural than substantive. That is, its function is to provide additional proof of the existence of and willingness to adhere to the unlawful agreement which is the nub of the offense. Because of this limited function, the overt act does not have to be unequivocal nor especially significant so long as it is in fact in furtherance of the conspiracy. To illustrate, an interview with a lawyer has been held to be a sufficient overt act to justify a conviction for a conspiracy to violate the Bankruptcy Act. See Kaplan v. U.S., 7 F.2d 594 (2d Cir.1925).

Implicit in the concept of agreement is that at least two people agree. Thus, most courts that have considered the problem have held that when one of the parties to the agreement was merely feigning acquiescence (perhaps to trap the other), or was incapable of agreeing, perhaps because of insanity, the other could not be guilty of conspiracy because there was no one with whom he could have made an agreement. See Regle v. S., 264 A.2d 119 (Md.Ct. Spec.App.1970). (Of course, this principal does not apply when there are three apparent conspirators, only one of whom is not serious or competent, because the other two could conspire with each other.) The M.P.C. and some courts [*e.g.,* S. v. Rambousek, 479 N.W.2d 832 (N.D.1992)] reject this position by defining conspiracy in terms of one person's agreeing with another rather than an agreement between two or more persons. M.P.C. § 5.03(1). The rule could also be rejected by defining agreement objectively, thereby making both parties guilty even when one was subjectively not serious. The courts, however, have been unwilling to do this.

Another numerical type limitation on conspiracy is the so-called "Wharton's Rule" which applies to conspiracies to commit crimes that necessarily require two people to commit, such as bribery or adultery. Under "Wharton's Rule," two people cannot conspire to commit such a crime since there is no added danger in numbers in this type of agreement. When there are more than the minimum number (*e.g.,* two bribers and a bribee conspiring to commit bribery) the prevailing (but not universal) rule is that a conspiracy conviction is appropriate. See U.S. v. Cogan, 266 F.Supp. 374 (S.D.N.Y.1967). Sometimes the court will construe legislation as intending to abrogate Wharton's Rule, Iannelli v. U.S., 420 U.S. 770 (1975). The M.P.C. rejects "Wharton's Rule" on the ground that any inchoate agreement to commit a crime should be punished as a conspiracy. M.P.C. Tent. Draft 10, pp. 172–73.

Ascertaining whether there is sufficient evidence to justify a finding of agreement is not easy. Obviously conspirators seldom enter into formal agreements and the law imposes no such requirement. A tacit agreement is sufficient so long as there really is an agreement. Since R. v. Murphy, 173 Eng.Rep. 502 (1837), many courts have been willing to allow juries to infer agreement from the fact of more than one person pursuing a course of action with an apparent singleness of purpose which would have been unlikely in the absence of an agreement. For this to occur, however, the circumstances must be quite compelling [*e.g.,* Griffin v. S., 455 S.W.2d 882 (Ark.1970) where at least 100 people simultaneously assaulted a policeman], and even then, some courts will insist on more direct evidence of agreement. See, *e.g.,* Weniger v. U.S., 47 F.2d 692 (9th Cir.1931).

In the final analysis, a judge's concept of justice is likely to dictate the amount of direct evidence (if any) required to establish an agreement. This will of course vary substantially, depending on the nature of the conspiracy.

Once a defendant has been found to have conspired to commit a crime, courts tend to reject the defense of abandonment on the ground that the crime of conspiracy has already been completed. *E.g.,* Orear v. U.S., 261 Fed. 257 (5th Cir.1919). Compare §§ 14.04, 15.08 *supra.* The M.P.C. rejects this rule when the defendant "thwarted the success of the conspiracy, under circumstances manifesting a complete and voluntary renunciation of his criminal purpose." M.P.C. § 5.03(6). Even under the prevailing view, withdrawal is important since, among other things, it terminates any liability for subsequent crimes committed by a former co-conspirator. See § 16.03 *supra.* In order to be effective for this purpose, some courts say that the withdrawal must be either "the makings of a clean breast to the authorities ... or communication of the abandonment in a manner reasonably calculated to reach co-conspirators." U.S. v. Borelli, 336 F.2d 376, 388 (2d Cir.1964). Others imply that the sole manner of withdrawal is by communication of the intent to all other co-conspirators. Loser v. Superior Court in and for Alameda County, 177 P.2d 320 (Cal.Dist.Ct.App.1947).

§ 16.06   Scope of the Agreement—One Conspiracy or Many

In some cases, it is clear that a person is part of a conspiracy, but the scope of his conspiratorial liability is questionable. To illustrate the nature of this question, assume that A agrees with B to engage in criminal conduct and that B also agrees with C to engage in such conduct. Under what circumstances can A and C be deemed co-conspirators?

The United States Supreme Court addressed this question in Kotteakos v. U.S., 328 U.S. 750 (1946), in which B conspired with A and C individually to fraudulently obtain loans from the Federal Housing Administration. The Court held that under these circumstances A and C were not co-conspirators. The Court reasoned that B's relationship to the others was like the hub of a wheel to its spokes, and that at least on these facts the spokes had no relationship to one another.

Not all jurisdictions accept *Kotteakos*. For example, in Anderson v. Superior Ct. in and for Alameda County, 177 P.2d 315 (Cal.Dist.Ct.App.1947), discussed in § 16.03 *supra,* the court allowed one procurer of abortions to be treated as a co-conspirator with all other procurers for the same abortionist. Arguably this situation is different from *Kotteakos* since here each of the "spokes" was aiding the "hub" on a continuing basis rather than the "hub"

aiding the "spokes" on a limited basis. Still, the
willingness of the court to impose this kind of
liability seems inconsistent with *Kotteakos*.

The United States Supreme Court limited *Kotteakos* in Blumenthal v. U.S., 332 U.S. 539 (1947),
when it held that C who agreed with B to unlawfully sell A's liquor could be held to be a co-conspirator
with A even though he did not know A's identity,
but merely knew of his existence. The Court distinguished *Kotteakos* on the ground that here A, B and
C were each necessary "links" in the criminal chain
as opposed to merely "spokes" in a wheel.

The *Blumenthal* "link" theory also has its limitations. Most significantly, each link must be aware of
at least the existence if not the identity of the
others. Thus, in *Blumenthal,* if C had thought the
liquor belonged to B, there would be no basis for
inferring an agreement between C and A. *Cf.* U.S. v.
Peoni, 100 F.2d 401 (2d Cir.1938).

Another type of case in which the scope of the
conspiracy can be significant is when A and B agree
to commit several crimes. The question raised is
whether they are guilty of one conspiracy or several
(one for each contemplated crime). In Braverman v.
U.S., 317 U.S. 49 (1942), the Supreme Court opted
for limiting conspiratorial liability to one count on
the ground that there was only one agreement
regardless of the number of its objectives.

§ 16.07   Mens Rea

In spite (or perhaps because) of the relative ease
of establishing the actus reus of conspiracy, the

mens rea requirements traditionally have been rather stringent. For example, ignorance or mistake of the law is sometimes recognized as a defense to conspiracy, especially when the offense is malum prohibitum and the alleged conspirators' motives are pure. Thus, in P. v. Powell, 63 N.Y. 88 (1875) the court held: "[T]o make an agreement between two or more persons, to do an act innocent in itself, a criminal conspiracy, it is not enough that ... the act which was the object of the agreement [be] prohibited. *The confederation must be corrupt.* The agreement must have been entered into with an evil purpose, as distinguished from a purpose simply to do the act prohibited in ignorance of the meaning of the prohibition. *This is implied in the meaning of the word conspiracy.*" *Id*. at 92 (emphasis added). (Compare the requirement of knowledge of the law when one is accused of acting willfully. § 8.07, *supra*). Although Judge Learned Hand described this as an "anomalous doctrine," U.S. v. Mack, 112 F.2d 290, 292 (2d Cir.1940), it does appear to represent the traditional view.

More recently, the Supreme Court has questioned the need for special mens rea requirements in conspiracy cases. In the leading case, U.S. v. Feola, 420 U.S. 671 (1975), the Court reinstated the conviction of four men who agreed to and did assault a person whom they believed to be a prospective heroin purchaser. The "prospective purchaser" turned out to be a Federal law enforcement officer. The crime for which the defendants were convicted was conspiracy to assault a "Federal law enforcement officer."

The Circuit Court reversed their convictions because they had not specifically agreed to assault a law enforcement officer, but had only agreed to assault a prospective narcotics purchaser. The Supreme Court, after holding that the substantive crime of assaulting a Federal officer did not require knowledge of the victim's official status, (§ 8.06, *supra*) concluded that conspiracy to commit that crime should require no greater state of mind. The Court specifically declined to pass on the *Powell* corrupt motive rule, noting simply that an agreement to assault anybody was corrupt. Compare Bryan v. U.S., § 8.07, *supra*. Although it did not reject *Powell*, the Court seemed to indicate that it would look askance at any mens rea requirement beyond the intent to commit the act itself.

Feola is not without its detractors. One can legitimately treat certain elements of a crime as circumstances which do not require any particular intent (such as the official status of an assault victim) whereas in a prosecution for conspiracy which reaches so far back into preparation, more scienter ought to be required. Even this approach, however, has limits. For example, if two people agree to steal something worth $205 which they think is worth $195, the value of the property should be treated as a circumstance even for purposes of conspiracy and they should be guilty of conspiracy to commit grand larceny (assuming of course that $200 is the dividing line and that the jurisdiction distinguishes between felonious and non-felonious conspiracies).

A final mens rea problem in regard to conspiracy is the liability of one who has only an indirect interest in the crime. The illustrations in § 15.03 *supra* should be reconsidered here [(1) A sells B a gun and bullets, knowing that B intends to assassinate the President of the United States, (2) C rents a motel room to D, knowing that she intends to use it for purposes of prostitution, and (3) E, a tailor, makes F a coat with special pockets, knowing that he intends to use it for smuggling]. Determining whether A, C, and E are conspirators with B, D, and F respectively requires substantially the same analysis as determining whether they are aiders and abettors, except that in conspiracy, unlike aiding and abetting, it is necessary to establish an agreement.

In the two leading United States Supreme Court cases, the Court reached opposite conclusions. In U.S. v. Falcone, 311 U.S. 205 (1940), the selling of sugar and yeast to people whom the sellers knew were engaged in a moonshine making conspiracy was insufficient to make them part of the conspiracy. But in Direct Sales Co. v. U.S., 319 U.S. 703 (1943), the Court held otherwise where the items being sold were restricted (drugs) and were being sold in such a large quantity as to preclude the possibility of the sales being legitimate. Compare § 15.03 *supra.*

§ 16.08 Procedural Peculiarities

Although this is not a nutshell in criminal procedure, some understanding of the procedural pecu-

liarities of conspiracy is essential for a full appreciation of the character of the crime.

One of the more interesting peculiarities is that
all of the alleged conspirators can be tried in any
place where either the agreement or an overt act in
pursuance thereof occurred. Hyde v. U.S., 225 U.S.
347 (1912). Consequently, in a nationwide conspiracy, the United States may be able to try fifty people
in California, even though forty of them were never
west of the Mississippi River. Although one might
argue that this is inconsistent with the Sixth
Amendment's guarantee of a trial in "the state and
district wherein the crime shall have been committed," it is defended on the ground that conspiracy is
a multi-faceted crime and that the crime was indeed
committed at the locus of the agreement as well as
that of each of the overt acts.

Another procedural advantage for the prosecutor
is the co-conspirator exception to the hearsay rule.
Under the basic hearsay rule, no unsworn out of
court statement which has not been subjected to
cross-examination may be admitted to prove the
truth of the matter contained therein. Under this
exception, however, such unsworn statements by
one co-conspirator are admissible against her fellow
conspirators. To illustrate, if co-conspirator X told
witness W that she (X) along with Y and Z planned
to rob the Last National Bank, W could testify as to
that statement in court and it would be admissible
against Y and Z as well as X. This rule is frequently
limited to statements made *during* the actual conspiracy. Thus, a statement made by X *after* the

robbery was complete would not be admissible. See Krulewitch v. U.S., 336 U.S. 440 (1949). This limitation is not constitutionally required, however, and is not universally followed. See Dutton v. Evans, 400 U.S. 74 (1970).

One problem created by the co-conspirator hearsay exception is its circular nature. The evidence is admitted to prove that Y and Z are part of an XYZ conspiracy. Yet the evidence is not admissible unless Y and Z are in fact part of the very conspiracy whose existence the evidence seeks to establish. The obvious way out is to hold that some evidence, apart from the hearsay, tending to prove a conspiracy including X, Y, and Z must be introduced as a predicate to allowing the hearsay. This indeed has been the approach generally taken by the courts, although there is some disagreement as to the quantum of non-hearsay proof necessary to permit the introduction of the hearsay statements. Compare U.S. v. Geaney, 417 F.2d 1116 (2d Cir.1969) (fair preponderance of the evidence), with Carbo v. U.S., 314 F.2d 718 (9th Cir.1963) (prima facie case).

Not all of the procedures peculiar to conspiracy favor the prosecutor. One procedure which very much favors a conspiracy defendant is that an acquittal of all of his alleged co-conspirators requires his own acquittal. Thus, if X, Y, and Z are accused of conspiracy to rob a bank and bank robbery and X and Y are acquitted of both offenses, the conspiracy charge against Z must be dismissed. Z, however, may still be tried and convicted for bank robbery. This is because the acquittal of X and Y renders it theoretically impossible for Z to have conspired with anybody (although the result would be otherwise if he were alleged to have conspired with other unknown individuals), but it is not theoretically impossible for him to have robbed the bank alone.

The scope of this rule is not clear. For example, such questions as whether an acquittal of one of two co-conspirators following a conviction of the other requires that the first conviction be abated and whether the entrance of a nolle prosequi (refusal to prosecute) as to one alleged co-conspirator precludes the prosecution of the only other have split the courts. Compare Miller v. U.S., 277 Fed. 721 (4th Cir.1921), with S. v. Verdugo, 449 P.2d 781 (N.M.1969). When, however, the failure to prosecute one co-conspirator has nothing to do with guilt or innocence, the other co-conspirator will not be aided thereby. The most obvious illustration of this is when one co-conspirator cannot be brought to trial because of death or subsequent insanity. The trial and conviction of one co-conspirator has also been permitted when for one reason or another his fellow conspirator has been granted immunity. *E.g.*, Hurwitz v. S., 92 A.2d 575 (Md.1952).

§ **16.09** **Political Conspiracies and the First Amendment**

The term "political conspiracy" sounds like an oxymoron in a country dedicated to political freedom and free expression of minority positions, however distasteful they may be. Not all such activity is protected, however. For example, conspiracies to incite the violent overthrow of the government or aid in the evasion of the selective service laws are political in a sense, but have been held to be unlawful. It is precisely because of their political overtones, however, that they raise special problems. Were it not for these political overtones, the cases could be resolved on traditional conspiracy principles.

Several different approaches have been suggested in political conspiracy cases. Mr. Justice Jackson's concurring opinion in Dennis v. U.S., 341 U.S. 494 (1951) (in which the Court sustained a conviction for conspiracy to incite the violent overthrow of the government) treated the First Amendment's prohibition against laws abridging freedom of speech as an irrelevancy in this type of conspiracy case. As he put it: "The Constitution does not make conspiracy a civil right. ... It is not to be supposed that the power of Congress to protect the Nation's existence is more limited than its power to protect interstate commerce." *Id.* at 572–74.

Judge Coffin, on the other hand, appeared to severely limit the concept of political conspiracy in his partial dissent in U.S. v. Spock, 416 F.2d 165 (1st Cir.1969) (in which the majority reversed a conviction on other grounds, but sustained the theoretical concept of a conspiracy to aid in the evasion of selective service laws). He based this position on the First Amendment requirement that the government protect its interests in a manner calculated to minimize the impact on free expression. To make this requirement meaningful, Judge Coffin contended that the government should be required either to prosecute for specific selective service violations rather than a general conspiracy, or at least show why such a procedure would not effectively vindicate the government's interest.

The court in *Spock* took an intermediate position. It held that a political type conspiracy was possible, but that a conviction could be obtained in such a case only upon clear proof of the defendant's personal adherence to the illegal conduct. Consequently, proof that the defendant knew that his alleged conspirator specifically intended to do or did an unlawful act does not justify convicting that defendant even if he remains a member of the group. This stands in sharp contra-distinction to the usual conspiracy rules upon which such a conviction might have been proper. Compare § 16.03 *supra*.

The Supreme Court has not yet addressed this question specifically. It has considered a number of cases in which the First Amendment was raised as a defense to conspiratorial as well as substantive type crimes. But it has not specifically considered the interrelationship between conspiracy and the First Amendment.

§ 16.10 RICO

Congress enacted the Racketeer Influenced and Corrupt Organizations statute to punish those who invest money obtained from racketeering in an enterprise. Although the primary purpose of this statute, known affectionately (especially to prosecutors) as RICO, is to preclude criminal infiltration of legitimate business, the Supreme Court has held that the phrase "enterprise" is sufficiently broad to encompass illegitimate as well as legitimate enterprises. Consequently, a racketeer who invests his ill-gotten gains in a drug trafficking ring can be convicted of a RICO violation in the same manner as one who invests such funds in a pizza parlor. U.S. v. Turkette, 452 U.S. 576 (1981).

Because prosecutors have been attracted by RICO's anti-conspiracy provisions, RICO is frequently studied as an appendage to conspiracy. All of the prosecutorial advantages of conspiracy (see §§ 16.06, 16.08, *supra*) are magnified by a judicial determination to construe RICO as broadly as possible. For example, some courts have held that the *Kotteakos* limitations (see § 16.06, *supra*) are inapplicable to RICO prosecutions, thereby rendering it possible to ensnare in one large net, many people who don't even know of each other. See U.S. v. Elliott, 571 F.2d 880 (5th Cir.1978). *Elliott*, however, has not been universally followed, and has even been limited in its own circuit. U.S. v. Sutherland, 656 F.2d 1181 (5th Cir.1981).

RICO's potential to replace conspiracy as the prosecutor's darling was vividly illustrated in U.S. v. Licavoli, 725 F.2d 1040 (6th Cir.1984). To convict one of a RICO violation, the Government is required to prove two enumerated racketeering offenses. Licavoli's two offenses were murder and conspiracy to commit murder of the same person. Under Ohio law (where these crimes were allegedly committed), one cannot be convicted of both conspiracy to murder and murder of the same person. (Compare § 16.02, *supra*). Nevertheless, the court construed this limitation to be merely procedural and upheld Licavoli's conviction. Licavoli also argued that because he was acquitted of both murder and conspiracy to commit murder in state court there were no crimes upon which to predicate a RICO conviction. In rejecting this argument, the court concluded that a Federal Court was not bound by an acquittal in an Ohio Court.

Although the court in *Licavoli* may have been influenced by its first statement of fact ("Defendant Licavoli is a leader of organized crime in Cleveland"), the decision does much to strengthen RICO's popularity among prosecutors. Whether RICO will do more harm to organized crime than to the Constitution remains to be seen.

CHAPTER XVII

CORPORATE CRIMINAL LIABILITY

§ 17.01 Theoretical Problems

Several theoretical problems inure in the concept of corporate criminal liability. As John Coffee's article suggests, there is no soul to damn, no body to kick. 79 Mich. L. Rev. 386 (1981). Then there is the problem of how does a corporation act. Whose conduct can render a corporation criminally liable? Any corporate employees? Only executives? What if they disobey corporate orders? Some statutes refer to persons. Others to individuals. Do these include corporations? Finally, are corporations principals or agents, and can they conspire with their incorporators?

§ 17.02 Punishment

The most obvious way to punish a corporation is by a fine. Obviously fines can be applied to corporations and, given a corporation's reason for being, a sufficiently high fine can be quite effective. Other punishments, such as temporary suspension of a corporate charter, or, in extreme cases, the death penalty (permanent revocation) are possible. Obviously these kinds of limitations are problematic because it may leave unsatisfied creditors and the offending individuals may be able to reincorporate under a different name. Plausibly probation would also be a possibility.

Fines, however, are probably the best way to punish corporations, and, if large enough can be quite a deterrent.

§ 17.03 Whose Conduct Binds a Corporation

Ordinarily, an employee acting on his own can not bind the corporation. As one court put it in a fraud case, the agent must be acting in the scope of his employment, his fraudulent conduct must redound to the corporation's benefit, and the criminal acts must be "authorized, tolerated, or ratified by corporate management." S. v. Christy Pontiac–GMC, Inc., 354 N.W.2d 17 (Minn.1984).

This is somewhat different from tort liability, where classic concepts of *respondeat superior* impose liability even where the employee's act may have only been apparently authorized. Obviously criminal liability is more serious. Consequently, the tie in to the corporation must be greater.

§ 17.04 Statutory Construction Problem

If the relevant statutory language clearly indicated that corporations were covered or they weren't, this section wouldn't be necessary. Unfortunately sometimes they don't. Typically, courts indicate that if a crime can only be punished by imprisonment (as opposed to a fine), it does not apply to a corporation (although it does seem hard to believe that if, at a corporate board of directors meeting, the directors decided to kill a competitor, that the corporation wouldn't be liable).

Various semantic arguments have been attempted (usually unsuccessfully) to avoid corporate liability. For example, in C. v. McIlwain School Bus Lines, Inc., 423 A.2d 413 (Pa.Super.Ct.1980), a vehicular homicide statute, D argued that the statute referred to "a person *who* unintentionally causes the death of another person." It contended that if the statute meant to include corporations, it would have said "a person *who or which . . . .*" The court rightly rejected that argument, noting that the statute defines persons as including corporations and that, being a person (however artificially), it was appropriate to refer to it as "who."

A more serious semantic argument was raised in S. v. Richard Knutson, Inc., 537 N.W.2d 420 (Wis. Ct.App.1995). There, the negligent homicide statute defined the killer as whoever and the victim as "*another human being.*" Exacerbating the problem was the fact that the prior statute defined those that could be liable, and included corporations. The current statute simply said "whoever" and nowhere explicit indicated that corporations were included. The court ruled 2–1 that, despite the arguable ambiguity of the statute, that corporations could be liable. The dissenting judge read the statute as clearly excluding corporate liability, and consequently found no basis for construing it as the majority did.

§ 17.05 The Corporation and Its Alter Egos

Sometimes one, or a handful of individuals may perpetrate a fraud through a corporation. Obviously someone should be liable therefor. But how far should the liability extend? Suppose a single person perpetrates a fraud through his alter ego, the corporation. If he simply perpetrated the fraud, he would be subject to one punishment. But because he employed a corporation, he may be liable for *four* punishments: (1) for his own crime; (2) for the corporation's crime; (3) for conspiring with the corporation; and (4) for the corporation's conspiring with him. *Cf.* U.S. v. Cincotta, 689 F.2d 238 (1st Cir.1982).

Obviously. this isn't that the only time that prosecutors have been known to gild the lily (compare burglary [§ 14.06A, *supra*], kidnapping [§ 5.05, *supra*], and of course conspiracy itself [Ch. 16, *supra*]). Nevertheless, this seems to be an excessively gilded lily even by prosecutor's standards.

PART VII

LIMITATIONS OF THE CRIMINAL LAW

CHAPTER XVIII

LIMITATIONS OF THE CRIMINAL LAW

§ 18.01 Vagueness

The United States Constitution precludes punishing a person under a statute too vague to be understood. There are two reasons for this. First, a person cannot avoid engaging in criminal conduct, if, prior to engaging in it, he is unable to ascertain that his conduct is forbidden by law. Consequently, fair notice is an essential prerequisite of due process. The second basis for condemning vague statutes is that they lend themselves to arbitrary enforcement. If one cannot tell what conduct is forbidden by a statute, it is easy and not unnatural for the authorities, and/or the jury, to enforce it more stringently against those whom they do not like than against those whom they do like. The United States Supreme Court emphasized both of these reasons when it invalidated a series of vagrancy convictions. See Papachristou v. Jacksonville, 405 U.S. 156 (1972).

More recently, the Court put especial emphasis on excessive police discretion in invalidating Chicago's anti-gang ordinance. The statute punished failure to disperse on police command when two or more persons, at least one of whom was a member of a gang, was in a public place with "no apparent purpose." The Court, concerned with the level of police discretion inherent in the quoted phrase, found the ordinance unconstitutionally vague. Chicago v. Morales, 527 U.S. 41 (1999).

The Supreme Court has announced seemingly inconsistent tests by which to measure vagueness. In Lanzetta v. New Jersey, 306 U.S. 451, 453 (1939), the Court said that "a statute which either forbids or requires the doing of an act in terms so vague that men of common intelligence must necessarily guess at its meaning and differ as to its application, violates the first essential of due process of law." Some years earlier, however, the Court had said that "the law is full of instances where a man's fate depends on his estimating rightly, that is, as the jury subsequently estimates it, some matter of degree." Nash v. U.S., 229 U.S. 373, 377 (1913).

In practice, these apparently conflicting views can be reconciled. The *Nash* test is appropriate when one can ascertain the general sort of conduct to be avoided, even though the exact line is unclear. For example, an automobile driver does not know exactly how deviant her driving must be before it will constitute reckless driving. She does know, however, in general terms, the type of driving to avoid. If she is driving 65 m.p.h. in a 45 m.p.h. zone, she might contend that she didn't believe she was driving recklessly and that she must necessarily guess whether a jury would agree or disagree with her assessment. Nevertheless, her conviction most probably will be affirmed on the ground that, in a general way, she knew she was approaching the line, and as a law-abiding citizen could and should have avoided approaching the line and thereby the risk of crossing it. See S. v. Jacobsen, 477 P.2d 1 (Wash.1970).

On the other hand, sometimes the statutory standard is so vague that a would-be law-abiding citizen of common intelligence can look at the statute and be unable to ascertain, in even a general sort of way, the kind of conduct he is supposed to avoid. In *Lanzetta supra*, for example, the statute punished as a "gangster" any person without a lawful occupation who had previously been convicted of a crime and was "known to be a member of any gang consisting of two or more persons." 306 U.S. at 452. The meaning of "gang" in this statute is so unclear that a person desiring to follow the statute would not know, even generally, what sort of conduct to avoid.

Although courts frequently (but not always) follow this dichotomy (if you can tell when you're approaching the line the statute is constitutional, but if you can't it is unconstitutional), there is sometimes only a small difference between the two categories of cases. For instance, in *Nash supra*, the Supreme Court held the phrase "undue restraint of trade" to be a permissible standard. But two years later, the same Court in an opinion by the same Justice (Holmes) held that the phrase "real value," as applied to a prospective price fixer, was unconstitutionally vague because it was so unclear that one could not ascertain in advance the prices to be avoided. International Harvester Co. v. Kentucky, 234 U.S. 216 (1914).

Sometimes the element of scienter has been held to be sufficient to render an otherwise vague statute constitutionally acceptable. The theory behind this practice is that if a person is in fact aware that he is violating a standard, he has overcome any difficulty of understanding that may be present for others. To illustrate, if the defendant in *International Harvester* had knowingly sold its products at less than "real value" (in the sense that their executives had personally determined that whatever real value was, their price was clearly below it), a persuasive argument could be made that as to the defendant, the statute was not vague. See Boyce Motor Lines v. U.S., 342 U.S. 337 (1952).

When the First Amendment is implicated, courts have demanded significantly greater statutory precision than has been indicated above. For example, in Winters v. New York, 333 U.S. 507 (1948), the Supreme Court reversed a book dealer's conviction for selling magazines with pictures and stories of bloodshed "so massed as to become vehicles for inciting violent and depraved crimes against the person." Had the Court applied the *Nash* test, it could have concluded that a magazine seller is aware, in a general way, when he is approaching the line and can avoid conviction by steering clear of the line. The Court, however, over Justice Frankfurter's strong dissent, refused to do this.

The reason for the distinction is that in *Winters*, unlike *Nash*, the defendant had a constitutional right to approach the line because the First Amendment guarantees freedom of speech and press. A less than perfectly precise statute necessarily deters more than it forbids. The *Nash* statute, for example, deters people from restraining trade even a little bit for fear that a court or jury will consider that restraint "undue." Similarly, the *Winters* statute deters the sale of stories of bloodshed that do not incite violent and depraved crime out of fear that a trier of fact might find that they do so incite. Since the right to restrain trade is not constitutionally protected, the fact that some people won't restrain trade at all is no great loss to society. On the other hand, deterring people from publishing constitutionally protected material is quite serious. Consequently, a stricter standard of vagueness in the First Amendment area is essential.

This same principle can apply to other constitutionally protected areas. For example, during the 1920's, when the Court believed that there was a heavy constitutional presumption against price regulations, it tended to hold such regulations to a strict standard of certainty. See, *e.g.*, Cline v. Frink Dairy Co., 274 U.S. 445 (1927).

§ 18.02   Ex Post Facto Laws

The United States Constitution forbids either the Federal Government (Art. I, § 9, cl. 3) or the states (Art. I, § 10, cl. 1) to enact an ex post facto law. In Calder v. Bull, 3 U.S. (3 Dall.) 386, 390 (1798), the Supreme Court defined an ex post facto law as: "1st. Every law that makes an action done before the passing of the law, and which was innocent when done, criminal; and punishes such action. 2d. Every law that aggravates a crime, or makes it greater than it was when committed. 3d. Every law that changes the punishment, and inflicts a greater punishment, than the law annexed to the crime, when committed. 4th. Every law that alters the legal rules of evidence, and receives less, or different, testimony, than the law required at the time of the commission of the offence, in order to convict the offender." (emphasis deleted)

Precisely what constitutes "less or different testimony" is not always clear. For example, in Carmell v. Texas, 529 U.S. 513 (2000), defendant was convicted of several counts of aggravated sexual assault against his stepdaughter. At the time that he committed some of his crimes, the law of Texas rendered a victim's testimony incompetent unless she was either under 14 at the time of the assaults or had informed another of the assault within six months of its occurrence. Subsequent to the defendant's crime, but before his trial, Texas changed its law to abolish the informing another requirement for victims who were under 18. Thus, *Carmell* presented the question of whether a conviction predicated on the testimony of an under 18, but over 14, year old victim constituted a violation of the ex post facto clause. By a 5–4 vote, the United States Supreme Court reversed the conviction, concluding that the new rule permitted a conviction on less or different testimony.

The purposes of the ex post facto prohibitions are substantially the same as those supporting the void for vagueness doctrine (§ 18.01 *supra*): fair notice to the defendant and prevention of arbitrary action by the government. Thus, the ex post facto prohibitions are not applicable to changes in the law which favor the defendant (*e.g.*, a law reducing a certain kind of killing from murder to manslaughter). Indeed, in the absence of a "saving clause" to the contrary (which are not uncommon), such a statute is presumed to intend such a retroactive effect. *E.g.*, S. v. Pardon, 157 S.E.2d 698 (N.C.1967).

It is often difficult to ascertain whether a given change in the law hurts the defendant, helps him, or is neutral. [A neutral change, like one that helps him, is not ex post facto. *E.g.*, Wetzel v. Wiggins, 85 So.2d 469 (Miss.1956).] Such cases have occasionally divided courts. For example, in S. v. Masino, 43 So.2d 685 (La.1949), the defendants failed to properly encase gas pipes which caused an explosion resulting in death. Between the time of the negligent failure and the time of the explosion, Louisiana adopted a negligent homicide statute under which the defendants were charged. Deeming the critical date to be the date the building was completed (although a dissenting judge thought that there was a continuing duty to encase the pipes up until the date of the explosion, thereby rendering the ex post facto analysis irrelevant), the majority concluded that the law was ex post facto and affirmed the quashing of the indictment. A dissent, however, argued that under the old law, the defendants would have been guilty of involuntary manslaughter and therefore benefitted from the change. The majority rejected this reasoning on the ground that the reason for the enactment of the new law was the difficulty of obtaining an involuntary manslaughter conviction in a case such as the one at bar.

The ex post facto prohibitions apply only to legislation. They do not apply to judicial decisions as such. Frank v. Mangum, 237 U.S. 309 (1915). Indeed, the principal function of the judiciary is to construe statutes and the common law, sometimes for the first time, and apply them to the case at hand. Nevertheless, a totally unexpected construction of a statute can have the same pernicious effects as an ex post facto law or an unconstitutionally vague statute—lack of notice to a prospective defendant and governmental opportunity for discriminatory enforcement.

In Bouie v. Columbia, 378 U.S. 347 (1964), the South Carolina Supreme Court had held a statute which forbade "entry upon the lands of another ... after notice from the owner or tenant prohibiting such entry" to be applicable to a sit-in demonstrator (prior to the 1964 Federal Civil Rights Act) who did not enter the drug store without permission, but rather refused to leave when asked to do so. The United States Supreme Court reversed on the ground that this construction of the statute was so extraordinary that the defendants (who testified that they expected to be arrested) could not have foreseen that the statute might apply to their conduct.

There are those who read *Bouie* as something of a constitutional sport, principally designed to avoid a more difficult fundamental question (whether restaurants are constitutionally forbidden to discriminate on the basis of race). Indeed, it has not been uniformly followed. For example in Ginzburg v. U.S., 383 U.S. 463 (1966), the defendant sold magazines that he believed were not obscene within theretofore announced Supreme Court guidelines. The Supreme Court assumed, *arguendo*, that Ginzburg's argument was correct, but added a new element to the test for determining obscenity (pandering to the interest in obscenity) which was sufficient and necessary to sustain Ginzburg's conviction.

The limitations of Bouie were also apparent in Rogers v. Tennessee, 532 U.S. 451 (2001), where the Tennessee Supreme Court had judicially overturned the year and a day rule (see § 3.04, *supra*), thereby allowing a man to be convicted of murder for the stabbing of a victim that resulted in his death fifteen months later. Arguing that this judicial change in the law would have been an ex post facto law had the legislature so changed the law, Rogers argued that *Bouie* compelled the reversal of his conviction. Although accepting *arguendo* that a similar change by the legislature would have been ex post facto, the Court held that *Bouie* did not apply all of the ex post facto jurisprudence to judicial change in the common law. Rather, the Court held that the test was unfair surprise, and that under that test, Rogers lost.

§ 18.03   Common Law Crimes

Although most Americans think of their criminal laws as having been codified, many states recognize common law crimes. Even in those that do not, it is necessary to resort to the common law to ascertain the meaning of statutory crimes. For example, a statute might say that rape is punishable by five to twenty years imprisonment, but fail to define rape, thereby leaving the definition to the common law.

The major problem with common law crimes is notice. If the specific activity was punishable at early common law, or under a prior decision of the State Supreme Court, no significant problem is presented. When, however, the activity has not been held to be criminal prior to the conduct, a serious argument of no fair notice can be made.

C. v. Mochan, 110 A.2d 788 (Pa.Super.Ct.1955), is a good illustration. Mochan had made several obscene telephone calls to a woman of the highest repute. Unfortunately, at that time Pennsylvania neither had a statute outlawing that sort of conduct, nor any common law precedent directly in point. Thus, the court was forced to either expand the common law or allow this reprehensible conduct to go unpunished.

The majority chose the former, holding that " '[t]he common law is sufficiently broad to punish as a misdemeanor, although there may be no exact precedent, any act which directly injures or tends to injure the public to such an extent as to require the state to interfere and punish the wrongdoer, as in the case of acts which injuriously affect public morality, or obstruct, or pervert public justice, or the administration of government.' " *Id.* at 790.

A vigorous dissent, however, suggested that "[u]nder the division of powers in our constitution it is for the legislature to determine what 'injures or tends to injure the public.' " *Id.* at 791. The dissent contended that with legislatures now sitting regularly, it is no longer necessary for the judiciary to make the law as it once did.

Under Musser v. Utah, 333 U.S. 95 (1948), the dissent's position may be constitutionally compelled. *Musser* held that a statute punishing a statutory conspiracy "to commit any act injurious to the public health, the public morals, or to trade or commerce, or for the perversion or obstruction of justice or the due administration of the laws" was unconstitutionally vague unless it could be narrowed by the state courts. *Id.* at 96. See § 16.04 *supra*. If such a standard is vague when set out in a statute, a fortiori it would seem to be vague without a statute.

§ 18.04 Victimless Crimes

A. NON–CONSTITUTIONAL LIMITATIONS

One of the great debates among criminologists is the extent to which the criminal law ought to concern itself with "victimless crime." To some extent the debate is tautological in that practically all would agree that if there truly were no victim, the act should not be punished. Some would argue, however, that the "victim" need not be any particular individual. They would argue that tort law compensates individual victims, whereas the criminal law is designed to punish those who victimize society. (See § 1.01 *supra*). The real question facing legislatures in this area is whether the societal gain from punishing particular conduct is worth the cost. Typical of the kinds of crimes generally denominated "victimless" are those dealing with such subjects as sex (excluding forcible sex, *e.g.*, rape), drugs, and gambling.

In support of punishment, some people believe that adultery is harmful because of its potential destructive effect on families. Drugs can seriously damage individuals as well as alter their personalities so as to increase the danger to society. Similarly, gambling can keep a man and his family in perpetual debt while lining the pockets of professional gamblers and criminals.

On the other hand, when all of the parties involved in these activities are consenting adults, the harm to society does not approach the level of crimes with true personal victims. Furthermore, capturing these "criminals" is difficult and frequently requires devious means (compare §§ 11.05, 11.06, *supra*). Consequently, selective enforcement is not uncommon, thereby creating the opportunity for arbitrariness. Moreover, the criminality of narcotics, gambling, and commercialized sex precludes quasi-legitimate business from entering these areas, thereby assuring their control by organized crime.

Perhaps the strongest argument against this largely unsuccessful attempt to outlaw private consensual activities is the psychological impact on the populace. With so many of our citizens having committed "crimes", one or both of two interrelated undesirable reactions tends to emerge: first, a person might acquire a general disrespect for the law for making such pervasive conduct criminal; and second, he may acquire a disrespect for himself, viewing himself as a criminal. These attitudes are especially prevalent among college marijuana users whose friends have been arrested for marijuana use. Indeed, even those who do not use marijuana may lose respect for the law by seeing their friends, whom they respect as good people, arrested for using or possessing marijuana.

Finally, in regard to drugs, it is at least fair to ask whether the harm caused by drugs is greater than the harm caused by drugs being criminal. Drugs being criminal has contributed to its appeal to organized crime, to gang turf wars, to drug users becoming criminals to obtain the money necessary to pay drug dealers, and to many neighborhoods being less safe than they could be. Obviously, the solution to these problems is beyond the scope of this book.

B.   CONSTITUTIONAL LIMITATIONS

Prior to 1965, the Constitution did not appear to limit victimless crimes. In that year, Griswold v. Connecticut, 381 U.S. 479 (1965), held that the penumbras of several provisions of the Bill of Rights precluded punishment of married people for using contraceptive devices. The immediate impact of *Griswold* was not significant. Contraceptive use had been legal in all of the other states and their sale was not unlawful in Connecticut. Thus, it seems reasonable to assume that there were many married "criminals" living in Connecticut prior to *Griswold*. As Mr. Justice Stewart said: "[T]his is an uncommonly silly law. As a practical matter, the law is obviously unenforceable, except in the oblique context of the present case [prosecution of a birth control clinic]." *Id.* at 527 (dissenting opinion). Nevertheless, *Griswold* is significant because of its refusal to sustain every victimless crime, regardless of how silly it may be.

Four years later, in Stanley v. Georgia, 394 U.S. 557 (1969), the Court held that a person has the right to possess obscenity in the privacy of his home. Later decisions, however, have held that *Stanley* does not preclude punishment for sending obscenity to willing purchasers through the mail

[U.S. v. Reidel, 402 U.S. 351 (1971)], bringing obscene materials into the United States from foreign countries [U.S. v. 12 200–Ft. Reels of Super 8mm. Film, 413 U.S. 123 (1973)], or even moving in interstate commerce an obscene film intended for private use. [U.S. v. Orito, 413 U.S. 139 (1973)]. As Mr. Justice Black sardonically said: "[P]erhaps in the future [*Stanley*] will be recognized as good law only when a man writes salacious books in his attic, prints them in has basement, and reads them in his living room." U.S. v. Thirty–Seven Photographs, 402 U.S. 363, 382 (1971) (dissenting opinion).

In Roe v. Wade, 410 U.S. 113 (1973), the Supreme Court held the right to abortion, prior to viability, to be a part of the constitutional right to privacy for both married and unmarried women. The scope of this right is being constantly revisited by the Court, but, at least for now, it appears that the core of the right will remain Constitutionally protected.

Perhaps the Court's most significant and far-reaching decision in this area is Lawrence v. Texas, 539 U.S. 558 (2003). In *Lawrence*, in the course of invalidating a law forbidding private homosexual conduct, the Court held that private sexual behavior between consenting adults, whether married or not, is constitutionally protected. The full scope of *Lawrence*, like most ground-breaking decisions remains open. For example, it is unclear whether *Lawrence* applies to adultery inasmuch as that crime involves a victim.

On different grounds, the Court has held that the Constitution prohibits punishment for drug addiction (cruel and unusual punishment, see § 12.04 *supra*) and vagrancy (vagueness, see § 18.01 *supra*) cannot be punished consistent with the Constitution.

PERSPECTIVE

Just as Columbus discovered that the world is round, the criminal law student should discover that this subject does not fall off the end of the last page of this or any other book. Rather, like the world, it continues at the beginning. To illustrate, the last part (Part VII) of this book is concerned with two major limitations on the criminal law, lack of notice and lack of harm. The rationale for these limitations are apparent when one examines Part I of the book and becomes familiar with the purposes of punishing one as a criminal. There is obviously no utility in reforming, restraining, wreaking vengeance upon, or deterring one who had received no prior notice of the illegality of his conduct. Similarly, when no significant harm has been done, there is no need to resort to the punitive ends of the criminal law.

The remainder of the book should also be evaluated in light of the reason for the criminal law as developed in Part I. Thus, in examining the homicidal crimes in Chapter II, the other crimes against the person in Chapters IV and V, and the crimes against property in Chapter VII, the student should constantly try to ascertain the criminological basis for each of the distinctions presented. Do premeditated killers really require more reformation, re-

311

straint, retribution or deterrence than other types of killers? Is a felon who inadvertently causes death significantly different from one who does not? Why is robbery punished so much more severely than grand larceny? A student who has thought through these and other similar questions can be expected to have a significant edge in understanding the criminal law as contrasted to a less diligent classmate.

Part III (Ingredients of Crime) relates directly to the purposes of punishment. To punish a person who acts with no mens rea at all is normally as purposeless and at least as counter-productive as punishing a person under a vague statute. If by hypothesis, a person is trying to adhere to the law and is diligent in his effort to do so, restraint, reformation, retribution, and deterrence are all inappropriate. The strict liability type of crime, discussed in § 8.04, is an exception to this principle, but the reasons for and limitations of this exception should be clearly understood.

Actus reus is necessary to avoid punishing a person for mere thoughts. Once he has taken significant steps towards commission of a crime, the reasons for punishment become appropriate. The actus reus need not be the completed crime, however. It can be a substantial step towards the completion of a crime (attempt) or even a mere agreement (conspiracy), but it cannot be a bare desire or wish.

In Part IV, we study special defenses which go to the heart of the reasons for punishment. An insane person, for example, is substantially undeterrable, and while it may be true that she needs to be reformed (more accurately cured) and restrained, these things can be accomplished civilly. Self-defense (Ch. VI) illustrates the dovetailing of rule and theory even more. We do not punish one who kills in self-defense because society accepts his conduct. Thus, he does not need to be reformed, restrained, or deterred because of his conduct.

Part V presents the burden of proof which provides an opportunity to rethink the relative place of all of these concepts. When we require the State to prove something beyond a reasonable doubt, we do so because the point at issue is so important that we do not want to risk a conviction if the point is in doubt. The examination of Part VI focuses on inchoate criminality which is relatively high in mens rea and low in actus reus. It also examines the dangers of group criminality which are such that special complicity and conspiracy laws have been thought necessary to deter such activities as well as to reform and restrain those who would engage in them. The great problem here is in ascertaining who, other than the first degree principal, has demonstrated sufficient culpability to warrant condemnation as an accomplice or co-conspirator. (Chapters XV and XVI.)

Finally, we return to the limitations on the criminal law, which is where this perspective began. Thus, the study of criminal law goes round and round, and the diligent student should stay on for several cycles.

*

INDEX

References are to Pages

315

BLACKMAIL
See Extortion, this index

BREAKING
Burglary element, 123

BURDEN OF PROOF
Generally, 207 et seq.
Affirmative defenses, 214
Automatism, 215
Death penalty sentencing factors, 218
Due process requirements, 209
Duress, 215
Element by element reasonable doubt, 212
Entrapment defense, 215
Inferences
    Generally, 220
  Constitutional requirements, 222
Insanity defense
    Generally, 215
  Mens rea, insanity negativing, 185
Intoxication, 216
Mens rea element
    Generally, 215
  Insanity, intent negativing, 185
Possible and reasonable doubt, 211
Presumptions
    Generally, 220
  Constitutional requirements, 222
Provocation defense, 213
Proximate cause, 207
Reasonable doubt standard
    Generally, 208
  Due process requirements, 209
  Element by element, 212
  Hate crimes, 217
  Instructions, 210
  Policy of, 313
  Self-defense, 215
Self-defense, 215, 221
Sentencing factors, 217
Shifting
    Generally, 214, 216
  Presumptions, burden shifting, 221
Standard of proof distinguished, 216

LARCENY—Cont'd
Stealth, larceny by, 98
Trade secrets, theft of, 94
Trees, theft of, 94
Trespassory taking element, 92
Trick, larceny by
        Generally, 102, 106
    False pretenses distinguished, 107
Types of, 98
Value-less property, 95

MALICE
Arson, 126
Felony murder doctrine, 49, 51
Universal malice, 46

MALICE AFORETHOUGHT
        Generally, 27
Attempts, 227
Depraved heart murder, 44
Homicide, 27
Intent to cause serious bodily injury, 34
Outrageously reckless conduct, 44
Serious bodily injury, intent to cause, 34
Universal malice, 46

MALUM PROHIBITUM CRIMES
        Generally, 52
Conspiracy, 281
Misdemeanor manslaughter, 52

MANSLAUGHTER
        Generally, 27
Homicide, this index
Misdemeanor Manslaughter, this index

MAYHEM
        Generally, 71
Battery distinguished, 71
Intent, 72

MENS REA
        Generally, 129 et seq.
See also Intent, this index
Actus reus, concurrence of, 158
Aiding and abetting, conspiracy mens rea compared, 283

ROBBERY—Cont'd
Pickpocket activities, 117
Purse snatching as larceny or robbery, 117

SCIENTER
Conspiratorial agreements, 282
Larceny, 95
Vague statute defenses, 298

SELF-DEFENSE
Generally, 75 et seq.
Apprehension of criminals defense, 85
Battered-spouse syndrome, 77
Burden of proof, 215, 221
Castle exception to retreat rule, 80
Crime prevention, 89
Criminals, defense of apprehension of, 85
Deadly force, 75, 76
Homicide non self-defense defensive acts resulting in, 29
Imperfect, 80
Necessary force, 75
Necessity defense compared, 199
Others, defense of, 83
Property protection, 89
Provocation, imperfect self-defense compared, 80
Reasonably necessary force, 75
Resisting unlawful arrest, 84
Retreat rule
Generally, 78
Castle exception, 80
Unlawful arrest, resisting, 84

SERIOUS BODILY INJURY
Malice aforethought, 34

SODOMY
Victimless crimes, constitutional limitations, 309

SOLICITATIONS
Generally, 238
Abandonment by solicitor, 268
Attempted solicitation, 243
Attempts distinguished, 239
First Amendment protections, 238

STATUTORY RAPE
See Rape, this index

†